In Solitary Witness

In Solitary Witness:
The Life and Death
of Franz Jägerstätter

Gordon C. Zahn

Templegate Publishers

Springfield, Illinois

ISBN 0-87243-141-X

Templegate Publishers
302 E. Adams St., P.O. Box 5152
Springfield, Illinois 62705

ACKNOWLEDGMENTS A generous grant from the Penrose Fund of The American Philosophical Society made possible the research upon which this study is based. It is both appropriate and a personal pleasure that this Fund and its administrators are cited first among those to whom the author's profound gratitude is due.

Next, I would like to thank all the people—and especially the inhabitants of the village of St. Radegund—who were willing to give freely of their time and hospitality to discuss with me their personal memories of the man and the action with which this book is concerned. I am especially indebted to Pastor Josef Karobath and, needless to add, to Mrs. Jägerstätter and her three daughters. There can be no question but that, at least in the case of the family, this need to relive the events surrounding their personal loss must have brought with it an active renewal of all the sorrow they had somehow managed to bring under control. I can only hope that the results of this work will ultimately justify placing such an emotional burden upon them.

Finally, my sincere appreciation extends as well to all who had a part in the physical preparation of this book—typists, editors, proofreaders—and to all those friends and colleagues whose advice and encouragement were always at my disposal.

There is is no hiding the fact that it is much harder to be a Christian today than it was in the first centuries, and there is every reason to predict that it will be even more difficult in the near future. When it becomes the "sacred duty" of a man to commit sin, the Christian no longer knows how he should live. There remains nothing else for him to do but bear individual witness—alone. And where such witness is, there is the Kingdom of God.

Reinhold Schneider

This book is humbly dedicated to the memory of Franz Jägerstätter and to all the others who, like him, stood alone and said "No"—many of whose stories have been completely lost to history, at least as it is kept and written by men.

Preface

In December 1984, responding to a nationwide popular petition, the President of Austria formally issued a special posthumous Award of Honor to Franz Jägerstätter. Twenty years earlier when this book first appeared it had been quite a different story. Apart from his family and former friends and neighbors in the remote Upper Austrian village of St. Radegund, the man and his heroic witness were unknown and seemingly destined to be lost altogether after they along with their memories perished.

Today, this official recognition of Jägerstätter as a national hero is but the latest evidence of the tremendous impact he and his story have had and continues to have. In its several translations (German, French, Italian and Greek to this point), it has reached people all over the world, and readers have written his widow telling her of the inspiration they have drawn from his sacrifice. Often enough they beg for some small token to serve as a relic of the martyr they already revere as a saint.

Radio and television dramatizations based on the book have brought similar inspiration to millions more. Even today, the prize-winning docu-drama produced for Austrian television, circulated in this country by the Pax Christi USA Center on Conscience and War, provides audiences with what one viewer described as "an experience too good to be hoarded and yet too profound to be adequately expressed." A number of plays have been written about this simple man who defied Hitler's totalitarian power; sermons have been preached presenting him as a model to be admired and followed; pilgrims have travelled, often from distant lands, to visit and pray at his grave.

At the Second Vatican Council an English Archbishop submitted an intervention devoted entirely to the Jagerstatter story. He called upon his fellow bishops, assembled from the entire world, "to consider this man and his sacrifice in a spirit of gratitude" and let his example "inspire our deliberations" on the document which would become *The Pastoral Constitution on the Church in the Modern World.*"

There is no way of knowing what, if any, influence his plea may have had upon the Council's affirmation of the legitimacy of conscientious objection. What can be said with absolute confidence, though, is that Jägerstätter has provided such inspiration to an untold number of individuals faced with the same moral challenge that led to his martyrdom. In the United States, opponents of the war in Vietnam linked their protests and acts of resistance to the example he set in his refusal to serve in a war his conscience told him was unjust and immoral. None were called upon to suffer the penalty of death, of course, but many accepted prison as the price for following in his footsteps.

It is not too much to suggest that this humble peasant changed the course of our history a generation later and an ocean away. On several occasions, speaking to college audiences, Daniel Ellsberg has revealed that this account of moral resistance unto death was one of the factors leading to his decision to release the Pentagon Papers. There is little doubt that this act and its effect upon public opinion hastened the end of this nation's involvement in that inglorious struggle.

If today there is reason to fear that the memory of Vietnam and all it meant has faded to the point where many now forget its shame and tragedy and regard the whole experience in a more "heroic" light; if, worse still, this nation's leaders seem intent upon risking similar adventures in central America, it is well that we turn again to the Jägerstätter story and the lesson it teaches. Simply stated, it is this: no matter how hopeless the situation or seemingly futile the effort, the Christian need not and must not despair. Instead, the believer can and *should* be prepared to accept and assert moral responsibility for his or her actions. If nothing else, as Jägerstätter wrote, it is always possible to save one's own soul *and perhaps some others as well* by bearing individual witness against evil.

We may take some comfort in knowing the lesson has been learned, at least in part. In his 1965 intervention to the Council Fathers Archbishop Roberts described what he regarded as "the major scandal of Christianity", namely "that almost every national hierarchy in almost every war has allowed itself to become the moral arm of its own government, even in wars later recognized as palpably unjust." It would be foolhardy to assume this pattern no longer holds or that the Archbishop's criticism has lost its force. Nevertheless the promise is there that future wars will find the Church less susceptible to nationalism's appeals and lures. Indeed, the 1983 pastoral letter of the U. S. hierarchy may be read as a fulfillment of the Roberts plea: "Let us break with this tragic past by making a clear and unambiguous affirmation of the right and the obligation of each Christian to obey the voice of his informed conscience before and during a time of war."

The Jägerstätter story and its aftermath provides still another lesson from which we can draw strength and inspiration. *No witness is lost or wasted.* He went to his death convinced that few would ever know or remember what happened to him. As far as he was concerned that made no difference. It was enough that *he* knew and that *his* God knew — and he gave thanks for the privilege of dying for the Faith. As it turned out he was wrong. The world *did* learn; he *is* remembered — and honored for the heroism of his witness. With more honors yet to come there is good reason to believe. A recent news item from Austria speaks of increasing interest "within church circles" in efforts to promote his canonization.

True, there are others who did suffer the fate he envisioned for himself. They perished unknown and unrecorded, not to be "discovered" years later through a happy series of providential accidents. Even so, we can be confident their witness and their reward have not been diminished by that sad fact. In the divine economy — however great or slight the sacrifice involved or the response stirred — every such witness sincerely given is sufficient unto itself.

Already named a national hero and possibly still to be proclaimed a saint! It is, of course, a source of much gratification to the author to have been privileged to contribute to his "discovery", even if only (as I am inclined to believe) as simply the *instrument* of discovery. More satisfying still, however, is the knowledge that the Jägerstätter story continues to serve as a source of strength and inspiration to young people in many countries who are united in their determination to rid the world of war and all that makes for war. In this sense it can be said his witness is still incomplete. If, as I most fervently hope, this new edition helps recruit others to join in that truly holy crusade and bring his witness to fuller completion, it will have fulfilled its purpose.

Boston, Mass.
February 1986

Gordon C. Zahn

Contents

Franz Jägerstätter: An Introduction

Franz Jägerstätter was born on May 20, 1907, in St. Radegund, a small village in Upper Austria. His natural father was killed in World War I when he was still a child, and when his mother married, her child was adopted by her husband.

In his youth, Franz had gained a reputation for being a wild fellow, but, in general, his daily life was like that of most Austrian peasants.

In 1936, he married a girl from a nearby village, and they went to Rome on their honeymoon. A Catholic by birth, he experienced a religious awakening—apparently about the time of his marriage—and later served as sexton of his parish church.

When Hitler's troops moved into Austria in 1938, Jägerstätter was the only man in the village to vote against the *Anschluss*. Although he was not involved with any political organization, and did undergo one brief period of military training, he remained openly anti-Nazi, and publicly declared he would not fight in Hitler's war.

After many delays, Jägerstätter was called to active duty in February, 1943; by this time he had three daughters, the eldest not quite six. He maintained his position against fighting for the Third Reich, and was imprisoned, first at Linz, then at Berlin. After a military trial, he was beheaded on August 9, 1943.

The facts of Franz Jägerstätter's life may be stated briefly, but how does one begin to tell his real story? What was there about this man that, alone among his friends and neighbors, perhaps alone among all his Austrian coreligionists, made it possible for him to come to his fateful decision? Perhaps even more important, what impact did his action have upon those who knew him, what meaning did they give to it, what significance does it have for them today?

3

It is almost an accident that we know anything at all about Franz Jägerstätter, about his prison letters, about the intensely moving, pious, and incisive commentaries he wrote before his final arrest. There are some who have said he must have been deranged; others have compared his rebellion to that of Thomas More and have suggested that he may some day be looked upon as a saint for our time. None of those whose judgments have been recorded have had the opportunity to investigate the whole record.

My own introduction to the story of Franz Jägerstätter was quite by chance. In 1956, while conducting research in Germany for an earlier book, I was taken to visit a former prison chaplain, Heinrich Kreuzberg, who had written a book about an Austrian priest, Franz Reinisch, who had been executed for refusing to take the required military oath of unconditional obedience to Adolf Hitler.

Inspiring as I found the Reinisch story to be, I was even more deeply impressed by a brief appendix chapter which told of another man, "Franz II" as the author identified him, who was executed a year later for a similar "crime" against the Third Reich. What made this case exceptionally interesting, I felt, was the fact that Franz Jägerstätter came from a social background that one would ordinarily not associate with such an overtly rebellious act. He was a relatively untutored man from a remote and isolated rural village. Even more important, he, unlike the priest who had preceded him to the executioner's block, was a married man with a wife and children for whom he was responsible and whose future welfare he was morally bound to consider.

Some months after reading Kreuzberg's book, I made a point of visiting Franz Jägerstätter's widow and his local pastor to get a more direct account of the affair and its aftermath. The visit was brief—a few hours of a single afternoon, in fact—but it was enough to convince me that this was indeed an amazing story, one deserving the widest possible attention. At that time I resolved that I would return someday to make a more complete investigation of this act of heroism and its sources.

Questions relating to community opinion and evaluation, important to me as a sociologist, immediately came to mind: what did the people of this little village think about Jägerstätter's action at the time? How do they look back on it today? In 1961, thanks largely to the generous assistance provided by The American Philosophical Society, it became possible for me to spend the months of June and July in this village of St. Radegund, making observations, conducting interviews, and following occasional leads to others—some far removed from the village setting—who might be able to furnish significant bits of information about the man, his life, and his death.

In studying something of this nature, a great deal of methodological improvisation is in order. It was necessary to begin by gathering together whatever material of a documentary nature might be available. There was practically none. Then I had to track down any secondary accounts that might have been published about the case. A few of these were found, but they were highly repetitious in their content. Finally, I conducted personal and very loosely structured interviews with the people whom Jägerstätter had known as friend and neighbor, as relative, as pastor and confidant, as his attorney when he was tried for his life. It was even possible, though again not anticipated, to locate both firsthand and secondhand descriptions of his behavior in prison up to the hours immediately preceding his execution. These interviews and other reminiscences, needless to say, constitute the core of this research effort.

However, another most significant and certainly most unexpected source of information was found in Jägerstätter's own writings. Some of the secondary accounts I had come across referred to and used two such documents—a final farewell letter, and a lengthy statement in which Jägerstätter explained his position; this had been written in prison at the request of the prison chaplain. It was not until relatively late in the course of my research summer that I learned for the first time, again by accident, of the existence of other writings, including seventeen letters to his wife written during the period of his imprisonment, and a most remarkable set of nine brief essays, or "commentaries" (as I will call them), dealing generally with the times he lived in, and written down sometime prior to his arrest. By means of these always moving and at times frankly inspirational personal documents, it became possible to

5

introduce a whole new dimension to the Jägerstätter story by recording his subjective awareness and evaluation of the events as they developed. Taken together, these writings constitute a graphic statement of his Christian witness.

The completion of the research led to an even more troubling problem in the preparation of its results for publication. It is always difficult, of course, to organize the facts one has gathered and to set forth the interpretation of those facts in a manner deemed most meaningful for the reader. The problem was greatly intensified in this instance. To me, as a sociologist, the story of Franz Jägerstätter was important as a case study of the martyr, or rebel, as an extreme social deviant; indeed, my original research prospectus had centered upon this as the approach I would be taking. It was not very long, however, before it became quite clear that I was "involved" in the unfolding story in at least two other respects. First, as a Catholic I could not fail to be impressed by the spiritual content and implications of this man's sacrifice, especially as revealed in his own writings. Indeed, I could not escape the suspicion that I might be dealing with an even more extreme form of social deviance than I had thought, that is, with a martyr-saint. Furthermore, as a Catholic who was also a conscientious objector, I began to see in his actions— and, in particular, the manner in which they were received and are still regarded by his fellow parishioners and the diocesan authorities —an occasion for a careful re-examination of the religious community's potential as a source of dissent with particular reference to modern war.

This is not to say, of course, that these are completely separate or conflicting considerations. As the final chapters will develop in some detail, they actually tend to converge, so that each has some direct bearing upon the others. But the problem remained: how to treat the material so that it would retain its sociological significance and still illuminate the other important areas of concern.

Even more compelling in this respect was another problem of presentation. If, as I hoped, this story was to reach the audience it deserved, it had to be told in a manner that would appeal as well to the reader who did not happen to be a sociologist, or a Catholic, or a conscientious objector. Such readers, one had to assume, would be primarily interested in the story of Franz Jägerstätter *as such*, and it would be grossly unfair to them, as well as to the memory of the man himself, to lessen or dull its impact by sacrificing its narrative appeal to these other considerations, important though they are to the author.

Secondary materials, official documents, the writings of Jägerstätter, the results of my interviews in St. Radegund, have been organized in such a way as to reconstruct the life of Franz Jägerstätter. In this regard it is important to stress the dedicated work of two priests. The first, Josef Karobath, the village pastor of St. Radegund, has collected materials pertaining to his late parishioner, including such things as letters and newspaper and magazine clippings. His collection, which I have called the St. Radegund Jägerstätter files, has been very helpful. Fr. Karobath has also made notes concerning Jägerstätter, to which several of the articles already written about him can be traced.

The second priest, Heinrich Kreuzberg, was chaplain at the prison where Jägerstätter was held during the period of his trial. After the war he wrote several articles about the peasant. These include his own reminiscences of the man and the events, especially in their final stages.

Many broader implications can be drawn from Jägerstätter's history. Sociological observations have not been eliminated from this study, but an effort has been made to limit such discussion to the end of the story. Two appendices have been added, one dealing with and containing some of the more important writings of Jägerstätter himself; the other details the methodology I employed in preparing this book, presents a survey of documents, articles, and books dealing with Jägerstätter, and offers a bibliographical listing of these works and others that may be of interest to the reader.

I recognize the danger in trying to please too many people at once. All I can do, in such a case, is to plead with each reader to give the story I have tried to tell—however deficient in the telling—his most serious consideration. I strongly suspect that if he does, he will find in it dimensions of meaning that may surpass the capacity of any author to capture on the printed page. If such there are, they must be left for the sensitive reader to glean for himself.

St. Radegund

Time settles softly on places like the village of St. Radegund in Upper Austria. Today one can stand near the village church looking down across the valley of the Salzach, his back to the ancient churchyard wall, and enjoy the same picturesque glimpse of the river below and the Titmoning church steeple five miles or so away in Bavaria that must have been familiar to the man whose ashes are buried in the St. Radegund churchyard. And that man, too, in his lifetime, was probably aware that through all the generations stretching back across the centuries since the tiny church was first established, many men must have stood near it and looked down upon the same peaceful view. For the transient researcher—little more than a summertime visitor and much more accustomed to the spirit, sounds, and frantic pace of a modern metropolis—this all-pervasive sense of peace and continuity with the remote past was at first something strange, a romantic curiosity. Later, slowly but surely, it revealed itself as something more, a way of life that, however much it may be weakening under the impact of lessening isolation and increasing mechanization, still exercises a mastery over the lives of the hundred or so households that make up the community of St. Radegund.

The parish church is perched just under the brow of the hill overlooking the river. All that one sees of it from the lower roadway at the center of town is its quaint onion-shaped steeple, familiar in this area. The graveyard circles its whitewashed walls; and it, too, has probably not changed much through the generations: the same narrow graves receive the last remains of sons and fathers, as they did of grandfathers and their grandfathers before them. The grave in which Franz Jägerstätter's ashes are buried is marked by a large crucifix and a marble block and is located against the west wall of the church itself. Somewhat apart from the regular burial plots stands a moderately large memorial originally built to honor the memory of the men of St. Radegund who had fallen in the First World War. It has now been modernized and expanded to include the names of the fifty-seven men of the parish who lost their lives in World War II.

Directly across from the churchyard gate, a larger building houses several family groups who do not have farms of their own, but who work the farms of others or perform various services for the community's residents. Here Jägerstätter's cousin, the town's only *Bibelforscher*, a member of the Jehovah's Witnesses, lived with his wife. Otherwise, St. Radegund is a totally Catholic village. In front of this building, Jägerstätter and his cousin spent many hours in earnest discussion, which later assumed an importance in the explanations of Jägerstätter's final decision.

A gravel path leads upward from the church to a more stolidly imposing building, which serves as both elementary school and official registry. Here begins what may be considered the village center. Apart from the church, it is in the four or five buildings clustered here that the major social and official events and activities of the community take place. Because of Sunday Mass, the church serves as the one meeting place where almost all citizens gather at least once a week. Consequently, most public announcements of any importance are made outside the church on Sunday after Mass; printed or written notices are posted on a board affixed to the side of a building across from the church. The yellow school building serves as local government headquarters. The third building, the pastor's residence and rectory office, also contains the community library, which the pastor operates. Adjoining his house is a general store and postal substation. The village has no post office of its own; instead, it is served by the Ostermiething office approximately ten miles away. Directly across from the pastor's house is the principal village inn. Known originally as the *Mesnerwirt*, for at least the past two generations it has been known as *Gasthaus Hofbauer*, carrying the family name of its owner-operators. A short path leads behind the inn to the residence and office of the town clerk, the only full-time governmental official hired by the community.

The main highway, which connects such towns and cities as Braunau, Ach, Ostermiething, Wildshut and, ultimately, Salzburg, lies about a mile away from this town center. There is another, but clearly secondary, concentration of buildings—bakery, another general store, two or three small dwellings—along the last half-mile of the gravel lane leading to the highway. Here one finds the second of the two local inns, the *Gasthaus Habl*, and behind it the large, weathered, barnlike building which had been built to house the Passion Play that once was performed annually and (if we are to accept the nostalgic memories of some of the residents) spread the fame of St. Radegund throughout the surrounding countryside and over into the border area of Bavaria as well. There have been no performances, however, since 1930. As a result, the playhouse stands empty and unused, little more than a deteriorating memory of the community's past glories. The visitor to St. Radegund will sometimes be told of the friendly raillery which still continues as the local residents are identified with the roles they played in the last performances: this milkmaid, the Virgin; that rough-looking farmer, St. Joseph. By a strange twist of irony, young Franz Jägerstätter had played the part of a soldier in the last season in which the Passion Play was given.

How can one measure change and continuity in a place like this? Certainly, in many respects—perhaps in most of the really important ones—the village one visits today is much the same as it was that February night more than twenty years ago when Franz Jägerstätter prepared to leave it for the last time.

No one reported seeing him there, but since he was a faithful sexton, it is safe to assume that in his last day in St. Radegund he made a final visit to the church; he would have wanted one last check to make sure that he was leaving everything in proper order. Because he loved the old church and the quiet village with such deep passion, it would not have been a hasty farewell. The cold and snows of the February winter would not have kept him from that last lingering look toward Titmoning, barely visible on the other side of the Salzach, or from making one more round of the graves squeezed so tightly between the church and its enclosing wall. Nor is it too much to imagine that there would have been an extra edge of sadness to his thoughts, since he must long since have abandoned all hope that his body would find its resting place in this beloved setting. Certainly he could not have foreseen that his ashes would one day be given a ceremonial burial in a place of honor here, or that his name would be included in the roster of local heroes of World War II listed on the community war memorial. Indeed, considering the step he was about to take, it is quite possible that he might even have protested the inscription of his name on such a memorial.

After saying good-bye to the church, he would have gone home, following the path that leads past the parish rectory. It is unlikely that he would have stopped for a farewell visit at the rectory. Perhaps if his regular pastor had been there, he might have done so, but Fr. Karobath had been "exiled" from the community in 1940 for being critical of the Nazi regime in one of his sermons. Forbidden to return to the village or to perform pastoral duties for his parishioners, his place had been taken by a younger priest who served as his vicar. Jägerstätter's relationship with this man was apparently satisfactory, but the depth of understanding he had found in his own pastor was lacking. This was particularly true with respect to his opposition to the Nazis, which accounts for the fact that it was to his absent pastor that the troubled sexton addressed the first report of the step he had decided to take.

He would also have passed the inn without stopping, although he may have thought of pausing for a glass of cider—people said he had stopped drinking beer and wine when he became "fanatically" devout—and for a last chance to see whatever friends and neighbors might happen to be gathered around the tables in the tavern.

11

Jägerstätter had long since avoided the inn because of the political arguments in which he always seemed to become involved and which would have become especially heated if the step he planned to take the following day were known. Besides, the moments and hours left to spend with his family were too few and too precious to be spent with others. His mother and his three little girls would not know until later that this was the last evening he would ever share with them; only his wife was aware of the decision he was about to take, and it was up to him to ease the terrible burden of this knowledge for her.

The following morning Jägerstätter left, quietly and early. A neighbor's wife recalls looking out the window and seeing him, quite by accident, as he walked slowly away from his house until he reached something of an elevation. She describes how he stopped and turned a full circle to take a long, sweeping, last look before taking the road to Titmoning. Moments later, another accidental meeting was to be his last contact with the people of St. Radegund, except for a single visit to his Berlin jail by his wife and the town's young vicar. It so happened that Jägerstätter's closest friend and most frequent companion in the escapades which, as a young man, had earned him the reputation of being "a wild one" stood outside his farm as Jägerstätter passed by. The friend called out the customary greeting, *Pfuat di' Gott, Franzl* ("Go with God, Franz"), but the response was nothing more than a sad shake of the head and the simple statement, "You'll see no more of me." And so it was.

If Jägerstätter could revisit St. Radegund today, he would probably be especially struck by the changes that have taken place. True, most of the houses are basically the same as they were: massive square structures with enclosed courtyards, designed originally to secure their inhabitants against marauding bands. The houses are electrified now, and so are the great barns which form one side of the square. The milking machine and the omnipresent tractor have brought great changes in the techniques of farming. Indeed, the major local event of the summer of 1961 was the introduction of a mower-thresher-binder combine purchased co-operatively by a group of villagers.

The greathouses are still occupied, for the most part, by the same families, although these families are now presided over by men, some of whom may have been among those youngsters whose occasionally unruly behavior in church had been one of the former sexton's more trying problems. But here, too, some changes of growing significance are to be seen. More and more of the local youth cross the river to find lucrative part-time work in the industries located on the Bavarian side; some leave permanently. As is usually the case, this is partly the result of the increased mechanization of the farm and partly a response to the lures of the "better life" offered by the world outside. The values of that other world have broken through the insularity of St. Radegund, too. A few of the men who have stayed and have taken over the operation of the farms that have been tilled by unnumbered generations of closely knit Radegund families are talking of building new houses to replace the ancient homes of their forefathers—and they plan their changes in terms of efficient kitchens, modern plumbing, and even picture windows.

Great as these changes are, however, the influence of the past is still dominant. It is difficult to establish with certainty the ancient origins of St. Radegund. Local interpretations of place names claim a link with the period of Roman conquest and migrations. The fact that house addresses still carry the name *Hadermarkt*, for example, is advanced by some as evidence that St. Radegund was once a way station along a trade route dating back to the time of Hadrian. Some support for this is found in other, more tangible, proofs of the village's antiquity. Two stone crosses, one standing before the school building and the other lying next to a nearby path, are very likely of early Roman origin. Similarly, some of the private roadside shrines which dot the area once featured sculpture and other decorations clearly traceable to early medieval times.

The most formal clue to the community's age is a document in the local pastor's possession, complete even to the ducal seal, which testifies to the presence of a church there as early as 1370. The present church—as the pastor tells it—was built in 1420 by members of a Bavarian community of Cistercian monks, and consecrated two years later. The pastor reasons, however, that a church of some kind, probably nothing more elaborate than a wood-frame building, must have been there even before this date. In this document, its author, Stephen the Elder, Duke of Bavaria, provides for the daily offering of Mass in St. Radegund for himself and his son. Since this was to be the responsibility of the Abbot of the Raithenhaslach community, and since it is unlikely that a priest would have made such a trip every day, the pastor concludes—with some reason—that there must have been a church on that spot when the document was issued in 1370.

Whether this community and its church have existed for six hundred years or more, of course, is of merely incidental interest. It seems to have been little touched by the sweep of historical events and currents that have shaped our age. If it has produced great thinkers in the past, no record remains of the fact. Its only widely recognized figure—apart from the man with whom this book is concerned—is also of relatively recent vintage, a self-taught artist who specialized in highly romanticized paintings of religious and devotional themes. This man, Johann Baptiste Wengler, seems to have gained recognition and favor in the art centers of the world, some as far away as America. His works are found in several important museums, and students of regional art in Austria still come to the village seeking material for scholarly monographs. But apart from him, the generations of Radegunders have come and gone without leaving any lasting mark upon the world.

In this remote village setting a simple peasant became a rebel: "A man," in Albert Camus' words, "who says no, but whose refusal does not imply a renunciation . . . who also says yes, from the moment he makes his first gesture of rebellion." A man who "is willing to sacrifice himself for the sake of a common good which he considers more important than his own destiny." Franz Jägerstätter, presented with his orders to serve in a war he considered unjust—a war, moreover, which he felt would serve the evil purposes of an intrinsically immoral political regime—refused to comply, and in his refusal accepted the death he knew would follow.

Perhaps we, whose days are filled with reports of world-shaking deeds by powerful national leaders, will find it hard to read, or even see, the lesson set forth for us by a humble peasant giving solitary witness in a community so small that it lacks almost all the custom-

14

ary civil autonomies; so remote that it is not to be found on ordinary maps of the country, or even those of the Upper Austrian province. Yet in this unlikely setting, an extraordinary act of rebellion took place. What we find recorded there is nothing less than a repetition of an old story, the ever-recurring confrontation between Christ and Caesar.

In his real life version of the Passion Play, the rough soldier of the 1930 performances threw down his sword and assumed instead the role of the committed and dedicated martyr for his faith. This is how a believer—and certainly Franz Jägerstätter himself—would choose to set forth the tragic events that took their course in the short period of six months between February and August 1943. And if one is prepared to accept, or at least entertain, this formulation, then other historical ironies of time and place begin to assume a significance verging upon the mystical.

Approximately thirty kilometers distant from St. Radegund is the "county seat," the *Kreisstadt*, Braunau-am-Inn. This is a town which can claim the distinction of being the birthplace of a powerful man who, for a time at least, determined the course of world history. In the impassioned introduction to a 1940 tourist handbook it was described as being "sacred to every German, for here is the birthplace of our *Führer*, Adolf Hitler, where in 1889 as the son of a customs official he first saw the light of day." Nor is this all. The provincial capital, Linz-an-der-Donau, is the city where Hitler spent most of his childhood and which always remained so much a favorite of his that he voiced grandiose dreams of making it one of the great centers of world culture and learning, once the Third Reich had achieved its final victory over the world. Linz can claim another dubious honor, since it was also the childhood home of Adolf Eichmann, the administrator of the infamous "final solution of the Jewish question."

Three men with their roots in the same soil: Hitler, Eichmann, and Jägerstätter. In a sense, one might read the whole history of the supreme tragedy of the Nazi era in the lives of these three men from the same corner of Austria: Hitler, the latter-day Caesar; Eichmann, his willing and perhaps all-too-eager servant; and, finally, Jägerstätter, the rebel-peasant who rejected the *Führer* and refused

15

his orders. Again with Camus, we may say, "On the day when crime dons the apparel of inocence . . . it is innocence that is called upon to justify itself." Perhaps it was precisely this, the justification of innocence, that Jägerstätter accomplished in his solitary witness.

St. Radegund is a village too small to have its own post office, almost too remote to be reached by normally scheduled means of transportation. Yet in the tiny graveyard surrounding its centuries-old church are buried the ashes of a simple peasant who, in his heroic act of true rebellion, defied the tyrant who had brought all Europe to its knees. It is a quiet place—some might say a holy place. Someday it may even be a place of pilgrimage.

16

The Young Ruffian

I came to the village of St. Radegund almost twenty years after the death of Franz Jägerstätter to hear from the inhabitants of the village about his life and to determine what his fellow townsfolk think of him today. Gaining an accurate picture of the opinions of the villagers was not a simple matter. I came as an outsider into a remote village to question its people about someone who had lived among them and who had a just claim to be protected against such scrutiny. Differences in background and status between the villagers and a foreign college professor created many hazards to communication. Nevertheless, with perhaps one exception, the villagers of St. Radegund were as generous and as sincere in their co-operation as anyone could have wished. The exception occurred when I arrived for an interview with a woman who had been mentioned as a classmate of the boy Franz, to find that she was not at home and had left word for me that she had never been to school with him and could give me no information.

In general, I was accepted into the homes of the villagers freely, and accorded all the hospitality of an honored guest. After I began speaking to people, the purpose and procedures of my visits must have become known throughout the community. This perhaps accounts for similarities in answers to certain questions from different people, although I do not believe any "story" was agreed upon in advance. In fact, the discussions among the townsfolk, generated by my arrival, seem to have helped to remind them of things they might otherwise have overlooked.

Usually I would speak to a townsman in the large family room of his home. In some cases, only one person was present; more often, however, other members of the family would be listening and adding comments and recollections at appropriate points. After an exchange of pleasantries about the weather, the state of the crops, and my reactions to St. Radegund, I would introduce my professional interest in the Jägerstätter case as an instance of a man "acting alone." I made every effort to avoid imposing, through my comments, either a favorable or unfavorable connotation to Jägerstätter's actions. For this reason, I usually began my interview by asking what kind of man Jägerstätter had been.

The general pattern of response—whether from an intimate friend or from someone who knew the man as a neighbor and fellow parishioner—revealed a remarkably high level of consistency in both content and tone. Slight discrepancies in recollection were nothing more than incidental variations on an underlying theme, and actually served to emphasize its fundamental unity. It is with confidence, then, that these responses can be presented as an accurate reflection of the man as he exists today in the memory of the community to which he belonged. In some respects, that memory may be faulty or misleading and will be subject to the corrections made possible by recourse to his own writings or his more intimate revelations to others, but this does not diminish the importance of the fact that such a community consensus does exist.

Franz Jägerstätter is generally remembered kindly, even lovingly. This does not mean that the villagers were ready to give any significant approval to his actions. Few were willing even to entertain the possibility that he acted as a man in his position should. It is revealing that when I was asked in Vienna, while interviewing someone there about Jägerstätter, how many people in St. Radegund bothered to say an occasional prayer at Jägerstätter's grave, I had to answer, based on my observations during my stay in St. Radegund, that there were only very few, perhaps only two or three. Yet almost everyone I approached began with the unquestionably sincere assertion that he had been a *liaba Mensch* (a wonderful guy) and that his death had been a terrible tragedy.

It is not entirely correct, however, to speak of the man in the singular. From the very first interview, and throughout the entire sequence, it became inescapably clear that the people of St. Radegund knew—and remember—two Jägerstätters: an "early" Franz, and a "new" man, who appeared after a sudden and complete change about the time of his marriage. It was equally clear that it is the early Franz who is more warmly regarded, although the other is remembered for his good qualities, in spite of the misfortune he brought upon himself and his family. Once again, whatever variations were encountered about the change did not disturb the essential unanimity. Some felt the change had not been quite as sudden or as complete as prevailing opinion held it to be, but even such dissenters (for the most part men who had been his closest friends) did not deny that a change had taken place.

Because of this agreement—and especially because of the important bearing this change has upon any attempt to gain a deeper understanding of the man—the "two Jägerstätters" must be considered. The early Franz has been described as something of a rowdy in some of the postwar articles written about him; it has been gently observed that there were times in his youth when he "kicked over the traces," in reference to episodes related by the Radegunders. Such observations, it should be noted, appear in, or are based on, reports of priests who were, understandably, more interested in stressing the high moral dedication of the martyr and in presenting him to their readers as a worthy model for Christians to follow. It is not surprising, then, that they skipped somewhat lightly over the indiscretions of his younger, and wilder, days. For them, the important part of Franz's story lay in the description of the climactic sequence of events culminating in his execution. In this context, the early Jägerstätter was irrelevant—or at most peripheral—to the story; and the more extreme the difference between him and the man who was put to death, the more irrelevant the young Franz would seem.

It is impossible, however, to describe or analyze the community's evaluations of Jägerstätter without reporting in fuller detail a phase in the man's life that plays so large and crucial a part in determining its recollections. The fact that the villagers were willing to talk about the lusty youth's indiscretions should not be construed as an effort on their part to deflate the reputation of the later Jägerstätter as a dedicated Christian. There was no instance in which one might have suspected even the slightest trace of malice or vindictiveness in their reports. They were matter-of-fact references made by people who were interested only in being helpful and co-operative in giving information. It is worth noting, too, that the more serious indiscretions were revealed only by those villagers who had been closest to Franz.

Jägerstätter's draft registration form of April 18, 1939, the only document relating to his case to be found in the Vienna military archives, contained two items that required, and found, clarification in the information of the villagers. The first concerned his own family background. On this form he identified his father as one "Franz Bachmeier, a farmer's son" and reported that he had died in 1915, a casualty of World War I. There was no difficulty at all in obtaining clarification of this, for it was generally known, and reported without the slightest hesitation, that Franz had been an illegitimate child whose mother married Herr Jägerstätter, proprietor of the *Leherbauer* land, in 1917. Since their marriage was without issue, the husband adopted his wife's son and "gave over" the farm to Franz after Franz's marriage in 1936, in the manner prevailing in this part of Austria: that is, parents turn over responsibility for the farm to a son or daughter, who then assumes full status in the community, while the parents themselves live on the farm with the status of *Altenteil* as dependents of the new owner-operator.[1]

None of the townspeople indicated any resentment of Franz

[1] This practice is often a source of tension between the generations. The elders seek to postpone a drastic change in their status as long as possible, while the younger generation is often impatient to take over the farm.

20

because of his illegitimate birth. The only hint of such an attitude was a comment made by the sister of his adoptive father, in which she referred to the adoption as "buying the Jägerstätter name" for the child. However, this statement was made in the context of her explanation that she was the last living representative of the Jägerstätter family line, and was not intended to carry the adverse connotations one might read into it.

In rural Austria the public attitude toward illegitimacy differs somewhat from what it is in the United States; it does not constitute quite as serious a moral scandal. A distinction is made between a child conceived and born out of wedlock, whose natural parents never marry (*unehliche*), and a child whose parents do marry subsequently (*vorehliche*). The latter situation is preferable, obviously, but there are indications that even the former—which would apply to Jägerstätter—is regarded as something to be expected in the normal course of events. Young people have been known to conceive a child as a means of forcing reluctant elders to consent to their marriage and "give over" the family holdings to them. Similarly, mothers have been known to encourage their daughters to engage in premarital intercourse with a particularly desirable young man in the hope of forcing a good marriage. This apparently relaxed sexual morality is limited by the fact that the putative father is generally held to be under obligation to marry the prospective mother and can be subjected to severe community sanctions if he decides to "let the girl sit," that is, not marry her.

Anyone familiar with the patterns of rural humor (or with more sophisticated parodies of rural manners and mores) will have encountered references to this relaxed sex morality, especially as it relates to *Fensterl*-ing. This "window-visiting" practice is a dating-and-courtship pattern in which the young man gets himself a ladder and climbs up to the bedchamber of the girl of his choice. As the local practice was described to me by a St. Radegund man, it is really innocent enough and has its own rules of etiquette. Thus, if one young man is visiting in this fashion (that is, conducting a conversation with the girl at her window while he is perched on a ladder outside) and another young man comes by with similar intentions, the newcomer is free to ask, "Is there room

21

for me up there?" If the girl gives him an affirmative answer, the first caller is supposed to take his ladder and yield the place to the newcomer. Needless to add, this can and frequently does lead to words and other forms of strife between the rivals, if the rules are not promptly and cheerfully obeyed. Should a girl be particularly fond of a young man, she might invite him into her room, but this, too, would be for the purpose of continuing the conversation more comfortably—although, as the villager who told of the practice admitted, it did sometimes happen that the suitor might spend the whole night and that more than conversation might take place. Indeed, if a young man is offended by a girl, one way of "getting even" with her is to place a ladder under her window and go away, letting it be discovered there the following morning with the obvious conclusions to be drawn by anyone so inclined.

I had heard of these practices before my arrival at St. Radegund. A woman operating the pension at which I stayed in Vienna while preparing for this visit learned that I would be spending the summer in the vicinity of Ostermiething. This immediately elicited the warning from her that this was a "God-forsaken region" in which all sorts of unnerving things might happen. She recalled a visit there when she was a young girl. A man was found murdered, she said, for the trifling sum of twenty schillings. Wednesday and Saturday nights were particularly frightening, in that these were the nights for the young men to go *Fensterl*-ing. The whole place was in an uproar then, with dogs barking, parents scolding, and so forth. After more than two months of residence in St. Radegund, I can testify that her description was grossly exaggerated—or, at least, did not apply to that village. Whether this is to be interpreted in terms of an overly active memory, or as evidence of a change in basic courtship-and-dating patterns, or whether she was referring to the moorlands of the Mühlviertel area in the other direction from Ostermiething, I cannot determine.

As it developed from the information of the Radegunders, young Franz had lived for a time in the household of his natural father before being taken to his new home by his mother. There was no satisfactory explanation of why his parents did not marry. Fr. Karobath, the village pastor, advanced the possibility that the father's intentions to marry the mother were circumvented by his death in the war, but this ignores the fact that the boy was already seven or eight years old at the time of his father's death.

Only bits and snatches in my interviews bear upon these early years. As might be expected in so isolated a community, there are rather close kinship ties among the various families. Jägerstätter's proper family name would have been that of his mother, Huber. This is a name as common in the area as "Smith" or "Jones" in the United States. Franz's mother was the sister of Thomas Huber, the father of the two boys (Johann, who still farms in St. Radegund; and Franz, a Viennese attorney) who were the young lad's closest friends. The since deceased priest who preached the sermon at the burial of Franz's ashes in 1946 was a third son of this family. Another of the mother's brothers was the father of Jägerstätter's baptismal godchild. Finally, the former *Burgomeister*, who was Jägerstätter's baptismal sponsor, was also related, though somewhat more distantly, to Franz's mother. This man's son is now the village clerk. These familial relationships were outlined by the pastor, and whatever inaccuracy they might include would be due to faulty note taking. The important point, however, is the fact that such involved kinship ties do exist and not the exact manner in which these particular families and individuals are linked.

One of his closest friends, who also happened to be a relative on the maternal side, described the great influence Franz's maternal grandmother may have had on the youngster. This woman, he recalled, had the reputation of being exceptionally devout and was even known to have spent whole nights outdoors in prayer before one of the many roadside shrines. At the time young Franz lived in her home, a cousin who was later to become an active leader in the *Bibelforscher* sect lived with them. This villager felt that this relationship was to prove significant in two ways. First, it was the basis for a close association between the two cousins in their later lives. More important, he felt the grandmother's intense religiosity was reflected in the fact that both boys were later to go to religious extremes—Jägerstätter carrying his Catholicism to the point of martyrdom; the other involving himself actively in an "heretical" religious group.

23

Other memories of his boyhood years focused principally on his performance at the local school, and here there were differences of opinion. Among his former schoolmates, some rated him as "ordinary" or, as one woman put it, a diligent but not outstanding student. Another classmate, who has since left the community to practice law in Vienna (and who, it may be assumed, can look back with the added perspective furnished by his own advanced education), remembered Franz as being "better than average" and also as an avid reader. This latter fact becomes significant in the later Jägerstätter whose extensive reading of spiritual and devotional material presumably played a determining role in the formation of his conscience with regard to Nazism and its wars. Finally, a man who had been a next-door neighbor of Jägerstätter's from the days when they were schoolboys until the time of his arrest, stated that Franz had not been so much given to reading as a boy as he was in his later life, but that he was, nonetheless, an exceptionally good student.

Official school records both support and clarify the general impression left by these recollections of Franz's former schoolmates. The reports covering the boy's attendance at the St. Radegund school for the period from May 1, 1913, to May 20, 1921 (apparently terminating, as permitted by law, with his fourteenth birthday), grade his performances as "Good" in the following subjects: German language, Geography and History, Drawing, Writing, Singing, and Gymnastics. He was graded "Very Good" in Religion, Reading, Arithmetic, and Natural History. Conduct and deportment were rated "worthy of praise," whereas his application and effort were rated merely "Satisfactory." Finally, the "external form, or appearance, of his written work" was described as *gefällig* —apparently a slightly stronger than "Satisfactory" grade. It is clear from this, then, that he was a better than average student with some special strength in areas such as Reading and Religion, a fact which his schoolmates also stressed and which bears an obvious and direct relevance to the events of his later life with which we are concerned here.

It is the Franz of early manhood who emerges with sharpest clarity from the combined interviews of the townspeople. A great variety of affectionate terms describing a jolly, robust, fun-loving, hot-blooded, "he-man" type, such as *lustiger Bursche, kreuzfideler Kerl, lebenslustiger Mensch,* were advanced to describe the well-liked young man. Several people added the phrase "the way most young men are," to indicate that these characteristics were not carried to unusual extremes. On the other hand, two or three townspeople clearly indicated that he may indeed have been a little wilder than the general run of young men, although such observations were made in a tone of fond remembrance. Other characteristics, mentioned less often, were his intelligence, his bull-headedness (a family trait of the maternal Huber line, one villager was quick to add), and his tendency to be "ahead of the crowd" in his interests and in his desire to be first to try something new. Those friends who had known him best confirmed and amplified this general description by calling him "a little wild in his ways and in his style of living," always "ready for a fight," a young man who liked roughhousing and "had his weaknesses" (as everyone does, one very close friend added).

These characteristics were further emphasized in the recollections of his activities. His reputation as a dedicated and very proficient bowler and sportsman, his passion for dancing and card-playing, and his liking for girls were all described and, in many cases, elaborated upon for my benefit. One elderly woman, to make sure that I got the point, went through the pantomime of bowling, dancing, and fighting in her description of his interests. Perhaps the single item most frequently stressed was the fact that he brought the first motorcycle to the community; it was quite clear that this event holds an important place in the memories of his former friends and neighbors as evidence of his personal daring and his *fortschrittlich* ("progressive") tendencies. The neighbor whose wife happened to see Jägerstätter as he took final leave of the community recalled that the young man often left home for brief spells without telling anyone where he was going. Some of these visits may have been to places like Salzburg. At any rate, one St. Radegund woman who lived in Salzburg for a ten-year period remembered that Franz would occasionally drop in to visit for fun and conversation. She, too, remembered him somewhat wistfully as a gay young man at dances, harvest festivals, and similar social events.

An even livelier note was offered by an older member of the community who recalled the time when a neighbor's wife begged him for help in persuading the young man to be a little less ardent and insistent in the attentions he was paying her daughter. It seems that the rowdiness and disturbance associated with these attentions knew no bounds, regardless of how late the hour might be. This incident, it should be noted, was offered as illustration of what a fine fellow the young Franz had been.

Young Jägerstätter's religious behavior appeared to follow the normal pattern for boys of his age and station. Certainly there was nothing to foreshadow the sexton of later years or to give a hint of the intense commitment found in the writings the condemned man was to leave behind. Everyone hastened to point out, of course, that he was not "irreligious," that he attended Mass regularly and fulfilled his other religious obligations as well. In the light of later developments, another incident apparently stemming from this early period may be of special significance. It seems that Pastor Karobath's predecessor once instituted a program of adult religious instruction in the schoolhouse, and Jägerstätter attended these classes. He is reported to have raised a question concerning the possibility of other children having been born to the mother of Jesus, and he proceeded to justify his inquiry by quoting some biblical texts. As the incident was recalled, the priest was somewhat embarrassed by the insistent character of the young man's questions and finally terminated the discussion by asserting that there were some things a priest was not supposed to explain. (The instruction classes came to an abrupt end a short time thereafter, I was told.) Since Pastor Karobath assumed his St. Radegund post in 1934, the incident obviously relates to Jägerstätter's early life. Two aspects of this incident deserve special note. First, the question reveals an interest in religious matters on the part of the young man; indeed, his very attendance must be taken as a sign of such interest. Second, a tendency toward independent confrontation of religious issues is indicated even before the great change which was to bring Franz to the point of total dedication to the ascetic ideal of Christianity.

One villager, who had been a close friend of Franz, remarked that Franz had a "following" in his ever-present readiness for a fight. A similar implication can be found in the recollection of a local woman that he had the reputation of being one of the most accomplished fighters in town in the frequent battles with the young fellows (Burschen) of neighboring villages. This distinction of his probably related to his activities as a member of a "gang" consisting of the unmarried young men in the village at that time. Such groups are not uncommon in the rural communities of the area. They are known to have their own social codes, complete with informal means of punishing a deviant individual or family, whom they usually torment on special holidays when everyone is permitted to let his hair down. These gangs of young men are always ready to defend the honor of their village in battles with their counterparts in neighboring communities. The woman who had remembered Jägerstätter as a good fighter spoke of terrible brawls that then took place between young men from St. Radegund and from the slightly larger village of Tarsdorf, a few miles away. Such groups of youths also often assume the right to punish any violator of community mores—such as a man who gets a girl pregnant and then "lets her sit," or an elderly widower who marries a girl considered too young for him.

Gang activities such as these reportedly continued as late as the early years following World War II, but have since subsided to a point approaching insignificance. One explanation advanced for their decline was the fact that the popularity of organized soccer leagues has displaced them (an interesting confirmation of William James's proposal to institute such games as an alternative to war). A grim reminder of the heyday of this type of gang warfare can be found in the display of gang weapons at the Heimat Museum in Braunau. An assortment of heavy chains, thick leather thongs filled with sand and edged with knife blades, etc., equals the weaponry associated with the most fearsome street gangs of the modern American metropolis. Incidentally, an interesting sidelight to my trip to the museum in Braunau occurred while speaking to the

27

curator. It developed that he was a native of Mrs. Jägerstätter's home village. When I described the research in which I was engaged, he said he had known her husband, at least by name. He was shocked (*erschüttert* was the word he used) to learn from me the manner and cause of the man's death. He had "heard" that Jägerstätter had "fallen" in battle.

The fact that young Franz is reputed to have been so accomplished and enthusiastic a fighter, coupled with occasional references to the personal following he had among the other young men of St. Radegund, seems to indicate that he took a prominent part in the gang activities of his time. Further evidence of this association may be found in an escapade recalled by a man who was perhaps Franz's closest companion in those youthful days. In 1934 the *Heimwehr*, originally an unofficial home guard, which later became quasi-official in defending border areas such as the vicinity of St. Radegund, earned the displeasure of the local *Burschen*. This displeasure was partly due to the *Heimwehr* members being outsiders, but it was compounded when they began competing for the attention of the local girls. The situation led to a pitched battle in which Jägerstätter and his friend participated prominently, and for which they were both arrested. The friend recalls that they were obliged to pay a fifty-schilling fine for this escapade; Jägerstätter's widow reported that her husband told her that this affair had led to his imprisonment for a few days.

His involvement, indeed his leadership, in the gang activities of this period is undoubtedly also related to an intriguing episode which was to lead to his temporary exile from St. Radegund. Unfortunately, the whole affair is surrounded by confusion and mystery. The only thing known for certain is that the young man spent several years—the actual length of time could not be determined—working in the iron mines of the Steiermark area. That his absence was imposed on him was fairly well established in the course of my interviews with the townsmen, although two or three claimed that it was a voluntary and not an imposed exile. These assured me that he merely left for a time, because there were enough hands to do the farm work, and Franz wanted to earn some cash. The famous first motorcycle came into the picture again, for it was the cash he earned during his absence that enabled him to buy it and introduce it to the community upon his return.

The weight of the evidence, however, as well as the aura of mystery surrounding his period of absence, argue against this minority interpretation. Two of those who hold this view may actually have been far enough removed so as not to know the full story: one was a farmer whose land lies in a somewhat detached section of the community; the other was the woman who was living in Salzburg at the time. The third who denied the "exile" implications was a schoolmate of Jägerstätter's and one of the few residents who were observed to give a sign of remembrance or respect at his grave. She might be inclined to hold back on this affair in order to protect a departed friend's reputation. Or, since she is related to the family that had been involved in a dispute with the Jägerstätters which was also advanced as one of the possible causes of the exile, there might be other personal bases for her reticence.

On the other hand, those who stress the involuntary aspect of his temporary departure from town have the advantage of being in a position where they would know more. Some were Franz's close friends; others were men of position in the community. That his exile was serious may be gathered from the fact that although he did occasionally visit his home, he always did so stealthily—arriving at night and leaving early in the morning before his presence could be noticed. This information was furnished by a neighbor who apparently maintained a friendly relationship with Jägerstätter's mother; she could not, or perhaps would not, give any better explanation for the young man's exile than to say he had gotten himself into "some trouble."

One of the more specific versions of the "trouble" had to do with a fight between families over a woodland boundary. It was said that Jägerstätter had cut down a tree on the other family's property, a frequent but not insignificant cause for conflict when there is a community division of woodland rights. The resulting controversy grew so intense that a "cooling-off" period was necessary, and this was the occasion for the young man's departure to the iron mines. This story was offered by a close friend of Jäger-stätter and should, therefore, be reliable. However, when the question was put to a member of the family who was supposedly the wronged party, the whole affair was dismissed as unimportant. Furthermore, she added, the elder Jägerstätter, not Franz, cut down the tree in question.

Another of the young man's former close friends could only say that the trouble centered on some kind of a fight over a girl—one man admitted that he "just assumed" this was the case. A more detailed explanation was given by an older man who said that Franz and another local boy had argued over a girl. Both young men, as he described the situation, could claim a substantial personal following, and what began as an argument between the two of them soon expanded into a kind of civil war in which anyone who was friendly with someone on one side was automatically regarded as an enemy by those on the other side. Both boys' families got involved, and it was finally decided that the only solution would be for the two boys to leave and stay away from the village for a while. This was done, he said, and both ultimately returned after the affair cooled down. Unfortunately, the other participant, like Franz, has since died, making it impossible to obtain a firsthand report on the controversy or its cause.

A clue to the whole affair may lie in a cryptic second entry on the 1939 *Wehrstammblatt*, Franz's military registration form. In completing his answers to that document, Jägerstätter reported himself as the father of three children, whereas the youngest of his three daughters was not born until May, 1940. A quite unexpected clarification of this discrepancy came in the course of my first formally scheduled visit at St. Radegund, in which an almost casual reference was made to the fact that Franz had fathered an illegitimate child. Indeed, the information was so casually given that it was necessary to check back to see whether the person I had been talking to had said that young Franz had *been* an illegitimate child (something already known to me) or had *had* one.

An interesting pattern developed. Every person who volunteered information concerning Franz's illegitimate child was someone who had been close to Jägerstätter. One man even began his description of his old friend by saying, "Well, of course, he had an illegitimate child"—and then went on to express his personal doubts that Franz had been the father. A former friend, who still can be occasionally observed helping with some of the heavier work on the Jägerstätter farm, referred to Franz having had "his weaknesses" like everyone else, and then responded to a further probe by volunteering the information about the child to illustrate what he meant by "weakness." Even the friend who had explained the exile in terms of the controversy over a tree once made some rather obscure reference in the course of a group conversation to certain youthful activities, which seemed to indicate this particular indiscretion. During a later conversation, at which this same friend was present, he interrupted my reference to the illegitimate child by insisting that although it was true that Franz had paid support money, he really had not been the father.

Interestingly, although all who discussed the matter assured me that it was common knowledge in St. Radegund, none of those who had not been particularly close to Franz volunteered any information about the child. A few did respond to my intentionally indirect probes, but even these responses tended to be marked by cautious restraint. One man admitted knowing the story, but he added that the affair had never been legally adjudicated and that whatever payments Franz made to support the child were voluntary. In another instance the question of the child was raised when I tried to elicit a townswoman's description of the community's judgment of Jägerstätter and his actions, with particular reference to a remark that the man may have been a saint. Some people, this woman replied, felt that this youthful offense was enough to exclude such a possibility; however, she (with the agreement of her husband, who was present) felt this was not necessarily true, that there had been many saints who had done far worse things in their youth. Both she and her husband admitted that the affair was a matter of general knowledge, though they were not sure if the Jägerstätter daughters knew the story. Mrs. Jägerstätter told me later that they did, adding that "of course" they had not learned it from her.

No attempt was made to check the truth of Jägerstätter's alleged paternity, even assuming the unlikely possibility that such an attempt could have been successful. The testimony of his close friends seems conclusive evidence that even if—as at least two of them maintained—he had not actually fathered the child, the possibility of such paternity was consistent with the behavior of the "early" Jägerstätter as they had known him. The fact—confirmed by Jägerstätter's widow and by a reference in one of his prison letters—that he had made financial contributions to the support of the child would also seem to be conclusive.

The incident is important because it throws some light on the mystery surrounding the young man's exile from the community. The child was born in 1934, which, according to most accounts, would place the event in or near the period of Franz's exile. Unfortunately, there was some indefiniteness and variation about the date and the period of exile, a fact which makes a more definite conclusion impossible. If this is the case, however, the "trouble" may well have been a matter of challenged paternity—or an effort on the part of some of the local *Burschen* under a rival's leadership to "punish" him for "letting a girl sit."

Some may feel that this whole affair is so peripheral to the principal focus of interest in Jägerstätter's history that it should not have been included, that doing so has given unnecessary exposure to the youthful indiscretion of a heroic man. But to omit so significant an episode in the past life of the man, merely to avoid tarnishing an otherwise shining image, would be a betrayal of integrity and objectivity. More important is the very fact that such a thing could happen: that a young man whose weaknesses had earned him a reputation for wildness could discover within himself the spiritual insight and moral commitment that would lead him to the executioner's block.

Later in life, Jägerstätter was to give evidence of regret for his past. The woman neighbor who had been close to his mother recalled once hearing an exchange between mother and son in which she complained that he had changed so much she found it hard to communicate with him. He replied by asking her if she would really be happier "if I were the way I used to be." Some further hints of his own evaluation of his past—and by that same token, confirmation of the community's recollections—can be seen in some of his writings. From time to time, he would argue a point in the framework of an almost puritanical sex morality. In his second commentary, written in St. Radegund before his fateful decision, he draws an extended parallel between Austria's unwillingness to take the risk of breaking her tie with an immoral Nazi regime and **a still halfway decent girl who has fallen under the spell of an adventurer** interested only in seduction, but who finds it difficult to make the sacrifice a total break would involve. **Such a girl, he declares, can pray day and night and still not have her prayers heard until she ends the relationship; and she may not shrink back from any hardship even if he should threaten to kill her or ruin her reputation.**[2] Other references to abortion and contraception as crimes inviting a horrible judgment upon German culture appear later in the same commentary, and may be further indication of an attitude which was, in part, a reflection of contrition for his own past.

Dissatisfaction with his past is also expressed in one of his farewell messages in these words: **I can say from my own experience how painful life often is when one lives as a halfway Christian; it is more like vegetating than living.** But the most explicit statement in this regard is to be found in the lengthy letter he wrote to his godchild. This letter, undated but seemingly written in 1936, was an effort on Jägerstätter's part to take the place of the boy's dead father in providing the spiritual counsel a boy of fifteen or sixteen would need. He notes that youngsters of that age are often reported to have committed suicide because of disappointments in love and he wryly adds, **It would be more accurate if these reports were to say these acts were also rooted in [lack of] faith; for if it were true that disappointment in love is a prime cause of suicide, few people would reach the age of thirty.**

He continues by stressing the value of giving children sound instruction in the truths of their faith, and the grave harm done when they are deprived of this needed direction. **Soon, he warns, you, too, will be experiencing the storms of youth—if you have**

---

[2] Throughout this and succeeding chapters, whenever direct quotations from Jägerstätter's writings are introduced, they will appear in boldface type.

not already felt them—since in this respect we humans are not all the same. To some they come sooner, to others later; to some they burst forth in full fury, while to others the onset is weak. Should it be that temptation is ever so strong that you feel you must give in to sin, give some thought then to eternity. For it often happens that a man risks his temporal and eternal happiness for a few seconds of pleasure. No one can know whether he will ever again have an opportunity to confess or if God will give him the grace to repent of his sin. Death can surprise us at any minute, and in an accident one very seldom has time enough to awaken repentance and sorrow. This much I can tell you from my own experience.

The bulk of the letter is a sermon on temptation and sins against the Sixth Commandment. It is a moving document in many respects, especially when one reads it in the context of its author's own reputation as a young man. Still speaking in terms of the need to rise above the taunts and ridicule one might have to endure for living chastely and refusing to go along with others in sowing wild oats, he moves on to a discussion that foreshadows his own future. He suggests that maybe the punishing hand of God is already far nearer to us than we expect.

Therefore, we must do everything in our power to strive toward the Eternal Homeland and to preserve a good conscience. Then, even if our enemies attack us and even if they are armed, they will not be able to tear us away from this Homeland. Though we must bear our daily sorrows and reap little reward in this world for doing so, we can still become richer than millionaires—for those who need not fear death are the richest and happiest of all. And these riches are there for the asking.

Or again: Since the death of Christ, almost every century has seen the persecution of Christians; there have always been heroes and martyrs who gave their lives—often in horrible ways—for Christ and their faith. If we hope to reach our goal some day, then we, too, must become heroes of the faith. For as long as we fear men more than God, we will never make the grade. O this cowardly fear of men! Because of a few jeering words spoken by our neighbor, all our good intentions are thrown overboard. Of course, even the most courageous and best Christians can and will fall, but they will not lie for long in the filth of sin. Instead they will pull themselves together and draw new strength from the sacraments of Penance and Holy Communion and strive on to their goal. And should anxious days come upon us when we feel we are being crushed under the weight of our troubles, let us remember that God burdens none of us with a heavier cross than he can bear.

The "New" Man

The quotations from the letter to his godchild may have put us too far ahead in telling the Jägerstätter story. For unless we can dismiss his sentiments as nothing more than the platitudinous moralizings of a hypocrite, these few lines suggest that we are no longer dealing with the "early" Jägerstätter but rather with a second and altogether new man.

As the story was told by those who knew him, a sudden and total change came over Franz Jägerstätter. Only one villager and some of the people who had been his closest friends did not completely agree, but the area of disagreement related only to the pace of the great change; they recalled it as more gradual. Except for these few dissenters, most of the recollections concerning the alteration in Franz described it in such phrases as "so sudden that people just couldn't understand it," "from one extreme to the other," and "it was almost as if he had been possessed by a higher power."

As far as the direction and content of this change are concerned, there was complete agreement. But there were some variations in the explanations offered, and these variations may provide some important clues to the extent to which "the Jägerstätter myth"— that is, the man as he is remembered in the community—may fall short of the reality. For most of the villagers, and even most of his closest friends, the event which brought about the difference in Franz was his marriage in 1936 and his honeymoon trip to Rome, in the course of which the newlyweds received the papal blessing in a public audience. Some people felt that Franz had been so impressed by seeing the pope that he decided then and there to reform his ways completely; however, the townspeople generally stressed the marriage itself. For them, the critical element was the intense religiosity of the woman he chose to marry. More than one person told me that she had always been exceptionally devout and had intended to enter the religious life before her marriage to Franz— a belief, incidentally, that was not confirmed in my interviews with the widow. One man who offered many cautious reservations, since he had been away from St. Radegund during these years, even remarked that when people had described the change that had taken place in Jägerstätter, they all believed that Mrs. Jägerstätter had much to do with it—an explanation he was obviously willing to accept.

This is not just a matter of acknowledging the influence of a good woman in the reformation of a wild youth, for this explanation must be seen in the context of what was to follow and how those events are looked upon by the community. In a very real sense, this explanation of the change, to the extent that it is a *causal* explanation (as it is in the minds of most who accept it), may be converted into a charge that the widow is to be held responsible for the later tragic developments in the Jägerstätter story. His new religiosity is viewed as having led him to the "fanaticism" which brought about his death. To the extent that the belief is held—and it is widely held in the community—that Jägerstätter's actions were a sign of mental derangement, this attributing the change in him to his wife's influence could mask an element of animosity, probably unconscious, toward her. An example of this may be found in the frequently heard observation that she made no real effort to get her husband to alter his final decision and accept military service, a statement she took pains to deny when I spoke to her. It would be wrong to magnify this possibility of latent hostility. Just as there were no openly vindictive or malicious judgments passed on Franz by the persons interviewed, so, too, there were no openly adverse or un-favorable comments voiced about his widow. The references to her religiosity, even to her presumed influence on her husband, were always highly complimentary. Nevertheless, the effect of these opinions was to give her a major share of the responsibility for a change which did not meet with community approval, and for the results of that change, which are regarded as a senseless tragedy.

Two bits of evidence would seem to disprove the explanation of the change in Franz in terms of his marriage. The first, and most explicit, is Fr. Karobath's information that Jägerstätter had previously indicated a desire to enter a religious order. The priest had counseled against this step by pointing out that the young man had an obligation to his parents to take over the operation of the farm. This obviously indicates that some change had already taken place before his marriage, probably before he had even considered marriage or met the girl who was to become his wife.

The other evidence is found, of course, in the letter to his godchild. It is not dated, but the recipient remembers that it came when he was sixteen. If he is correct, the letter would have been written in 1936, the year of Jägerstätter's wedding. But the failure to mention this event—or to refer to the trip to Rome and the experience of seeing the pope—clearly indicates that it must have been written before these events took place. Yet the tone of the excerpts quoted from this letter shows that the change had already taken place.

This puts things in quite a different light. For one thing, it would now be permissible to explain his choice of a bride in terms of his recognition of characteristics in her that would be in keeping with his new spiritual outlook. This could still mean that it was his marriage which brought the *visible* change in his behavior: His marriage to a woman of like mind and equal depth of moral commitment would have provided him with the kind of support that would make it easier for him to reveal in his external behavior the interior change that had already taken place. The same is true of the trip to Rome. A Viennese woman who had been a regular visitor to St. Radegund at the time remembered being shown the honeymoon photographs taken in the Eternal City. She had been most impressed by the fact that an ordinary peasant from a remote rural village should even have had the idea of making such a journey. At that time, she told me, even the more sophisticated city dwellers were rarely given to foreign travel. She chose this incident to illustrate the independence of thought and interests that had characterized the man. But in the present context, another aspect may be of equal importance: the fact that he chose Rome for the visit at a time when such a trip was most unusual would testify to a very special interest in that place as the center of the religion to which his bride and he were so deeply devoted. If this were the case, the opportunity to see the pope and receive his blessing in a general audience would be another expression of a commitment he had already reached, and not the occasion of a conversion.

How and when did the change take place? This is a question that is crucial to the understanding of Jägerstätter's motivations, yet the best that can be done is to offer an alternative explanation, which seems to fit the facts, but which, unfortunately, cannot definitely be established. This hypothetical explanation relates the change to the incident involving the illegitimate child and the period of exile that followed. This might well have been the event which shocked the relatively wild youth into a personal conviction of sin and forced him into a totally new confrontation with Christianity as it affects one's moral obligations. This hypothesis seems to explain the tone of the letter to his godson. Jägerstätter's next-door neighbor, a boyhood chum with whom he had always had an extremely close relationship, does not subscribe to the theory that Franz's marriage explained the change in him. He says he had already noticed that Franz was much more religious when he returned from work in the iron mines. He "guessed" that this would have been in late 1934 or 1935, a date entirely in keeping with the suggestion offered here that the illegitimate child, the exile from St. Radegund, and the subsequent emergence of a "new" Jägerstätter are intimately linked.

The villagers' memories of the changed man emphasize two major points: his intense and open religiosity and his thoroughgoing opposition to the Nazi regime. These two characteristics of his later thought and behavior are so closely interwoven that it is sometimes difficult to treat them separately. The only discrepancies encountered in the descriptions of the "new" Jägerstätter involve the intensity of these two factors and some of the specific examples that were offered to illustrate them.

These discrepancies relate primarily to the religious fanaticism attributed to him by many—perhaps the great majority—of the villagers. There was, for example, the matter of his singing hymns while he worked or while on his way to and from the parish church. Several villagers mentioned this practice, and others went further than this by "remembering" that he could sometimes be observed saying the rosary while plowing—or even interrupting his farm work to say a few prayers or read a bit in the Bible. One man, who would have been a boy of eight at the time, told how Franz sang hymns while tending the cattle in the communal pasture, and then went on to add that he had even been known to object to mowing the fields because he would be "killing God's flowers" in the process. An outsider, but a regular visitor to the village, had "heard" the same story, with the added touch that the man had even gone so far as to "pray to the flowers." It is safe to say that the last two accounts were based on hearsay and had undoubtedly suffered some distortion and exaggeration by the time they were repeated. However, even though Mrs. Jägerstätter denied that her husband was given to such religious practices while at work, the young man who was Jägerstätter's godchild—and who apparently had been something of a protégé—confirmed that he had sometimes sung hymns in the fields. He could not recall any instances of his praying there, however.

Other illustrations of his purported extremism related to acts of self-denial and self-discipline. It seems quite clear, for instance, that he stopped playing cards and gave up certain other diversions which had given him pleasure as a youth. One neighbor told of an incident in which Franz, invited to join in a game of cards, refused, with the explanation that "gambling is a vice"; he was willing to join the game only after he was assured that they would not play for money. A similar story was related by the young priest who had replaced Fr. Karobath during the period of his exile: two priests had been visiting him and a fourth was needed for a game. Although the vicar knew that his sexton had given up such games, he asked Franz to play, and Jägerstätter agreed because he knew it would give the priests some pleasure.

It appears, too, that Franz did stop visiting the local inns, although the proprietor of one of them said he still continued to drop by for a drink or two from time to time. The villagers interpret this to mean that he had also given up alcoholic beverages. Here, again, we may have a matter of a false, but understandable, misinterpretation of the man's behavior. When Mrs. Jägerstätter was asked about this, she denied that her husband had become a teetotaler; he still continued to make and drink *Most*, a kind of strong cider, at home. His visits to the taverns stopped, she said, but this was so that he might avoid becoming involved in the political arguments that were sure to develop if he went there. This explanation was confirmed by the former wife of the *Bibelforscher* cousin; she and her husband had, in fact, followed Franz's example because their appearance usually set off a religious discussion that all too frequently led to open controversy.

Two other forms of self-denial deserve mention here. The first relates to Jägerstätter's practice of fasting. Dean Kreuzberg, who had been chaplain of the Berlin-Tegel prison where Jägerstätter was confined for a period of three months, referred to his long and intensely contemplative prayers, and added that "he took penances and fastings upon himself and implored heaven for enlightenment and strength." According to a neighbor, it was Jägerstätter's practice, after he had begun to receive Holy Communion daily, to fast until noon every day as a special mark of respect for the Sacrament he had received at the morning service. Since the normal meal schedule for peasant families begins with a small breakfast at 5:30 A.M. or so, and is followed by a more substantial second breakfast at 9:00, such a pattern of fasting would involve a rather substantial sacrifice.

The other item concerns the practice of charity. An elderly woman recalled that in the trying years of the war, Jägerstätter would pack a knapsack with foodstuffs and meats and quietly distribute these to the poor of the area—even though, she added, he and his family did not have too much themselves and tended to live simply, almost, in fact, in poverty. This story was confirmed by his widow, who added that he did this because "he believed in it." This has a striking relevance to the brief aside in his second commentary written in St. Radegund sometime before his arrest. After stating the obligation of the Christian who would still be saved immediately [to] dissociate himself from the Nazi Folk Community and make no further contributions to it, he adds: Anyone who wishes to practice Christian charity in his deeds can manage to provide the poor with something for their sustenance without the WHW [Winter Relief Collection] or VWF [People's Welfare Fund].

It is, however, in his intense devotion and dedication to the Church that we find the most telling evidence of the change in the man. There is an intriguing disparity between stories told by Fr. Karobath and Franz's widow. Pastor Karobath insists that Franz made regular pilgrimages to the Altötting shrine before he indicated a desire to become a lay brother; the widow, however, insists that his first visit there took place after their marriage. Whichever is the correct version (and I incline to favor the pastor's account in this instance), it is certain that regular and frequent visits to this pilgrimage center in nearby Bavaria did take place throughout their married life, husband and wife going together on the famous motorcycle. One villager also made the point that Jägerstätter made the pilgrimage (probably a 20- to 30-mile trip) on foot, just before his refusal to serve in the army.

One of Franz's "closest friends" remembered getting a ride from Jägerstätter to a garage some distance away in Bavaria to pick up his own motorcycle, which had undergone some repairs. They passed no church on the route, he recalled, without stopping so that Franz could go inside to look around and say a few prayers. He described this trip to show the contrast with the "early" Jägerstätter who, he insisted, was an average and regular churchgoer but was by no means exceptionally religious.

This the "new" Jägerstätter certainly was. The clearest evidence, of course, is his activities with respect to his home parish. He became sexton sometime in 1940, holding that post until his final departure from the community. Indeed, in view of the instructions and encouragement contained in some of his prison letters, it appears that Mrs. Jägerstätter continued for a time to act as his proxy.

At the time Jägerstätter assumed these responsibilities, his friend and regular pastor had been removed from the community by official order. His replacement as vicar, a young priest named Fürthauer, was to have the immediate responsibility of dealing with the practical and spiritual aspects of the problem Jägerstätter and his rebellion were to raise. It is difficult to calculate the full effect this change in personnel had upon later events, but certain impressions gained in the community interviews would suggest the intriguing possibility that events might have taken a somewhat different course had another priest been on the scene. It is felt, in retrospect, that the young vicar was not too well qualified to meet so unusual a challenge. First of all, his youth and the fact that he was a newcomer to the community—and, undoubtedly a major consideration to a man of Jägerstätter's political inclinations, that he had come as a replacement for the exiled pastor—put him at a serious disadvantage from the very beginning. The general consensus seems to have been that his intellectual capacity was unimpressive and that he had no overwhelming sense of commitment to his job. In addition, the reservations the parishioners had as far as their new pastor was concerned were greatly intensified by the low regard of the community for his sister, who had come along to serve as his housekeeper and who is still the object of very critical comments regarding her performance in that job.

I spoke with this priest at a village rectory some distance from St. Radegund, where he now serves as house chaplain to a nobleman. The two hours or more spent with him did not reveal any of the failings which had been intimated. He was cautious and evidently disinclined to volunteer information not specifically requested, but this did not obstruct the flow of conversation or limit the value of the information he gave.

As he remembered it, Jägerstätter was away from the village (presumably during an earlier period of military training) at the time of his arrival in St. Radegund. Shortly thereafter, the man who had been serving as sexton became ill and died. When Jägerstätter returned and began to attend Mass and receive Holy Communion daily—and Fr. Fürthauer put great stress on the word *daily*—the young vicar decided to ask him if he would be willing to take over the vacant post. Since Jägerstätter did not know any of the Latin prayers, he had to learn them all by heart, and he did so in what the priest described as an amazingly short time. But before he would take over the job, Jägerstätter asked his predecessor's daughter, who had been filling in since her father's death, if she had any objection. Although he had not known him then, the priest was able to refer to his sexton's "wild" past. This information was apparently based on hearsay, for he was most scrupulous throughout our interview not to reveal anything that might involve his obligation to keep silent about what he might have learned in the confessional. But for the whole period of their personal relationship, he added, Jägerstätter was a thoroughly devout man, an exemplary Christian. Franz was not given to idle talk, nor would he speak ill of others, unless such opinions stemmed from his political opposition to the Nazis. He had already foresworn mundane pleasures, and it was in this connection that he mentioned the exception Franz made when he had agreed to join the card game with Fr. Fürthauer and two visiting priests.

Asked whether he would have characterized Jägerstätter's religiosity as excessive, he insisted that the contrary was true, that the man had been thoroughly sound in his approach to religious matters. To support this evaluation, he offered several incidents which, he felt, would illustrate the depth and the orthodoxy of the peasant's religious commitment. They also shed considerable light upon the relationship between the vicar and his sexton. For one thing, Jägerstätter objected strongly to people talking and gossiping in the sacristy, and he made a hard and fast rule that anyone who did not belong there had to stay out. This is reminiscent of stories told by others in the community of how Franz used to close the doors as soon as Mass started so that latecomers would have to face the embarrassment of being let in separately.

Two other incidents concern more serious matters and relate more closely to later events. Jägerstätter once told the priest that he ought to preach more about the sufferings to be endured in purgatory, and call for a greater striving for perfection on the part of his parishioners so that they might learn that the lesser and temporary tortures of purgatory should also be avoided as far as possible. The suggestion, Fürthauer added, was followed. The second incident involved the burial of a soldier, at which Fürthauer officiated and preached a little sermon stressing the heroism and valor displayed by the deceased in giving his life for the Fatherland. Afterwards he was approached by his sexton, who chided him for being so ceremonious (*festlich*) in lauding the virtues of the military life, and reminded him that this life brought with it many occasions of sin for soldiers, particularly the younger ones.

This readiness to criticize and make recommendations about the spiritual life of the parish shows that Jägerstätter's view of his involvement went far deeper than merely attending to the physical care of church buildings, assisting in the services, keeping unruly altar boys under strict control, and assuming some organizational tasks. His involvement appears to have been recognized and is still remembered by Fürthauer and the parishioners; none of them failed to credit him with being a thoroughly dedicated sexton who had done his work exceptionally well. In recognition of his devotion to his church, a marble marker on his grave identifies him as both "*Leherbauer* and sexton." *Leherbauer* is the name by which Jägerstätter is best known and remembered in the community. In the rural areas of Upper Austria, the practice is for the owner of a piece of farmland to be known by the name given to the land. In this way, it passes on from generation to generation with the owner-occupants always known by the same name, even though the actual familial name may change many times, for lack of male issue or some other reason. Thus today, Jägerstätter's widow has turned ownership of the farm over to her eldest daughter and her husband; the new owners bear the husband's family name, but he will henceforth be known as *Leherbauer*, just as Jägerstätter was known in his lifetime.

Many evidences of the impressive religiosity of the "new" Jägerstätter relate more specifically to the period after he had made his refusal to serve in the army, or to the grounds on which he made that refusal, and will be treated later. One final item, though, belongs here, because, in the minds of the people of St. Radegund it seems to be one of the most striking memories of the man as sexton. It is customary, I was told, for mourners to arrange for prayers to be said for departed relatives or friends, and for a stipend to be left with the sexton and kept by him as compensation for making the

45

necessary arrangements. Jägerstätter, however, refused to accept these donations and made a practice, moreover, of not only leading the prayers, as would be expected, but joining in as one of the bereaved. It was rare when one began to ask about Jägerstätter as sexton that this practice was not mentioned as a prime example of his sincerity and dedication.

The second note which characterized the change from the "early" to the "new" Jägerstätter was, again, his total opposition to the Nazi regime and its policies. It was an outspoken opposition, surprisingly so if one considers the penalties that could, and often did, follow any expression of criticism or opposition. The fact that Franz stopped going to the local inns because he expected to get into political arguments suggests that this had often occurred. The townspeople were unwilling to indicate that they had supported the Nazis in such arguments, but even if inner opposition to the regime was as widespread as is claimed now, it must have been trying to be continually reminded by someone like Jägerstätter that such inner opposition should have outward expression too. Not everyone could be expected to imitate Jägerstätter in responding "Pfui Hitler!" whenever he was greeted by the usual "Heil Hitler!" But one may take it for granted that some of the disillusionment expressed throughout Jägerstätter's commentaries about the unwillingness on the part of Austrian Catholics to dissociate themselves from Nazi policies and programs must have been inspired by experiences in his own little community.

Jägerstätter's opposition began even before the Nazi troops crossed the Austrian border. The elderly former *Burgomeister*, who had been replaced by the Nazis, and had then resumed his position under the postwar Occupation, remembered Jägerstätter's annoyance with Chancellor Schuschnigg for his attempt to come to terms with Hitler. This same *Burgomeister* had been head of the local segment of a powerful peasants' organization, the *Bauernbund*, and he recalls that Franz threatened to withdraw from the organization if it were to weaken in its opposition to the Nazi movement—a threat he carried out when it did. This protest resignation was mentioned in the course of other interviews as well, an indication that it did constitute a significant action in the eyes of the community.

On March 11, 1938, the forces of Adolf Hitler crossed the border and occupied Austria; two days later, Austria was incorporated into *Grossdeutschland*, and on April 10, the plebiscite was held which gave approval to this *fait accompli* by majorities approaching unanimity. This was, without question, one of the darkest days in Jägerstätter's life. Not only did he see his fellow citizens **voluntarily capitulate to the National Socialists**, as he was to describe the event four years later, but he even had to witness how the *Anschluss* with Germany was approved and supported by the leaders of the Catholic Church in Austria. Admitting that few priests would have continued to enjoy their freedom and perform their spiritual functions **if the Austrian Catholic clergy, from the very beginning at the time of the April 10 plebiscite, had set themselves firmly in opposition, instead of actually praising the Party for its many good works in order to help it win an almost unanimous victory at the polls,** he nevertheless insisted that a tragic mistake (for the Church) had been made. At another point in his commentaries, he introduces a dramatic simile which reveals the true measure of his disappointment: **I believe that what took place in the spring of 1938 was not much different from that Maundy Thursday nineteen-hundred years ago when the Jewish crowd was given a free choice between the innocent Saviour and the criminal Barabbas.**

It is a matter of common knowledge in St. Radegund that Jägerstätter did not cast one of the *Ja* votes which, in his opinion, represented a betrayal of Church and nation. It is equally clear that he had been put under some friendly social pressure to persuade him to do so, if only on grounds of prudence. Fr. Karobath, himself an opponent of the Nazis, argued that it would be pointless to cast a negative vote; that this would actually help the Nazis by identifying their potential opposition for them; and, finally, that the more total the measure of approval recorded, the more evident it would be to the outside world that the whole thing was a farce. Other friends, including the present mayor, whose farm borders the *Leherbauer* land, urged him to cast a vote in favor of the unification because "there was really nothing else to do." As it was, he pointed out, the published vote did register one hundred per cent approval in St. Radegund, in spite of the fact that Franz had cast a negative vote. This differs somewhat from other reports that the peasant had not voted against the proposal but had, instead, cast an intentionally "void" ballot.

This marked the first step in a continuing series of refusals to co-operate that was to culminate in the action which cost him his life. From time to time in his commentaries, he refers scornfully to the little red collection boxes which apparently were always being circulated to gather funds for various Nazi-sponsored welfare or patriotic organizations. His refusal to make any contribution to these drives was so consistent and so public that, as one man who had passed those boxes around as a boy remarked, no one bothered to ask him any more. Only once, a close friend recalled, did he make an exception. As the collection box circulated around a group in which he was present, Franz asked what the purpose of this collection was. Told that it was to benefit the police, he surprised everyone by contributing—adding, one may assume rather shamefacedly, that he owed them something because he had given them "some trouble" in the past.

His godchild, having then come to St. Radegund to work on the *Leherbauer* farm, reported that it was due to Jägerstätter that he never had anything to do with the Hitler Youth or similar Nazi organizations, a fact which was to stand him in good stead at the time of the postwar Occupation, he added. Another incident recalled by this young man shows that Jägerstätter did not restrict his expressions of opposition to St. Radegund where he could count on the protection or tolerance of his friends and neighbors. Once, he and Franz had taken a short pleasure trip and stopped for refreshment at Freilässing, the Bavarian-Austrian rail junction near Salzburg. While there, Franz and the innkeeper got into a discussion in which the former gave full vent to what he felt were the principal faults of the National Socialist regime.

The peasant's refusal to contribute to the Nazi movement and its regime was matched by a refusal to accept its benefits. He renounced all claims to the official family assistance program under which he would have been entitled to cash allotments for his children. The man who had assumed the office of mayor during the Nazi period offered another illustration on this point: shortly after the Nazi takeover, the area suffered a severe hailstorm which destroyed most of the crops. The government instituted a program of emergency cash subsidies to the farmers, but Jägerstätter—alone among all the others—refused to take the money.

In a letter received by Dean Kreuzberg, a reader of one of his articles in praise of the peasant objected that Jägerstätter must have collaborated with the Nazis, if only in the very important area of continuing the food production so necessary to the success of any regime. The objection undoubtedly has some validity. There is no record of Jägerstätter getting into any difficulties because he refused to comply with production or market regulations. But it must be taken for granted that argricultural practices were not significantly changed under the Nazi rule, so that he was merely continuing what he had always done, and that he would be inclined to see these activities as fulfilling the duties associated with his "state in life" and not as (what, of course, it was in part) a contribution to the stability and success of the Nazi order. Two other considerations may also have some bearing on this. First, the family was living at a level described as near the point of poverty, and second, Jägerstätter nevertheless distributed foodstuffs to the poor. Both facts might indicate a level of production geared to the minimal needs of subsistence and an avoidance of higher levels of farm production. If so, this would tie in with a widely held opinion that the "new" Jägerstätter, especially toward the end, permitted his religious extremism to interfere with his farming responsibilities.

This judgment, however, is not universally held. Certainly the widow (and others, including her sister and the young man who was her husband's godchild, both of whom lived with the family and helped with the farm work) insisted that Franz was a good farmer, and remained so until the end. The woman who had been his cousin's wife supported this, adding the interesting observation that, because Franz's religious activities forced him to reorganize his work activities, others might have felt he was neglecting some tasks. Actually, she said, the new organization was probably more efficient.

Sharply contrasting opinions were voiced by most townspeople, many of whom specifically said that Franz began to spend so much time and energy on religious concerns that his farm work had to suffer. This would be no minor failing in the eyes of a peasant community! Anything which is permitted to interfere with the proper performance of one's farm duties is certain to be criticized most severely; this is doubly so if these shortcomings can be traced to "excessive piety" (*Frömmigkeit*). The peasant views religion as part of the established order of his life, and not as something that interferes with it. As a consequence, he tends to distrust the overly pious, just as he would distrust an unbeliever. Peasants who independently concern themselves with questions of faith and speak their minds accordingly are exceptions.

It would not be surprising, then, that any real or even suspected decline in Jägerstätter's farming proficiency would attract the notice of his neighbors and make a lasting impression upon them. Sometimes the point was made in general terms: "He just didn't care about his farming toward the end." Or, to cushion the criticism a bit, someone might say, "He was a good farmer until the end when his religious interests took up so much of his time." The complaint was given more precise content in the reports that he had begun to neglect his duties: "He spent the mornings reading and studying." Or, as another put it, "He was seen reading and studying the Bible when he should have been plowing, and this took time from his farm work, which suffered as a result."

This latter comment was made by a man who had not been living in the community but who had "heard all about it" from his father-in-law. He had also been told of an incident in which some friends chided Jägerstätter about his neglect of farm duties, only to get the response from him that "my few kernels" would not "save Austria." This secondhand account was given me in the presence of the schoolmaster (who also, incidentally, had not been a member of the community at the time in question), and both the teller of the tale and the schoolmaster, interestingly enough, suggested conflicting interpretations of this remark. The schoolmaster suggested that it could have been an indication by Jägerstätter that he was not going to make any special effort to aid the national cause; to the other, it merely meant that Jägerstätter had the idea that he could contribute more to the "saving" of Austria by prayer and Bible reading than by working on his farm. Obviously, both interpretations would easily fit Jägerstätter's point of view, depending upon whether one viewed it in a religious or in a purely political framework.

Information obtained from the peasant's closest friends never resolved the question of whether or not he had permitted his farm to run down. There had been comments, for example, that Franz had shown a loss of interest in farming when he sold a noncontiguous section of the *Leherbauer* holdings. Asked about this, one of his former friends confirmed the fact, and said that he had actually tried to sell another piece of the land, this time part of the farm itself, but that his mother had intervened to block that unwise move. Another close friend supported this testimony and went on to say that there was a distinct decrease in Franz's interest and competence in the operation of the farm. Yet two other friends, equally close, registered mild dissents; they both said that as far as they knew—and both were themselves away in service at the time of his arrest—Franz continued to do his work well. One of these did add, however, that Franz may have planted one section unwisely, but he indicated that this was the kind of thing that could happen to anyone.

Although the weight of the testimony would seem to support the generally held impression, quite a different story is told by Franz's letters from prison which reveal a continuing interest in the farm and its welfare. In his third letter (March 12, 1943) he already notes, **Now it is almost time to be sowing the oats. The weather must really be glorious. Whenever you have questions about the farm, write me so that I can help you with my advice. Needless to say, I am always ready to do so—though I would much rather be helping you in person.** Later that same month, he expresses his concern about the problems his wife must be having over the water supply and his hope that it would soon rain. This letter continues, **If it were possible for me to get a leave to clear away some trees, you would also have the straw in the cow barn changed. If the weather stays like this you will begin mowing the hay by Easter and will be able to have fresh feed. Yesterday we already saw apricot blossoms in our [prison] garden.**

Other comments in these letters refer to new changes in market arrangements; to the birth of new livestock apparently reported in one of the letters from his wife; to the new scythe she should get for the mowing, and so forth. A touching comment appears in the letter of May 2, in which Franz notes the start of a month that is particularly beautiful for those who live on the land, because it usually does not bring so much work with it as do the summer months. Nature, he adds, has not taken much account of the misery that has descended upon mankind—even though I cannot see much of it, it seems to me, nevertheless, as if everything has grown and blossomed much lovelier this year. Even in the July letter, written from Berlin after he had been sentenced, he includes a few lines for his father-in-law, who had volunteered to help Mrs. Jägerstätter with the work. This year God has sent weather for those who perspire easily: if you have no better weather than we do here, I fear you will not even be finished with the hay harvest by now. True, it does not rain very much, but I believe that there has hardly been a time all summer when two beautiful days have followed one another—and July hasn't started out any better. Let us hope it will improve by harvest time. Then he adds a bit of tactful advice: It would be good if you don't drive my people too hard at their work so that they may have at least a little time left over for thinking—and for praying too.

These few references are not, of course, a final refutation of the opinions voiced by those whose judgments were based on observation. But if he had really completely lost interest in doing a respectable job of farming in the few months preceding his arrest, one would hardly expect him to have devoted so much thought in prison to the farm or so many of the precious few lines he was able to write to his beloved family.

There is one other memory of the "new" Jägerstätter that must be mentioned. It, too, concerns the effects of his extremism, especially his *political* extremism. There is a widely held notion in Radegund that he did not give the needs of his family sufficient priority. His—to some, at least—distorted religious and political commitment was seen as producing a callous lack of concern for their future welfare. One man, for instance, holds him responsible for the physical handicap of his second daughter; the apparently congenital hip malformation from which she still suffers could have been observed and cured early, this man believes, if Franz had not been so stubborn about not accepting any medical or financial assistance from the Nazi regime. In view of the fact that this child was only four and a half years old at the time of her father's arrest, however, and what was probably viewed as a minor problem of gait did not show its real severity until her school years, this seems to be a rather farfetched charge to bring against him now.

There were other criticisms based on more tenable grounds, at least in the context of the critics' values. A priest who had been born in St. Radegund, and who later was to preach the sermon at the ceremonial burial of Jägerstätter's ashes in the parish churchyard, appears to have been a particularly severe critic. He has since died, but at least two villagers referred to statements he had made, indicating his belief that Jägerstätter had become so self-centered in his religious and political thinking before his final decision that he had given insufficient thought to those who were dependent upon him. Other testimony was obtained from people who recalled that when anyone tried to talk Jägerstätter into thinking more about his children and not going through with his hopeless stand, he would reply that he would pray for them "from the other side."

Recollections of this kind are undoubtedly quite correct, for the same position is taken in several of the peasant's writings. In an undated farewell message, for instance, we find the lines, **If one argues from the standpoint of the family, you need not be troubled here either; for it is not permitted to lie, even for the sake of the family. And if I had ten children, the greatest demand upon me is still the one I must make of myself.** The prison statement prepared at the request of the chaplain strikes the same note: **Again and again people stress the obligations of conscience as they concern my wife and children. Yet I cannot believe that, just because one has a wife and children, he is free to offend God by lying (not to mention all the other things he would be called upon to do). Did not Christ Himself say, "He who loves father, mother, or children more than Me is not deserving of My love"?** Along with references like this, there runs another consistent theme of confident hope and expectation of a happy reunion, if not in this world, in a future world of blessedness. In the letter written a few hours before his death, the passage specifically addressed to his children promises, **I will surely beg the dear God, if I am permitted to enter heaven soon, that he may also set aside a little place in heaven for all of you.**

To a man of unshakable faith and perfect abandonment to the will of God, the assurance of help and care for his family "from the other side" makes complete sense. But such a pattern of behavior might well appear to be deluded and unconcerned, or even a callous disregard of family obligations and responsibilities, to most of Franz Jägerstätter's friends and neighbors.

This recounting of the community's recollections of the man must not end without stressing once again the favorable cast of those memories. There was general agreement that he was an exemplary neighbor, the statement being volunteered time and time again that he left nothing to be desired in this respect and that he was always on hand whenever help of any kind was needed. One neighbor recalled an incident in which Franz came to his assistance and worked well into the night to help him shore up a cellar wall which had collapsed. Even the criticisms concerning his farming or his failure to consider the welfare of his family stressed that he was a very good farmer and an excellent husband and father; indeed, the criticisms were set in these terms: because he was such a fine man in these respects, his failings were convincing proof that his religious and political extremism had brought him to the point where fanaticism shaded into mental derangement.

From Enns to Berlin

Today I am going to take the difficult step. This simple declaration in a letter written to his wife from Enns, the location of the induction center to which he had been ordered to report, marks the beginning of the critical stage in the Jägerstätter story. The letter is dated March 1, 1943. The day before had been spent in the company of a priest with whom he had become acquainted, apparently during an earlier period of military training. He had not revealed his intentions to his host: **it would only have led to an argument, for I would not have found any understanding there, either, for something like this.** Whether out of candor or bitterness, he couples the factual observation that the priest was then receiving a monthly allowance of one hundred marks from the government, with the statement that **if one were to speak today of the spirit of penance and detachment, he would not find much understanding for that, either.**

His act of rebellion was a "difficult step" for others, too. The purpose of his writing was not only to pass on the news of his own decision but, beyond that, to thank his wife **from the bottom of my heart for all the love and fidelity which you have brought me and the whole family. And for all the sacrifices you must still undergo** on my account. Among those hardships, he warns his wife, will be the fact that she will not be able to reply in kind to those who will abuse her on his account, for love requires that we strive ever harder toward perfection—a striving, he goes on to assure her, that will get easier as time goes on. At least you know where you can find understanding and who can help you too, when your sorrows come upon you. For Christ, too, prayed on the Mount of Olives that the Heavenly Father might permit the chalice of sorrow to pass from His lips—but we must never forget this part of His prayer: Lord, not my will be done but rather Thine. He writes her to continue to help the poor as long as she is able; to take the father's place for their children; and, referring to one source of opposition that must have been a particular hardship for him, not to become angry with his mother if she does not understand us.

In what was apparently intended to be the closing sentence, he sounds a note which was to be repeated many times in the following five months: Should it be God's will that I do not see you again in this world, let us then hope to meet soon again in heaven. But he adds a double postscript, in itself perhaps a significant index to the frame of mind in which this letter was composed. First he asks her to greet the children once more for me. Tell them often about the Child Jesus and heaven. Even this was not enough. Like a lover unwilling to bring a lingering farewell to an end, he adds another message, a message which gives moving testimony to his real assessment of his situation. To all my loved ones: I must send you all my sincerest greetings as long as I am still in freedom. Learn to become a family loving one another and forgiving whatever may come. Forgive all those who might cause you hardship, and me, too. Goodbye until we meet again.

Of course, this was not really the beginning of the end after all. The real beginning would have to be traced to that previous period of military training, during which the incompatibility between his opposition to the Nazi regime and his service in the Nazi forces first became clear to him. Once Franz was released from that training—whether on an agricultural or family deferment, no one seemed to know—he returned to St. Radegund with the firm conviction that if he were ever called to service again, he would have to refuse. He made no secret of his intention. Virtually all of the people I spoke to admitted having heard him state his intentions, and many went on to describe their own efforts or the efforts of others to dissuade him from so hopeless and, to them, meaningless a course of action. In our conversations, Pastor Karobath admitted that he, too, had tried to counsel Jägerstätter against taking such a stand. The immediate responsibility for such spiritual guidance, of course, lay with his replacement, Fr. Fürthauer. Fürthauer apparently recognized that he was not quite up to the task—he admitted at one point that he had advised the man to consult other priests, and he knew that Jägerstätter had done so. As far as their own discussions were concerned, the peasant was unshakable in his insistence that the war was unjust. Although the priest did not deny the validity of that conviction, he tried to make Jägerstätter see that it would serve no useful purpose for him to sacrifice himself. His efforts were unavailing: Jägerstätter continued to insist that he would never again report for military service, partly because of his certainty that the war was unjust and partly because he believed that life in the army presented too great an occasion for sin (especially, Fürthauer added, sins against the Sixth Commandment). When the final induction order arrived, Jägerstätter came to him again for advice —and the advice he gave was that he should report for service. The peasant refused to accept it, and, according to the former vicar, had then consulted other priests. He did not know that his parishioner had gone so far as to seek advice from the bishop himself, nor was he inclined even now to believe that such was the case.

Fr. Krenn, the priest with whom Franz stayed in Enns, died some time before I began my inquiries, so I cannot know for certain to what extent, if any, Jägerstätter had sought counsel from him. However, it was possible to meet and interview Fr. Taimer, the pastor of Ach, a village located between St. Radegund and Braunau. The meeting was arranged by Pastor Karobath, who knew that this priest had been approached by his onetime parishioner. Taimer's account of his contact with Jägerstätter throws considerable light upon the climate of those days. He remembered this strange man suddenly appearing at his church one day in 1941. He could be sure about the year, he added, because he was then in the midst of some extensive repairs to the church. Jägerstätter had come to seek advice as to whether or not it would be morally permissible for him to fight in the war. Since the priest had never seen the man before and was fully aware of the possibility that he could be a Gestapo agent seeking to force him into treasonous remarks, he treated the questioner with the utmost caution. He told him to put his problem in writing and then leave it under one of the statues in the church where no one else would be likely to find it. As the priest now remembers it, the statement delivered in this manner covered several pages and set forth in detail a position against serving in an unjust war—a position which he could only describe as unchallengeably sound in theory and logical development. Nevertheless, he, too, gave the man the same advice: he should report for service as ordered.

Little definite information could be found about the visit to Bishop Fliesser of Linz. Inquiries at the Linz diocese were not particularly fruitful. It is clear, however, that such a visit took place, for, in a postwar letter to another priest, the Bishop was directly quoted as saying, "I knew Jägerstätter personally, since he spent more than an hour with me before his scheduled induction. To no avail I spelled out for him the moral principles defining the degree of responsibility borne by citizens and private individuals for the acts of the civil authority. I reminded him of his far greater responsibility for his own state of life, in particular for his family." This is the only clear indication of what transpired between the two. All Mrs. Jägerstätter could add was that her husband told her he had been kept waiting in an outer office for a very long time, but that he was inclined to explain this, too, as a concession to prudence, forced by the possibility that he might have been a Gestapo agent.

Pastor Taimer's account indicates that the man was already committed to his stand as early as 1941; Jägerstätter's commentaries written to set forth the rationale behind that stand were apparently written in 1942. It follows, then, that the actual event found him fully resigned to what was to come. And so it was that he was able to state the situation so simply in his letter to Pastor Karobath, dated February 22, 1943:

Reverend Father: I greet you from the bottom of my heart and thank you sincerely for your note. I must tell you that you will probably be losing another of your parishioners soon. Today I received the induction notice and am ordered to report (on the 25th) at Enns. However, since no one can dispense me from what I view as the danger to the health of my soul that this gang [the Nazis] presents, I cannot change my decision, which you already know. As it is, it is so hard to come even one step closer to perfection. Is it even conceivable to try in such an outfit?

Christ did not praise Peter for denying Him merely out of fear of men. How often would I probably have to repeat that denial, serving with this outfit—for if one were not to do so, he could be almost certain that he would never see his dear ones on earth again. Everyone tells me, of course, that I should not do what I am doing because of the danger of death; but it seems to me that the others who do fight are not completely free of the same danger of death. People say that four or five men from St. Radegund were in the Stalingrad battle. May God reward these poor fellows in the hereafter for all that they have had to bear in soul and body—for, truly, as far as this world is concerned, it is generally taken for granted that their sacrifices were made in vain. If so many terrible things are permitted by this terrible gang, I believe it is better to sacrifice one's life right away than to place oneself in the grave danger of committing sin and then dying.

I beg you to remember me at Mass as long as you are permitted to offer Mass. And from my heart I ask you to pray for me, too, and to forgive me any trouble I may ever have caused you. May God not abandon me in the last hour! God and the Blessed Virgin will surely not abandon my family when I can no longer protect them myself. Things will be very hard for my dear ones. This leave-taking will be most difficult. Your deeply indebted sexton greets you from his heart. May God protect you and all other priests.

One may suppose that the appeals to Franz to change his mind became much more intense and insistent. His reference in the letter from Enns to his mother's not being able to understand him is undoubtedly related to the fact that she opposed his taking such a stand, and tried to get as many people as possible to talk him out of it. His stepfather's sister recalled that his mother pleaded with him not to worry about whether the war was just or unjust, reminding him that going into the army did not necessarily mean that he would have to kill anyone. In what must have been an act of desperation, his mother even appealed to the mayor to talk her son into changing his mind. As the representative of the hated regime, this man would probably have been the last person to have any influence on Jägerstätter; indeed, a close friend of his has suggested that Franz held this official responsible for his being called up in the first place. Recalling Franz's mother's appeal, this former mayor told me he knew he could do nothing himself, but that he had talked with the local police official and asked him to see what he could accomplish.

Two or three other villagers also referred to the police official in this connection. He was described as a kindly, fatherly man who was deeply concerned about Franz and his prospective fate. Not only did he talk to him; he promised to write an official letter to the military authorities requesting noncombatant service for Jägerstätter if he would only agree to report as ordered. He pleaded with Jägerstätter not to force him to make an arrest that would cause him, the arresting officer, such deep sorrow. Assuming that Franz shared the community's favorable impression of this policeman, such an appeal may explain his decision to make his refusal away from the home community. However, a more pressing consideration probably was the desire to spare his family as much difficulty as possible.

Within the family circle, it appears that one more force was being exerted to no avail. Although the people of St. Radegund believe otherwise, the peasant's widow insists that she, too, tried her best to get her husband to change his mind. He had told her of his intention from the very first, and when she saw he was determined in his stand, she apparently resigned herself to the inevitable, but she did not encourage it.

None of these pressures was enough to bring him to the decision that he could accept military service again. There were other alternatives, of course, and there is evidence that he gave them some thought. Fürthauer, for instance, said that he had considered hiding out in the woods, but had abandoned that possibility because of his fear of reprisals against his family. By a rather striking coincidence, there was a case of a local military deserter hiding out in St. Radegund and the surrounding countryside shortly before the end of the war. The pastor and the others who discussed this case with me admitted that everyone in the village knew about it at the time but that there was never any likelihood that he would be betrayed to the authorities. Instead, he was given food and other necessities and, on one occasion, a dentist was even brought to his hiding place to perform a tooth extraction. It is interesting to speculate on whether this pattern of the rural community caring for and protecting "one of its own" might not have made it possible for Jägerstätter to have done likewise. It is doubtful that Franz ever seriously considered such a step, for deeply woven into his intention was another objective, one described by the priest as a desire to offer his life so that he could say to the regime that it was unjust in its war and in its persecution of the Church. When the moment of rebellion came, Jägerstätter stood completely alone.

Except for the single instance of the visit to Berlin by Mrs. Jägerstätter and Fr. Fürthauer—and this took place toward the end—the people of St. Radegund had no further contributions to make to the substance of the Jägerstätter story. From this point on, then, information had to be obtained from people who came in contact with him during the last few months of his life—prison chaplains, cellmates, and his defense attorney—and from the letters written to his wife and family. Both may be somewhat superficial sources: the first because these individuals had such brief contacts with him; the second because it is quite evident that he tried to spare his loved ones as much worry and concern about his welfare as he could.

It is clear that after his appearance at the Enns induction center (presumably on March 1, 1943) at which he stated his refusal to serve, he was placed under military arrest and taken the following day to the military prison at Linz. Most of the prisoners sent there had committed some serious offense against military discipline—the priest who served as chaplain recalls accompanying thirty-eight men to their execution. A few of them, it seems, were there for reasons similar to those involved in Jägerstätter's case. Though the rebel had no way of knowing it, Linz was to be just a way station for him. All he knew when he arrived there—and he must have seen this as a very real possibility—was that he was subject to summary execution at any moment.

The first letter bringing loving greetings from my new home was dated March 3, and was obviously intended to be a comforting assurance that all was going well so far. The food was not bad, and it was nourishing; there were five men in his cell; other conditions were satisfactory. Just don't forget me in your prayers and everything will turn out for the best according to God's will. If we seek to follow the will of God, everything will work out for the best for us. It is his wife's "name day" and he sends her the customary greetings, adding the wish: May God give you everything that you desire for yourself—as long as it is not likely to be a hindrance to your eternal welfare. For the sorrows of this world will quickly pass. The rest of the letter and a postscript ask for some necessities: a work shirt and trousers, toothbrush, soap, etc. But no foodstuffs may be sent, he tells his wife. Finally he asks that she enclose one of those little pamphlets about the visitation of the Blessed Mother in Portugal in her next letter.

Two days later he writes another, and longer, letter. The tone has changed to that of a man who now knows the ropes enough to express himself more openly about the ideas which had brought him there. He has been exchanging thoughts and experiences with other prisoners, and some of the things he has learned have obviously encouraged him in his stand. For one thing, he heard of a farm woman in Enns who refused to permit her children to participate in Hitler Youth activities; this is a rarity, he observes, and a source of some comfort to know that there are others who can stand apart from the crowd. He has become convinced that he can accomplish much more religious good in his cell than he could ever hope to do in the army. The bitter and disillusioned men under arrest offer one such opportunity. Just what "spiritual accomplishments" he had in mind are not specified; it is interesting to note in this connection that one report refers to him converting two condemned men while in prison. No other evidence of this was uncovered, however.

62

It is frightful what they [the prisoners] can tell about all they have already done and suffered during these past five years. Some men have been given long-term sentences for even the most minor military offenses, but one can always gain his release by volunteering for service at the front. If they all turned over a new leaf, spiritually speaking, it could bring many bitter disappointments, but it would still be the right thing for them to do. Already there have been SS-men, so I have heard, who have been converted before their death. This thought about conversions leads him to send a closing message to the pastor, reminding him that people are often not as bad as one thinks. He advises him always to take the greatest pains to stress the teachings of Christ, for at least this effort will assure the salvation of his own soul.

Of more direct importance to his wife, perhaps, was his suggestion that she might soon be visited by a cellmate who had suddenly been released, although according to Mrs. Jägerstätter, no such visit ever took place. This leads him to the thought that she might be subjected to interrogation on his account, and his advice is, When people ask you if you agree with my decision not to fight, just tell them how you honestly feel. After all, he points out, there is little she can do to improve his situation and nothing that could make it much worse. The most important thing is to be honest: For if I did not have such a great horror of lies and double-dealing, I would not be sitting here. He tells her, too, that they tried all sorts of arguments in Enns to get him to become a soldier again and that it was not easy to stick to his decision. And it can be even harder in the future. But I have faith that God will still give me a sign if some other course would be better. He had been questioned, too, about what his pastor had to say, and he was glad to be able to report that the priest had advised him to accept service. If it had been necessary for me to keep silent about his spiritual counsel, it is certain he would not be free much longer.

The letter of March 11 marks what may have been the lowest point in Jägerstätter's morale. He is obviously much concerned about the situation at home. He feels he has to write a few lines, even though he has little to tell. I am always troubled by the fear that you have much to suffer on my account: forgive me everything if I bring injustice down upon you. Then a surprising bit of news follows. **I can also tell you that I have declared myself ready to serve in the medical corps.** He explains that one can do good and perform a kind of Christian charity in a practical sense in that branch of service, a fact that would ease his conscience somewhat **though I would still be punished.** It is not clear whether this refers to "punishment" by the authorities for his original refusal or—probably more likely in the context of his thought—a spiritual punishment to be suffered for compromising his conscience even to such a limited extent. But anything can be borne **if God so wills and it is possible for us to see each other again in this world.**

This is the only reference in all his writings to a willingness to accept even limited military service. The various articles published about him, and the personal interviews I had with the inhabitants of St. Radegund and elsewhere, revealed widely differing opinions on this score: there were some who reported that he did seek such service but that his request was denied by the authorities. Mrs. Jägerstätter indicated such a belief in a letter she wrote to Fr. Karobath after visiting her husband in Berlin. Other unquestionably reliable informants revealed that he was actually *promised* such an assignment and could have gained his freedom, even at the last moment, by accepting those offers. Taking all the available evidence together, it is best to conclude that Jägerstätter would not have accepted any form of military service, that he was sincere in his statement to his pastor and others that acceptance of limited service would only mean that he was replacing someone else who would be doing the killing for him. The fact that he apparently did make this one request for such service—of which, incidentally, nothing further is heard—is probably to be interpreted as a sign of a low point in his morale bordering upon despair.

The key to the explanation of his low morale is perhaps found in the opening lines of a letter written to his wife the very next day, in which he acknowledges receipt of the first communication from home, together with a package containing books and food. (Apparently an exception was made and the food was passed on to him, but he cautions her against violating any regulations in the future.) It should not be too difficult to imagine how long the intervening three weeks since his departure from St. Radegund must have seemed for him. The sadness of being away from his family was bad enough, and all of his letters reveal his desperate longing to maintain every possible link with them. But, even worse, he must have been troubled by the thought that his action had subjected his family to unpleasantness or even direct reprisal at the hands of the community or the Nazi authorities. This first letter from home substantially helped to reduce such fears.

The letters written to Jägerstätter during his months of imprisonment are, needless to say, no longer available. Yet, from time to time, one can catch a glimpse of their contents as they are reflected in his replies. In this case, one can assume that his wife had given full expression to her sorrow and concern, for he answers, **Dear wife, you should not be sad because of my present situation. For we cannot know God's mind, or which of the many paths he leaves us to travel and still reach the right goal. As long as a man has an untroubled conscience and knows that he is not really a criminal, he can live at peace even in prison.** The phrase, "not really a criminal," raises the interesting speculation that some people were saying he was. Though the widow was most reluctant to complain about the treatment shown her by the villagers (partly because "Franz always said one should remember the good and not the bad about people"), she did admit that there were some who had told her that her husband was getting just what he deserved.

Although far away from his little church and his duties as sexton, prison walls were not enough to make him unaware of the progress of the church year. Many of his letters make specific references to a relationship between his own situation and the wider liturgical context. For example, he writes: **Especially now in this season of Lent we should be mindful that, even though we may still have much to suffer, it is, nevertheless, nothing like what Christ and His mother suffered in their innocence.** He marvels, too, to learn that his eldest daughter (not yet six years old) has been making sacrifices for him. **They certainly will not be in vain. How could I feel abandoned here when so many are praying for me at home?**

From this point on, with two-way communication now established, Jägerstätter's prison letters begin to encourage and strengthen

65

those he had left behind and to assure them that they need not worry about his well-being. There are occasional requests—for envelopes, religious pamphlets—and frequent advice concerning farm matters. In almost every case there is a special little paragraph or postscript addressed to the children.

Sometimes the reader is struck by a note of poignant longing, as in the next letter, written on March 19, with its comment that he doubted there had been quite so lovely a St. Joseph's Day in a long while, especially for those who can still enjoy it in freedom. Or, again, there is a flash of humor that catches one unawares, as in another passage where, after mentioning the worry and care which burden his wife in addition to so much work, he suggests: **I think it would be good for us occasionally to trade places for a week; such a rest would be good for you.** But then he reiterates: **But I place my whole future in God's hands. He will certainly make everything turn out for the best for us: the important thing is to fear God more than man. This month, and especially today on his feast day, let us pray for St. Joseph's help. He will certainly come to our assistance—even if his assistance is not quite what we might be hoping for.**

In perhaps one of the most touching passages of all, he gives evidence of that thoughtfulness which had been praised by his former friends and neighbors. **Dearest wife,** he writes, **today I have another request to make of you. I wonder if maybe you could enclose a few edelweiss[1] in your next letter. One of my comrades here has asked if I might be able to get some for him. He is a young Frenchman who was sentenced last week, and he would like to send the edelweiss to his girl friend as a remembrance, since she is very fond of flowers.**

March 25 was the date of his seventh letter. As if to show that life in prison can have its blessings, he says, **Even though there is practically nothing to do here, this does not mean that a man has**

[1] Edelweiss is the national flower of Austria. Legend has it that it grows wild only on the highest mountain peaks and that a young man can prove his devotion to a sweetheart by making the daring climb to bring her a spray. Of course, these flowers can be domesticated. It is interesting to note that the Jägerstätter grave is decorated with them.

to let his days go by without putting them to some use. As long as he can pray—and there is plenty of time for that—life is not in vain. This leads him to inquire about the current year's festival of the Altötting Marian congregation and whether an invitation had come. He is writing, he notes, on the lovely Feast of the Annunciation in which Christ assumed human form out of love for us men. The King of Heaven has given us sinful men so much that we should always try to imitate Christ and forgive our fellow men, even though, miserable creatures that we are, we will never succeed completely because of our pride. Lest she miss the point, he spells it out more explicitly: Though difficulties may still lie ahead, whoever perseveres in love will someday find that everything has turned out for the best.

Early in the letter, apparently in answer to a question from her, he had written, I think it is better for you to tell the children where their father is than to have to lie to them. Now, after what appeared to have been the end of the letter, he opens a new paragraph, saying it was lucky he had saved some space, for I hoped I would still get a letter from you today, and one has just been delivered at supper. And now to my dear little ones! Dear Rösl, Maridl, and Loisl,[2] I thank you from the bottom of my heart for the greetings you sent me. It makes me very happy that you pray for me so often and that, as I hope, you have also become better children. I think of you very often and pray for you too. It would make me so happy if I could see you again—I would gather you all together so that you would soon learn not to fight among yourselves any more. Also, you must not lie, and at mealtime you should always be satisfied with what you get. Then, I believe, the Heavenly Father will grant that I can come home to you someday, even though it may not be right away. A further note of paternal instruction tells them not to trouble their mother too much and to be obedient to her, as well as to their grandmother and the aunt who was then living at the farm. He closes by saying, I greet you, my dear little girls. May the Child Jesus and the dear Mother of Heaven protect you until we see one another again.

[2] Diminutives for Rosalie (born September 1, 1937), Marie (born September 4, 1938), and Aloisia (born May 5, 1940).

The next letter, April 4, is particularly interesting for his effort to discourage his wife from visiting him at the Linz prison. *Concerning a visit about which you wrote, I would advise against it for the time being—maybe for Easter, for by then there may have been some decision about my case. As yet I have had no hearing.* Toward the end of the letter he reverts to the subject again, pointing out that all he knows is that the visiting period would not last longer than fifteen minutes. *It would certainly be a great joy to see you again, but I would still advise you to put it off for now. Dearest wife, let us carry our cross further with patience until God takes it from us.*

However valid his reasons may have been, one must question whether they really explain his position. As the letter was being written, he had been separated from his family for more than a month. He was still quite sure in his mind that he would never be permitted to rejoin them again. Linz, while not an everyday trip for a Radegund villager, was nevertheless close enough to permit an occasional journey for a special purpose. In this and similar answers to what must have been increasingly urgent pleas on the part of his wife, one can assume that other considerations carried at least equal weight. For one thing, he must have wanted to spare her the unpleasantness of seeing him in prison, and to spare them both the cutting sorrow of another personal leave-taking. Perhaps, too, his opposition to a visit may indicate a preference not to be faced with the severe temptation to violate his conscience that such a personal confrontation might possibly have occasioned. These reasons are never given, of course, but they must have played some part in his decision.

Reassurances of his well-being are again stressed in this letter. There is always enough to eat and it is well enough prepared. Again, a touch of wry humor: *Of course, you can easily understand that we are not getting fat on this diet, but that is not essential either, for they have not locked us in here in order to fatten us up.* Becoming more serious again, he reminds her that it would not matter too much if things did get worse since, as she already knows, he is not concerned with making life easier for himself. He assures her, furthermore, that *so long as the grace of God does not desert me* and I do not lose my faith, I really cannot be unhappy. Though the heart is sometimes sad, we still know that our sadness will one day be turned into joy. Even if we could live to be a hundred, what would that be compared to eternity? Not a half second!

The usual greetings conclude the letter, and in the special message to the children he tells them that the flowers their mother had sent from them had not arrived. He encourages them to gather bouquets to honor the Heavenly Father.

In many respects the letter of April 9 is the most beautiful and moving of all Jägerstätter's writings because it is an open and unquestionably sincere expression of a husband's devotion to his wife and the testimony of an abiding faith in a love that will continue despite separation and death. Some of the words are blotted, quite possibly by tears shed while the letter was being read—or, perhaps, even while it was being written.

It begins with the customary references to letters that had arrived, and Franz expands his usual expressions of gratitude:

In spite of all the work you have to do, you still take time to make your husband so happy—something which I probably do not deserve at all. Of course, every line you write interests me, and you will surely forgive me for not writing more often, since there is never much new to write about from here. I still have had no hearing.

Dearest wife, today it is seven years since we spoke our vows of love and fidelity before God and the priest, and I believe we have faithfully kept these vows to this day. I also believe that, even though we must now live apart, God will continue to give us the grace to keep them until the end of our lives. When I look back upon all this joy and the many graces that have been mine for these seven years, it seems at times almost to border on the miraculous. If someone were to tell me that there is no God or that God does not love us—and if I were to believe him—I would not be able to explain how all this has come to me. Dearest wife, this is why, no matter how we may dread the future, He who has upheld us and given us joy till now will not abandon us then either. If only we do not forget to give thanks and do not hold ourselves back in our striving for heaven, God will permit our joy to continue on for all eternity.

Though I sit behind prison walls, I still believe I can build further on your love and devotion in the days to come. And should I have to leave this life, I will still [rest easy in] my grave, for you know that I am not here as a criminal. It makes me very happy that you have had a Mass read for today, for I know you have given special thought to me while participating in it.

This is followed by a more lighthearted touch: Now your new husband greets you from his heart. For it is said that human beings are completely renewed every seven years—so from this day forth you have a new husband! The special note to the children mentions that the violets had arrived after all, and he thanks them. I see you do not forget your father, who will never forget you either, and who would like to be with you. But the Heavenly Father does not will it to be that way. That is why we will be able to be happy in heaven forever someday if you will only become truly good children. Then he reverts to his original theme. The children are to give thanks to God for giving them so good a mother and him so good a wife, and they must always love her very much and do whatever she asks. Apparently his wife was ill at the time, for he continues, If you are good and follow her wishes, mother will not die so soon and will get better again. There are so many children who do not have any father or mother—at least not a mother as good as yours.

The weather must have taken a drastic change, for he tells them in closing: Now you will no longer be able to run around bare-footed; early this morning we actually had some snow, and it is not likely that it is much warmer where you are. Your father who thinks of you very often sends his love.

His next letter (April 11) begins with a lament that "another sad Sunday" is coming to an end. He did not want it to pass by without at least writing a few lines. He tells of his great disappointment that a request he had made for permission to attend church on Sundays had been denied on the grounds that it would require two guards to accompany him. But, he says, he will try again for Easter, and maybe he will have better luck then. It would not be too much for me if I had to go a hundred kilometers on foot to attend a single Mass. But I guess one must have patience and leave his fate to God to dispose. And yet how true are the words Christ once spoke: "My Lord is sweet, and my burden is light." For when I compare my cross and sorrows with the sufferings of others, I must still say that God has always given me the lightest cross to bear.

To illustrate this rather surprising conclusion, he goes on to describe a happy event that had taken place the week before. Books were distributed in the cells, and he had been lucky enough to find among them a collection of sermons by St. John Chrysostom and other saints. Although most everyone here likes to read to kill time, they were perfectly happy to leave this book to me. A man first realizes the true value of our faith in a situation like this. Let us fervently pray that the light of faith will never be extinguished in us.

Once more the concerns of the good farmer are evidenced in comments on the bad weather and inquiries about the state of the hay and of some work the wagoner was to have done for his wife.

The beginning of Holy Week is the occasion for Jägerstätter's eleventh letter. He imagines what it must be like in their parish church; their children would probably be carrying palm branches in the procession. I do not believe that anyone could ask for better weather than we have again. Just to see the fresh green of the grass does one good—though we never really notice it when we have our freedom.

The major portion of the letter stresses the special meaning Holy Week should have for them: This week especially must bring us new courage and strength to lighten the burden of our fate, for what are our little sorrows compared with what Christ had to suffer during Holy Week? He who is not willing to suffer with and for Christ will also not share in His Resurrection. And even if the cross that God (or we ourselves) has laid upon us becomes a little heavy, it will never get as difficult and heavy as the one which Satan loads on his followers, many of whom have already broken under this burden and thrown their lives away. In an interesting interpolation about suicide, he adds that one should pass judgment only on the act of suicide and never on the suicide himself, and he follows this

71

with the statement, As far as my future is concerned, I am still not able to report anything—even this week I have still had no hearing. Inasmuch as other letters suggest that he was occasionally troubled by the thought (or, perhaps, by the accusation voiced by others) that his action and the certain death to which it would lead might be regarded as a form of suicide, the sequence of these last two thoughts could be a reflection of a moral concern that weighed heavily on his mind during his period of imprisonment.

He next expresses his sorrow that he cannot celebrate Easter with them, and makes the general observation that if there is still no chance this year for a peaceful Easter, we should not lose hope on this account. And if it should be God's will that we can never again in this world celebrate a joyous Easter together in our intimate family circle, we can still look ahead in the happy confidence that when the eternal Easter morning dawns, no one from our family circle shall be missing, so that we can then be permitted to rejoice together forever. Another interesting conjunction of thought leads him to follow this with: Concerning visits, I would prefer that you hold off for the time being; as long as I have had no hearing, it is not likely that I will be transferred to another prison. It will be recalled, of course, that he had himself suggested an Easter visit in the earlier letter in which he had urged a postponement of his wife's plans to come to Linz to see him.

The note to the children tells them that the warmer weather means that they can pick flowers again and roll Easter eggs (and, naturally, eat them when they break). He thanks Rosalie for the apple she sent him. I have saved it for today and will eat it this evening. Earlier he had sent them three oranges, along with a bundle of clothing, and he expresses the hope that they were still good, for I had saved them for quite a long time. And again the closing instructions that they should be good girls so that mother does not have to lose her temper with you.

Christ is risen—Allelujia! So the Church rejoices today. On this jubilant note the Easter Sunday letter opens. And if we must also experience hard times today, we still should and can rejoice with the church regardless. For what is there more joyous than the fact that Christ has risen again and has gone before us as victor over death and hell? What can give us Christians greater comfort than the knowledge that we need never again fear death?

Dearest wife, you can easily imagine what these holy days have been like for me in prison, but with God it is possible to overcome everything. One should not always fix his thoughts on the things he cannot have at the moment. No matter how great our sufferings in this world might become, I believe the poor souls in purgatory would still change places with us in an instant. That is why we help them as much as we can. And this man who would gladly walk one hundred kilometers to attend Mass has happy news to report. I am, I think, always a child of luck. On Holy Thursday morning I asked again about going to church on Easter—but, again, it was not approved for me. Instead, however, I was promised a visit from a priest who arrived that same afternoon. And thus I was able to fulfill my Easter duty even here, for the priest had brought the Blessed Sacrament along. On Friday, then, others asked again for the priest and, as a result, I was able to receive Holy Communion once more on Saturday morning.

Except for this momentous news he has nothing else to report. One week passes after another; the important thing is that we do not let a single day go by in vain without putting it to good use for eternity. He is happy to hear that his wife is still able to do some work for the parish church; soon she will be decorating the Mary altar for the May devotions. Do this in honor of our beloved Mother of God. She will surely not abandon us. Noting, then, that this Easter day is also slowly coming to an end, he asks, How many more will go by before another peaceful Easter Sunday will be ours? It is good that man cannot see into the future. This way we can take each day just as God sends it to us.

Easter thoughts carry over into the opening of his letter of May 2 as he notes that the third Sacred Heart Day that he has been unable to spend at home has arrived and the Easter holidays are over. Have our children, as I hope, learned the meaning of Easter? Once again he must tell her that he still has heard nothing as far as my future is concerned, that he has had no hearing. The only thing to do is to wait patiently and, besides, any change is hardly likely to be for the better.

A few comments on the lovely weather lead him to some spiritual reflections:

As soon as the dawn begins to break, one can hear the birds singing outside our windows. They seem to know more of freedom and joy even though they are only unreasoning animals than do we humans with our gift of intellect, and even though we know what a great reward awaits us after our brief existence on earth. Ought we, then, to be so greatly troubled when we must do without, or worry about those things which weigh upon our hearts, when these can still be repaid a thousand times over in eternity? If we only concern ourselves with the temporal things we can get, will we not be counted among those for whom, as one Gospel puts it, their stomach is their God?—that is, if our yearnings and worries are concerned more with food, drink and pleasure than with the eternal riches?

As he had done in previous months, he asks his wife to send him the texts of the communion intentions for May and June in her next letter. And he tells her to attend the May devotions regularly so that you may obtain the benefits not available to me here—for Mary has always helped and will help again. As far as he is concerned, I would much prefer it if I could hear the lovely Marian hymns instead of the popular "hits" one usually hears in these cells.

The rest of the letter is devoted to a wide range of questions about the condition of the farm, and this leads him to a half-hearted apology. You will think that I am not a little curious about how things are coming along at home. But, he adds, that is always the way it is when one loves his home.

Two days later the blow fell: Jägerstätter was suddenly transferred to Berlin. He had time to write only a brief note, which he said was one last greeting from Linz, giving the address of the Military Investigation Prison (Berlin-Tegel) where he would be held. After telling his wife she could write to that address, he closes his stay in Linz by saying, Do not worry any more about me. The Lord will not desert me in the future either.

These letters, fortunately, are not the only sources of information about this period of imprisonment at Linz. It was also possible to obtain the testimony of three men who had an opportunity to observe Jägerstätter: the prison chaplain and two of his fellow prisoners. In both instances, luck played a part in contacting them. A Linz newspaper, *Linzer Volksblatt*, was sufficiently interested in the study I was making to publish a story about it and its subject. At the end of its report, the suggestion was made that any reader who had information about Jägerstätter could send it to me at St. Radegund. Two very important letters resulted from this suggestion, the first of them from a Rev. Franz Baldinger, of Linz, who wrote:

I am sure that Franz Jägerstätter is the condemned prisoner in the military detention center at Linz whom I visited at that time in his cell, since, as the local pastor, I was providing spiritual assistance to the Catholics in the armed services. I remember that a relatively young father of a family from St. Radegund told me *he had been sentenced to death because he refused to take the military oath*—and this precisely on the grounds described in this morning's paper. At that time I made every effort to save this fine, upstanding and brave young man. I tried to make it clear to him that he must keep his own and his family's welfare in mind even in following his personal ideals and principles. At the time of my last visit, *he seemed to have come around to seeing my point and promised to follow my recommendation and take the oath.* I was shocked when I later learned that he had been executed in Berlin. [Italics added.]

As soon as the opportunity presented itself, I visited this priest. At this meeting he said that further thought had clarified his memory to some extent. He seemed to recall that the young man had been a sexton in his home parish. The fact that I could verify that point obviously pleased him. Further, he was now not sure whether the prisoner had already been condemned or was just being held for transfer elsewhere. Nor was he absolutely certain that a refusal to take the oath was the specific point at issue; he had just taken that for granted, since most of the unfortunate men who had come under his care had been charged with desertion, and he knew that Jägerstätter was an exception.

Other than that he remembered the man quite well. He had impressed him as a devout and dedicated man without the slightest hint of mental imbalance or religious fanaticism. In their discussions Franz had been clear and logical in his arguments and all but unshakable in his commitment. When I asked if the peasant's attitude toward him was at all antagonistic or disrespectful because he was performing his priestly duties in the context of a Nazi military prison, he replied that quite the opposite was true. Had there been the slightest hint of disrespect or rebelliousness, he would have taken an altogether different line of approach to the man.

Jägerstätter, he recalled, was fully aware of the fact that he had merely to indicate his willingness to serve and all would go well with him. Against this, however, stood his firm conviction that the regime was evil (and had been so designated by the Church), and that it was engaged in fighting an unjust war. Under the circumstances, he found it impossible to accept service.

In his role as chaplain and spiritual advisor, Baldinger had tried to convince him that he had no responsibility as a private citizen for the acts and policies of the government. Again the crucial distinction was proposed: in taking the oath and performing the service required of him, he would not be endorsing the Nazis and their objectives; instead, he would merely be following orders like millions of other Catholics, including seminarians. Furthermore, he had continued, the ordinary individual—and especially one in the peasant's restricted sphere of activity—had neither the facts nor the competence to pass a final judgment as to the justice or injustice of the war. His concluding argument, once he learned that the man had a wife and family, stressed his primary responsibility for them and their welfare, especially in view of the inescapable consequences of the course he had chosen. In an article published some years after this interview took place, Baldinger added another argument he had used at the time: the merciless military policies of "the other side," with its unjustifiable bombing of cities and their helpless populations, had reduced the whole war to the question of survival. Interestingly enough, he had not remembered this in our discussion.

Of course, these were all arguments with which Jägerstätter had long been familiar. As his last few letters from prison indicated, he certainly had not entertained any serious thought of changing his stand, however much the priest may have thought he had convinced him. The decision to accept limited military service mentioned in the letter of March 11 was not related to this talk with the chaplain, for they did not meet until more than a month later. Nevertheless, Father Baldinger's description is important, since it gives an outsider's view of the man at the time of his gravest trials.

The two men whose letters furnish the last material available for this period of imprisonment were conscripts from the Moselle-Rhineland border area (Lorraine) between Germany and France. At the period in question, they, too, were prisoners at Linz, and at least one was a cellmate of Jägerstätter for part of his stay there. In January, 1962, that is, after my stay in St. Radegund, one of these men wrote to Mrs. Jägerstätter to inquire whether she had ever been able to obtain official transcripts of her husband's case from the Linz military court. If she had, he was interested in obtaining his records, too. But he prefaced this inquiry by saying:

I have not forgotten your husband, and I never will forget him. For he gave me a rosary in the prison at Linz. All I know is that your husband was shot [sic] because he would not take the oath. I, too, was under sentence—ten years at hard labor—but I was fortunate enough to gain my freedom again. After that, I deserted from the army and hid myself in the woods until the Americans came. That is how I managed to escape death.

All passes over and goes by. Your children must be fully grown by now. These children can safely say that their father died in God's friendship. For he prayed day and night, and when he was not praying the rosary, he was reading a religious pamphlet.

77

Mrs. Jägerstätter's reply to this letter was apparently shown to his friend, Gregoire B., who was then inspired to write a few lines of his own to the widow. Since he had no other purpose, his letter dealt entirely and more explicitly with prison recollections:

> In January, 1943, along with three other Frenchmen . . . I was taken to the military prison in Linz and thus made the acquaintance of Mr. Franz Jägerstätter a few days later.[3] Since, like him, we would not take the oath, we developed a special friendship right away. I was in the same cell with Franz for a long time, and I can only assure you that we found a good friend in Franz who, in the darkest moments, was always able to find a word of comfort and always managed to give us his last piece of bread from the meager morning and evening meals we took in the cell, while he satisfied himself with a little black coffee.
>
> His faith in God and justice was beyond measure [*übergross*]— thus one saw him sunk in prayer the whole day through, his rosary his constant companion. In the same way, the Easter Communion we received together in April, 1943, brought him great happiness.

There follows a point of particular importance in the Jägerstätter story in terms of the controls and pressures operating to shake the determination of this man to follow the dictates of his conscience: "He was never afraid to confess his faith openly in spite of the taunts of the guards and his fellow prisoners." B. then closed with his own laudatory evaluation: "Franz belongs without question to the heroes of our time, to the heroes of your homeland alongside men like Andreas Hofer and Gustav Palm. For like them, he, too, was a fighter to the death for faith, peace, and justice."

In an attempt to obtain further information from these men, I wrote them each a letter suggesting a series of points I would like them to cover. The one who had initiated the contact with Mrs.

---

[3] Since Jägerstätter could not have joined this man in the Linz prison earlier than March, this correspondent's memory has no doubt grown hazy on this point—a fact not at all surprising in view of the length of time that has since elapsed.

Jägerstätter did not reply; the other, however, did furnish some additional, interesting, and most significant recollections. He wrote:

> I remember Jägerstätter as a man of profound faith, honest, very frank, and very helpful. He was my cellmate for some weeks during the time I was in prison at Linz, from February to June, 1943. Throughout this time I saw him every day, but it was not always possible to talk with him. In our morning walk (ten times around the corridor), I always saw Jägerstätter praying his rosary. His piety was the thing that impressed one most. As a cellmate, he would share his last morsel of bread, saying he did not need any more.

In my letter I had asked whether he felt there was any basis for the feeling on the part of many that Jägerstätter was mentally unsound. To this he replied that Franz was "very religious but in no sense demented," and that he possessed "a fanatical love for his country, Austria." As for Jägerstätter's stand against the war, he said it was similar to the grounds of his own imprisonment; both had refused to serve what they considered to be the enemy. "The only difference was, that as an Austrian, he had been considered a German since 1938, whereas Lorraine had not been annexed until 1940." Another recollection describes his cellmate's attitude toward Hitler:

> One day during a discussion, Jägerstätter explained his point of view concerning Hitler in the following way. He likened him to a man who finds a little worm while digging in his garden and holds in his hands the choice of letting it live or cutting it in two with a stroke of his spade—for no cause and without justice. Such was Hitler who wished to dispose of the lives of those he oppressed at his pleasure. According to Jägerstätter, the system could not last long and was opposed to his religious convictions.

The image of Franz, as it emerges from the letters written to his wife, finds striking confirmation in the memories of the man who shared the hardships of his prison life.

79

Jägerstätter was always very quiet, especially vis-à-vis the Germans. With me, both German and soldier against my will, he dropped some of his reserve. He confided to me that he refused to fight in a war that was senseless and doomed in advance. Furthermore, he told me, as a Christian he preferred to do his fighting with the word of God and not with arms. He loved Austria intensely, and he absolutely refused to serve the oppressor of his country. He always knew and said that he would be executed, but he preferred to die this way than to do evil to others and die anyway on the battle front.

One of God's
Special Friends

Jägerstätter's hasty note of departure had said he was leaving Linz at 10:15 A.M. Later that same afternoon he was able to send his wife another message from Regensburg, where he apparently had a brief stop.

I must write you still a few more lines from here. I hope you have received my note of this morning. The departure came as a complete surprise, so that there was not even time to take final leave of comrades. The Berliner who will be my companion when we leave for Berlin at 2:30 is a very nice fellow. I can tell you that, as far as my stand is concerned, I am still unable to come to any other decision. Through all the things that have happened, I cannot bring myself to act in any other way.

Apparently there had been a preliminary hearing, because he refers to an attempt in the proceedings to deny everything the Nazis had done against the Church and to show that people were, in fact, acting quite differently. This suggests that the familiar argument was advanced which would distinguish between the German military and the Nazi regime. This morning I was told by someone (whose father is a general, no less) that people in high places are saying: one must first fight the enemy outside, and

81

then the time will come for the enemy within (namely the N.).[1] As far as my spiritual condition is concerned, you have no cause for worry. Should things conceivably go worse for me in Berlin, I would not want you to be troubled for this reason either. The letter concludes: I am still as firm as ever in everything.

In a way it can be said that Jägerstätter wrote at least three "farewell" messages, in addition to the letter written just before his actual execution in August. When he wrote his first letter from Enns, he had reason to believe that he would never be in touch with his family again. So, too, with the note during his abrupt transfer to Berlin. For all he knew, nothing awaited him but the formalities of a final condemnation and execution. Perhaps he knew enough about the legal processes of the military to know he would have some privileges of communication there, too, but it is unlikely that he would have felt secure about that. One may suppose, then, that this was intended to be a final good-bye—just in case.

Three days later (May 7), however, he was able to write again. A good part of the letter is concerned with "small talk" about the trip and the new prison. They had arrived safely in Berlin the night of the 4th, and he is moved to comment that **had it been just a pleasure trip, it would have been a beautiful journey; the countryside and the cities through which we passed were, for the most part, very nice.** As for the amenities of the new location, **some things are a little different from Linz; but as far as I can see, one does not go hungry here. I also have a very nice little room all to myself.**

Of course, there were some drawbacks, one of which was the fact that a visit he and his wife had apparently arranged for June was now impossible, **for it would be too much of a strain for you to come to Berlin.** Another was the sad news that he could write only one letter a month. He could, however, receive mail as often as it came. Apparently the discussions mentioned in the note from Regensburg were informal, for he continues: **Needless to say, if I had had any idea that I would be sent away from Linz without**

1 Nazis.

a formal hearing, I would have had you come for a short visit long ago. Now resignation is counseled. If God so wills, there will still be a reunion in this world someday; and, if not, we can then look ahead to one in that other world where the visiting time will be much longer than fifteen minutes or a half hour.

He is, of course, fully aware of the realities of his new situation. Though I am now still farther separated from you, this should not be any reason for you to have a heavier heart on my account. You know very well under whose protection I stand. . . . It will certainly not be any worse for me that I have come here, for God does not intend that we be lost but, rather, that we may be happy with Him for all eternity. If one harbors no thought of vengeance against others and can forgive everyone, even when he sometimes is the object of a harsh word, he will be at peace in his heart— and what is there in all this world more lovely than peace? Let us pray to God, therefore, that a real and lasting peace may soon descend upon this world.

To the children he writes: Now your father is not able to write to you so often any more. I am also very far away, but, in spite of this, I can still be with you in my thoughts. And I can still pray for you and will do so most diligently so that you become truly good children. Be obedient to mother and to grandmother, and Aunt Resi too. Then the Heavenly Father and the Heavenly Mother will love you dearly, and you will be able to ask them for many things. Don't forget your father, and pray for him. Now, I put you all under the protection of your Heavenly Mother. Your father who always loves you greets you from his heart. Farewell to all until we meet again.

The reference to world peace finds a parallel in the June 6th letter in which he suggests that the family pray fervently to the Sacred Heart of Jesus so that He may bring an early peace to the world—if only all the people wanted it! It would be too much to believe that his interest in an early peace was inspired by concern for his own welfare, but it is probably true that he had come to recognize that peace would be his only hope of escape. At any rate, after mentioning that the month of June should be one of the loveliest months of the year (in a devotional sense), he returns to a familiar theme: Dearest wife, if it is God's will, there will still be the reunion I believe each of us is yearning for. Stay at peace, love one another, and be quick to forgive. Most men make life bitter for themselves by the hardness of their hearts.

In this connection, he speaks again of how sorely he missed the May devotions at church, but goes on to describe how I held a May devotion of my own each evening in my cell. As decoration for a picture of Mary, I still had the violets from Rosie you once sent me. Of course, it would have been much nicer if the father could have gathered his whole family about him for the prayers.

He also comments on some stomach trouble he has been having—These little stomach upsets are easy to bear, for things could easily be much worse—and offers some general observations on prison routine. He is still alone in his cell, but he has a half hour of outdoor exercise every day and a chance to work (making envelopes in his cell) as much as he pleases. Of course, I would much prefer to be able to take some of the heavy work off your shoulders, but free choice is gone for the time being and this cannot be changed. At least I can still pray for you. It is also a blessing from God when one is permitted to suffer a little for his faith. Here I can really make the best retreats. If I were at home, I would hardly be able to take a week off for this purpose, if retreats are still held. He assumes they are busy at home with the hay harvest—and in what is probably a humorous suggestion, he guesses that the two oldest girls (about five and six years of age) might already be "helping" in that effort. If they have had no more rain than the Berlin area, prospects would not be too good for the fruit crop or for the water supply.

As usual, he includes a special greeting for the children: You haven't forgotten your father, have you, just because he hasn't written for so long and doesn't come home at all? By now I suppose you are again picking strawberries and heidelberries and cherries from neighbor Lang's trees. This year little Aloisia will almost be able to do it too. Be very good and obedient children, and God will make everything turn out right again.

He still has nothing definite to say about his immediate future. He does tell his wife that he had appeared before the Reich's Military Tribunal on May 24, but he does not say what transpired there. Instead he makes purely incidental observations: The drive there covered a good distance by car, since the Tribunal is located in the city proper, while Tegel is on the outskirts. Only in this way does one begin to get a small idea of the size of such a great city.

If Jägerstätter's prison writings skip over some matters, we are fortunate in having another source from which the story can be obtained. A letter in Fr. Karobath's files was signed by an attorney, "F. L. Feldmann." It turned out that F. L. Feldmann had been assigned to defend Jägerstätter before the Reich's Military Tribunal, the *Reichskriegsgericht*. In the hope that the attorney's records might contain information or documentation vital to the story, I asked American embassy officials in Berlin to check into his present whereabouts. They were unable to locate anyone by that name in Berlin, but they noted that a directory of German lawyers did list a Friedrich Leo Feldmann in Düsseldorf. A letter to this address brought the welcome news that this man had been Jägerstätter's counsel and that he remembered the case very well. He stated his willingness to discuss the matter if his former client's widow was willing to sign a waiver releasing him from his obligations of professional secrecy. This Mrs. Jägerstätter was kind enough to do, thereby opening a most significant source of information. It turned out, too, that his connection with the case proved important to his later career, since it helped establish his personal and political reliability for the Occupation authorities during the denazification period. One of the chaplains serving the Berlin-Tegel prison had written a letter, still in the attorney's possession, specifically citing the energetic efforts he had made on behalf of "an Austrian peasant who refused military service on the grounds that he could not support a regime that was attacking his Church."

The opportunity to become the court-appointed attorney was given him through a friend who held a court post of some authority; no special interest had drawn him to the case. But once he became involved, he was prepared to make any attempt to save his client's life, no matter how desperate or farfetched it might appear. He looks back upon it all as an extremely tragic affair, but he

85

takes great satisfaction in knowing that he did everything in his power. He assured me that no official documents existed which would be of any value; but the case had made so deep an impression upon him that he was certain that his recollections were accurate in all crucial aspects.

He felt he was not qualified to judge the man's mental condition at the time—especially in view of the fact that the position he had taken was so extreme and he was so inflexible in his commitment to it. But in all of his contacts with him, the prisoner conversed in a "perfectly normal" way, and his manner gave no indication of mental instability or abnormality. One interesting fact was the attorney's apparent lack of familiarity with Jägerstätter's general religious behavior—the frequent devotions, constant prayer —and he was genuinely surprised to hear that the man had actually made a personal visit to his bishop to discuss his intention to refuse military service on grounds of conscience.

The description of the relationship between attorney and client was one more in the series in which the peasant was subjected to a battery of arguments to induce him to abandon his stand. The attorney recalled Jägerstätter's position: he could do nothing to support the regime or aid its cause, since the Nazis were persecuting his Church. When Feldmann sought to counter this argument, pointing out that millions of other Catholics found it possible to do their duty to the nation—and he, like so many others, gave particular emphasis to the seminarians and priests, some of whom were actually engaged in combat—the peasant merely replied, "They have not been given the grace" to see things otherwise. Pursuing his line of argument further, the attorney had challenged Jägerstätter to cite a single instance in which a bishop— in a pastoral letter, a sermon, or anything else—had called upon Catholics not to support the war or to refuse military service. The prisoner admitted that he knew of no such instance, adding again that this proved nothing more than the fact that they had not been "given the grace" either.

Turning next to arguments of more theological substance, the attorney cited the familiar scriptural injunction to "give unto Caesar the things that are Caesar's," and he asked by what right the peasant thought he could take a position that was "more Catholic" than that taken by priests and bishops who bore the responsibility for making theological judgments. Jägerstätter justified his stand by insisting that this was the kind of a moral judgment that ultimately has to be made by the individual conscience, especially since the point at issue concerned precisely the distinction between the "things that are Caesar's" and "the things that are God's." On a more practical plane, the attorney, like all the others who had tried to change his mind, stressed the prisoner's responsibilities toward his wife and family and the threat his action would pose to their welfare. This, too, met with the now familiar response that the dictates of conscience must always be given precedence even over such pressing personal considerations.

On the day of the trial, July 6, 1943, Attorney Feldmann was given an unexpected opportunity, which he converted into his first unusual effort to save the man's life. When he arrived on the scene, he found that the room assigned for Jägerstätter's trial was still in use. The attorney decided to use the delay to make a desperate plea to the court officials to see what they could do informally before the start of the actual hearing. He approached the presiding officer of the military tribunal and explained the special problem posed by this unquestionably sincere man with his fixed determination to refuse service. He suggested that if these officers would talk to the man, they might be more successful than he had been in changing his position.

To the attorney's surprise and gratification, the court agreed. Feldmann interrupted his story at this point to stress the uniqueness of this occurrence; he is still convinced that it had never happened before and that it probably never happened again. Certainly it was a moment of high drama: the peasant was confronted with two high-ranking military officers who represented the power he had chosen to reject and who were soon to pass final judgment upon him for his act of rebellion.

As the attorney recalled the course of this exceptional discussion, the meeting began with a rather stern lecture by the court officers on the prisoner's obligation to serve the Fatherland. They also reminded him that if he persisted in his stubborn refusal, they would have no alternative but to condemn him to death. To the lecture of the court officials, Jägerstätter's response was the calm and firm statement that he was fully aware of the penalty his action entailed, but that his conscience would not permit him to fight for a regime that was persecuting his Church. The argument progressed along already familiar lines, with the officers making the usual distinction between support for a given regime and the "defense of the Fatherland," and stressing the inability of the partially informed individual to make a competent judgment on such complicated issues. These exchanges served no purpose other than to establish the utter sincerity of the peasant's commitment. In the process, the attorney noted a distinct change taking place in the tone of the officers' appeals, until they finally reached the point where they were pleading with the prisoner not to "force" them to condemn him to death. They begged him, in effect, to modify his stand, at least to the degree that he would accept some form of noncombatant service. The attorney was most definite and explicit on this point; he recalled that his client was given a guarantee that he would never be called upon to bear arms if he would only withdraw his refusal to serve. But Jägerstätter rejected this offer, too. As he explained it, such an agreement would only complicate matters by adding to an already essentially immoral compromise, the sin of falsehood, through his only "seeming" to accept service as a means of avoiding the death penalty.

One can imagine how attractive this offer must have appeared to Franz. To some, his decision will serve as evidence of total abandonment to the will of God as he saw it, and of a state of perfect readiness to accept the fatal outcome that was now a certainty. Others will continue to see it as the ultimate display of stubborn fanaticism. No matter how his motives are interpreted, however, at this moment the rebel in Jägerstätter appeared most clearly.

After these dramatic encounters, the trial itself was a brief and formal affair. Although the attorney was certain that whatever records were made of the trial no longer exist, he assured me that all they could contain would be a formal reading of the charges, an acknowledgment of their validity on the part of the defendant in the form of a renewed statement of his refusal to serve, and the mandatory sentence of death. Legally, Attorney Feldmann informed me, Jägerstätter was being tried under a section of a wartime penal law that dealt with harming the war effort (Paragraph 5 [*Zersetzung der Wehrkraft*] of the 33. *Kriegssonderstrafrechtsverordnung v. August 1938*), which states: "The death penalty shall be levied against . . . anyone who publicly advocates or incites the refusal to perform the required service in the German army or one allied with it or who otherwise openly seeks to weaken or undermine the desire of the German people or any allied with it to maintain its military effectiveness."

Before moving on to the events of the last few weeks of Jägerstätter's life in prison, some comments should be made about this remarkable episode. One is struck at first by the fact that so much effort was made to save the life of a man who was certainly "an enemy of the State," according to Nazi definition. This is perhaps best explained by noting that Jägerstätter's case remained in the hands of the military authorities. As the attorney took great pains to stress, they operated according to vastly different principles and procedures than did the infamous People's Court, the civilian police, and security agencies. In this respect, too, he was quick to deny that Jägerstätter had been mistreated in prison. Dean Kreuzberg was later to make a similar denial, also distinguishing military justice from the behavior associated with Gestapo investigations and detention. But could not something else have been involved? It is clear, for one thing, that the officers had been favorably impressed by the man himself—an unusual turn in individuals who had devoted their lives to an order, and its virtues, repudiated by him. It is conceivable that Jägerstätter reached them as they were unable to reach him. At the time of this encounter, the dissatisfaction within military circles, which was to culminate in an ill-fated assassination attempt on Hitler about a year later, was undoubtedly already widely felt. It would be interesting to know to what extent Jägerstätter's rebellion struck chords already familiar to these officers, and not totally repugnant to them. Unfortunately, the attorney's notes do not contain the names of the officers involved. And even if their identities were known, it would be impossible to do more than speculate upon this possibility. We are forced, then, to leave the matter at its most obvious level of inference—that their concern was to save the life of a man whose sincerity and courage moved them deeply.

Two days after this meeting and the trial, Jägerstätter wrote his monthly letter to his wife and family. It is a remarkable document, not so much for what it says as for what it does not say, and for the way in which things are not said. The letter is clearly intended to spare them the grief the final decision was certain to bring them, yet it had the equally obvious purpose of strengthening them for the inevitable outcome. The "next letter" to which he refers would, he must have been sure, be the last letter he would ever write. In this context, then, the following lines provide a significant and revealing clue to the frame of mind which marked his final days on earth.

All of you will certainly be very curious to know if any decision has been reached concerning my future. Nevertheless I beg you to remain patient, at least until my next letter. I hope to have some final decision by then. Dearest wife, as long as I am not unhappy, there is no need for you to be heavy of heart or to weep. Only do not forget me in prayer, even as I will not forget you—and remember me especially at Mass. I can also give you the good news that I had a visit yesterday, and from a priest no less! Next Tuesday he will come with the Holy of Holies. Even here, one is not abandoned by God.

The letter began, At long last the time has come when I can again write you a few lines. First of all, my most fervent thanks for your letters which I have received with great joy and which I always look forward to with great longing. Heartfelt thanks, too, for the lovely photos which also brought me great joy—as well as moist eyes. I hardly recognized little Loisl any more: from her appearance she seems to be a lively child. It would be such a joy if one could spend the few short days of his life in his happy family circle. But if the dear Lord has decided otherwise for us, then that is also well and good. It is always a joy to be permitted to suffer for Jesus and our faith. Then, too, we have the joyous hope that these few days on earth during which we are forced to be apart will be repaid a thousand times over in eternity when we will be permitted to enjoy uninterrupted joy and happiness forever with God and our Heavenly Mother. If only we can stand fast in God's love: for it is possible that difficult tests of faith are still to come upon us this year. For all we know, we may be entering upon that time when, as it has been written, even the justest of the just can hardly be saved.

His wife had apparently violated the regulations against sending food, by sending his favorite dish which was still tasty when I received it on Pentecost Sunday and which had to do as dessert for two meals. He warns her not to do this again, adding: They let this little gift come through to me purely out of good will. He assures her that his health is good, and makes a few references to farm affairs and his fear that the summer might prove too much for the frail health of his wife and his mother, once the work starts in earnest. This leads him to add a special note for the latter, apparently in reply to the first message he had received from her. Dear Mother, I thank you, too, for your lines which made me very happy. I hope this means that you are no longer angry with me because of my disobedience. I beg you not to be so concerned and anxious about my physical welfare. Even if more difficult things come upon me, this means nothing. For the dear Lord will not send me more than I can bear.

The letter concludes with the usual note for the children: My dear little ones. Your photos brought me great happiness. Of course, it would be much better for me if I could see you again in person. But you should not let yourselves be disappointed just because your father never comes to tell you stories any more. Today there are many children whose fathers cannot come now or who will never come again. I am very happy to see from Mother's letter that you always pray diligently. I believe that you have already become much better and more obedient in other ways too. It would make me very happy if you grow into good and brave children. On Corpus Christi Sunday I thought of you especially. I would have loved to have seen you wearing your little crowns of flowers. Your devoted father greets you from far away. Stay healthy, all of you, and pray well until we meet again.

When we realize that sentence had already been passed on

Jägerstätter, we see the true depth of meaning behind the phrase: "these few days on earth"; the warning about "difficult tests of faith" still to come; the assurance to his mother that "the Lord will not send me more than I can bear"; or the sad reminder to his children that "there are many children whose fathers . . . will never come again."

Jägerstätter had carefully avoided telling his family about the death sentence, trying to spare them the tragic confirmation of all their worst fears until the very last moment. But things were to turn out differently. Attorney Feldmann was moved to make a second extraordinary effort to save Franz's life. In a letter dated July 6, 1943, and addressed to "the Catholic pastor of St. Radegund," he had already broken the news to the family:

> I assume that the case of one Jägerstätter from St. Radegund is known to you. I am the attorney assigned to defend Franz Jägerstätter. Today the hearing was held before the Reich's Military Tribunal in which, unfortunately, Jägerstätter did not abandon the position with which you are familiar but, on the contrary, continued to represent the point of view that, as a Catholic, he could not take up arms, since that would mean that he would be fighting for National Socialism—which he considers impossible for him.
>
> As a consequence, Jägerstätter was condemned to death . . .

But a faint ray of hope is offered at once:

> The sentence is not yet binding; it must still be formally confirmed by the officials of the Tribunal. Jägerstätter can still be saved, but only if he abandons his totally senseless position and declares himself ready to accept military service. Circumstances could then make it possible to base an appeal on this.
>
> I am permitted, very respected pastor, to notify you to inform Jägerstätter's family at home. Perhaps it would be possible for them to come here without delay and personally try once again to influence this man. In such event, I ask that you notify me by wire when the relatives can be here.

I would at once petition the military court to hold off the confirmation and the execution of the sentence.

In the meantime, he continued to do what he could on behalf of his client by enlisting the aid of others who might also have some influence upon him.

I have already tried all day to reach the Catholic military chaplain who serves as the prison chaplain. I will ask him to make a special point of visiting Jägerstätter and to prevail upon him to change his mind. He is doing no one any good and only jeopardizes his whole case.

The attorney's impatience with his stubborn client and his "totally senseless" position should probably not be taken too literally. Together with the customary "Heil Hitler!" which closed the letter, it might better be taken as a concession to prudence. He was, in a sense, "sticking his neck out" to an extent that could jeopardize his career, if not his personal safety. Perhaps that is why he adds the caution: "In addition, I beg you to treat the above letter as strictly confidential." After all, he had already tried his best and lost the case. The fact that he was prepared to make these desperate attempts at appeal, that he even went to the trouble of "trying all day" to enlist the aid of the prison chaplain, shows a real desire to leave no stone unturned.

The three principals in the subsequent visit to Berlin—Attorney Feldmann, Fr. Fürthauer, and Mrs. Jägerstätter—were all asked about their memories of the event. Of the three, the attorney had the least to say, and even this was not always reliable. For instance, he was under the impression that the visit had taken place before the trial; more surprisingly, he thought that the widow had already made an earlier visit to the Berlin prison on her own initiative and he "vaguely remembered" meeting her. He was more definite in his recollections of Fr. Fürthauer, describing him (almost twenty years after the event) as a typical "country bumpkin" whom a Berliner, especially, would associate with rural Bavaria and Austria. These discrepancies are not particularly vital, however, since it does not appear that he was present at the actual meeting of husband and wife.

The account furnished by the widow seems the most reliable. In a letter written shortly after her return, and dated July 15, she told Pastor Karobath that she had received the dreaded news of the trial and the sentence on Saturday and she had begged Fr. Fürthauer to go with her to Berlin. They left Titmoning, the nearest railway stop, the following morning and arrived in Berlin that evening. As she described the visit, her husband was not in the prison when they arrived; they were taken to a waiting room with windows overlooking the prison courtyard and left there for about half an hour. At length they saw a truck drive into the courtyard. When it came to a stop, the back was opened and some soldiers jumped out and formed a circle. Then Jägerstätter was pushed out so roughly that he fell to the ground, a sight which caused her to scream his name from the window. Hearing her voice, he jumped to his feet and looked wildly about him—as if, she added, he thought her voice had come from another world. He had not known they were coming to see him.

Another brief wait followed before she and the young vicar were taken to a cell where they sat across a table from her husband, who was flanked by guards on either side. Fürthauer remembered that when they saw Franz in the truck, he was in chains, but that they had been removed before he was brought to the visiting cell—although, he added, the prisoner was accompanied by an armed guard at all times. His wife had brought him some food, but was not permitted to give it to him. Both she and the priest tried to prevail upon him to change his mind, but it was useless. (As she put it in her letter to Karobath, "He could not bring himself to promise us he would become a soldier. He had suffered much, but in spite of this, he told me he felt generally happy. He certainly did not want to change his mind. He still has several days to think it over, but only the dear Lord knows how much longer he has to live.") She interrupted her narrative to add that she knew people thought that she did not try to get him to change his mind, but that this was simply not true. She knew he would die if he could not be persuaded to abandon his position, and she certainly did not want him to die.

There was not much more for her to tell. The whole visit lasted only twenty minutes until, as she wrote later, "with heavy hearts we had to take leave of each other."

She and the vicar left Berlin at 10 o'clock the following night. In words strikingly reminiscent of her husband's account of his own trip, she wrote Fr. Karobath: "It would have been a thoroughly enjoyable journey had it been just a pleasure trip. But as it was, it was a very sad journey, since we could not change his precarious condition, for the way the laws work today, this society is determined to carry them out to the bitter end. Maybe they will still find some other way out, for nothing will be gained by shooting him." Then follows an interesting bit of evidence, indicating that neither Jägerstätter nor the attorney had told the visitors the full story: "They could easily have assigned him to the medical corps, but they were naturally too proud for that, for it might have looked like a compromise on their part. I hope that with God's help, everything will still turn out for the best." The question therefore remains: why was she not told that he had been "begged" to accept such service? One might conclude that the attorney's story of the dramatic confrontation was an ingenious concoction, but there would be no real reason for him to falsify his account, and his manner in telling the story was thoroughly persuasive. The more likely explanation is that Jägerstätter preferred her not to know that he had been given the opportunity to save his life—and had rejected it. It is still somewhat surprising that the attorney had not told them, but the limitations of time in what must have been a thoroughly hectic day, or his own feeling that this was a matter of utmost secrecy that should be kept even from them, may be sufficient explanation.

Fürthauer's recollections of the visit added a few valuable insights. He said he had relayed the message, apparently from the attorney, that all charges would be dropped if he would only change his stand, and he added his own strong recommendation that the offer be accepted. Jägerstätter had replied with a question: Even if I were to agree now, do you think they would really keep their promise? They would almost certainly send me out to serve in a *Straf-legion* (a military unit reserved for particularly hazardous or even hopeless action, in which there would be virtually no chance of survival). The priest took this as proof that the man had already thought everything through to its last consequences and had reached the point of final certainty as to the only course open to him. Jägerstätter also mentioned that he had talked with a military chaplain and that this discussion had brought him a great sense of "inner peace." Even when Fürthauer suggested that the war would probably be over soon and that he might never have to face a situation which would call for actions he opposed, the argument had no visible effect upon him.

Apart from this, Fürthauer said that Franz had been overjoyed to see his wife again. As far as her contribution to the visit was concerned, he said that she had made little real effort to get him to change his mind since she, too, could see that he had already reached the point of commitment where all such attempts were hopeless. When the visit came to an end, Jägerstätter gave his wife a little piece of chocolate for each of the children—an event she did not remember, incidentally. Before leaving the cell, the priest again advised him to accept military service. Failing in this one last effort, he gave the prisoner his priestly blessing and assured him that he need not fear that he was committing a sin by following the dictates of his conscience .

With that, the visit was over. Franz Jägerstätter and his wife had now indeed seen one another for the last time on this earth.

The chaplain who had given the peasant his sense of "inner peace" was almost certainly Dean Kreuzberg. It must have been about this time that he had made his own three-hour-long attempt to change the condemned man's mind. Possibly this, too, was the result of the attorney's urging. However satisfying it would be, it is not possible to fix the exact order of events during the month of July. Kreuzberg had two visits with Franz. After the first, he left the condemned man to think it over and tell him his final decision when he returned. During the second visit, he received Jägerstätter's decision and then congratulated him on the strength of his moral commitment. It would seem that the second visit had not yet taken place when Franz's wife and the vicar made their fruitless journey to Berlin. This assumption rests on the fact that Kreuzberg, during his second visit to Franz, told him about Fr. Reinisch, a Pallotine priest who had gone to the scaffold the year before. In a book on Reinisch, written by Kreuzberg after the war—a book which includes the Jägerstätter story—the former chaplain describes the joy and relief with which Franz had received the news that someone else (a priest, no less) had traveled the same path. It seems reasonable to assume that Franz would have wanted his wife to share his joy in this news. The fact that he said nothing about it during the visit seems a clear indication that the second Kreuzberg visit had not yet taken place.

The question of time sequence has some importance with reference to one of the more significant Jägerstätter documents, the "statement of position," written in Tegel at Kreuzberg's request. This document is dated "July," with no further indication as to whether it was written before or after the trial, or before or after the visit of his wife. Internal evidence would suggest that it was written between the two. The first is a positive clue: the "sentence of death" reference in the opening lines and, even more significant perhaps, the note of scornful dismissal that pervades the whole first paragraph.

These few words are being set down here as they come from my mind and my heart. And if I must write them with my hands in chains, I find that much better than if my will were in chains. Neither prison nor chains nor sentence of death can rob a man of the Faith and his own free will. God gives so much strength that it is possible to bear any suffering, a strength far stronger than all the might of the world. The power of God cannot be overcome.

The very next sentence offers negative evidence. The absence of any reference to the visit in a context where such reference would have been all but unavoidable places the statement *before* his wife's journey to his Berlin cell; the arguments, even the quotations, have been used before by him.

If people took as much trouble to warn men against the serious sins which bring eternal death, and thus keep them from such sins, as they are taking to warn me against a dishonorable death, I think Satan could count on no more than a meager harvest in the last days. Again and again, people stress the obligations of conscience as they concern my wife and children. But I cannot believe that, just because a man has a wife and children, he is free to offend God by lying (not to mention all the other things he would be called upon to do). Did not Christ Himself say, "He who loves father, mother, or children more than Me is not deserving of My love"? Or, "Fear not those who can kill the body but not the soul; rather fear much more those who seek to destroy body and soul in hell"?

One portion of this statement is of particular importance here, since it relates to the finality of his commitment. It is a discussion, interestingly enough, that was anticipated at least seven years before in his letter of spiritual counsel to his godson. Now it is no longer a matter of theory; for him it has become a practical certainty. Then he wrote, **We must do everything in our power to strive toward the Eternal Homeland and to preserve a good conscience.** Now he writes:

Why do we give so little thought to eternity? Why is it so hard for us to make sacrifices for heaven? Yes, even though we cannot see it, we are sometimes clearly aware of the presence of an invisible power which makes every conceivable effort to lead man along the path to ruin. And that is the power of hell. Lucifer knows full well what joys and glories there are in heaven, but since he himself can never return to them, he cannot bear man to know such joy. For this reason, he and his companions use every means to bind our thoughts and desires to this world. The less we think of eternity and of God's love and mercy, the more likely Satan is to win his game. For us men there are only two possibilities in this world: either we become ever better or ever worse; there is simply no such thing as standing still. Yes, even for those who have worked hard to come closer to God, there can be many reverses, just as an army advancing toward its victory does not win all its battles but must endure many defeats. Nevertheless, this does not mean that the struggle should be given up as hopeless; instead, one must pick himself up with renewed strength and strive on again toward the desired goals.

Therefore, just as the man who thinks only of this world does everything possible to make life here easier and better, so must we, too, who believe in the eternal Kingdom risk everything in order to

receive a great reward there. Just as those who believe in National Socialism tell themselves that their struggle is for survival, so must we, too, convince ourselves that our struggle is for the eternal Kingdom. But with this difference: we need no rifles or pistols for our battle but, instead, spiritual weapons—and the foremost among these is prayer. For prayer, as St. Clare says, is the shield which the flaming arrows of the Evil One cannot pierce. Through prayer we constantly implore new grace from God, since without God's help and grace it would be impossible for us to preserve the Faith and be true to His commandments.

The true Christian is to be recognized more in his works and deeds than in his speech. The surest mark of all is found in deeds showing love of neighbor. To do unto one's neighbor what one would desire for himself is more than merely not doing to others what one would not want done to himself. Let us love our enemies, bless those who curse us, pray for those who persecute us. For love will conquer and will endure for all eternity. And happy are they who live and die in God's love.

Two more documents remain to complete the body of Jäger-stätter's prison writings. Both of them are "farewell" messages. There is a touch of mystery about the first because its date of composition is uncertain, as well as the means by which it came into Mrs. Jägerstätter's possession. The message is written on both sides of a large yellow card which had not been folded and, hence, could not have been sent through the mails. On the other hand, the most obvious explanation—that it was written and left behind at the time he left St. Radegund—is thrown into question by the fact that the handwriting is cramped and crowded to the point of being all but illegible, indicating that it had been written under circumstances requiring stealth and even camouflage, an unlikely situation if it had been written at home. The possibility that it may have been smuggled out of the Linz prison by the cellmate who was to have visited Mrs. Jägerstätter is unlikely because she can recall no such visit, and also because of a reference in the text to "my lonely cell," a bit of evidence which, of course, argues against the other tentative explanation, too. If, as it seems, it was written in Berlin, the mystery remains as to how it was delivered. Dean Kreuzberg assured me that he delivered no such message, and although he pointed out that at least two other chaplains had contact with the prisoner at the time, it is unlikely that they would have undertaken the personal delivery that its unfolded condition would indicate. It is most unlikely that Franz would have had a chance to write the message in the short period before he was taken to visit his wife or to hand it to her during that visit; it is scarcely possible that both she and Fr. Fürthauer would have forgotten so dramatic a part of the visit.

The most likely explanation, then, is that the card was written in the Berlin cell and later delivered to the widow, along with whatever clothing and other personal effects were returned to her after the execution. The message itself is interesting because it is more personal and much more expository than the "official" farewell letter written on the day of his death. His explanation of what has taken place is much more argumentative in tone; the advice he offers is more strongly colored by his own personal commitment. Actually, either side of the card could serve as the start of the message; I have chosen to present what I have designated as "Side A" first, because the message to the children (at the end of "Side B") had usually been a closing feature of his letters from prison. It is a most impressive display of the power and depth of the man's spiritual commitment and, therefore, is reproduced here in its entirety.

(SIDE A)

All my dear ones, the hour comes ever closer when I will be giving my soul back to God, the Master. I would have liked to say so many things to you in farewell so that it is hard not to be able to take leave of you any more. I would have liked, too, to spare you the pain and sorrow that you must bear because of me. But you know we must love God even more than family, and we must lose everything dear and worthwhile on earth rather than commit even the slightest offense against God. And if, for your sake, I had not shrunk back from offending God, how can we know what sufferings God might have sent us on my account? It must surely have been hard for our dear Saviour to bring such pain upon His dear Mother through His death: what, then, are our sorrows compared with what these two innocent hearts had to suffer—and all on account of us sinners?

And what kind of a leave-taking must it be for those who only halfway believe in an eternal life and, consequently, no longer have much hope of a reunion? If I did not have faith in God's mercy, that He would forgive me all my sins, I could scarcely have endured life in a lonely prison with such calm. Moreover, though people charge me with a crime and have condemned me to death as a criminal, I take comfort in the knowledge that not everything which this world considers a crime is a crime in the eyes of God. And I have hope that I need not fear the eternal Judge because of this crime.

Still this sentence of death should serve as a warning. For the Lord God will not deal much differently with us if we think we do not have to obey everything He commands us through His Church to believe and to do. Except that the eternal Judge will not only condemn us to mortal death but to everlasting death as well. For this reason, I have nothing pressing upon my heart more urgently than to make the firm decision to keep all the commandments and to avoid every sin. You must love God, your Lord, and your neighbor as yourself. On these two commandments rests the whole law. Keep these and we can look forward to an early reunion in heaven. For this reason, too, we must not think evil of others who act differently than I. It is much better to pray for everyone than to pass judgment upon them, for God desires that all become blessed.

(SIDE B)

Many actually believe quite simply that things have to be the way they are. If this should happen to mean that they are obliged to commit injustice, then they believe that others are responsible. The oath would not be a lie for someone who believes he can go along and is willing to do so. But if I know in advance that I cannot accept and obey everything I would promise under that oath, then I would be guilty of a lie. For this reason I am convinced that it is still best that I speak the truth, even if it costs me my life. For you will not find it written in any of the commandments of God or of the Church that a man is obliged under pain of sin to take an oath committing him to obey whatever might be commanded of him by his secular ruler. Therefore, you should not be heavy of heart if others see my decision as a sin, as some already have.

In the same way, if someone argues from the standpoint of the family, do not be troubled, for it is not permitted to lie even for the sake of the family. If I had ten children, the greatest demand upon me would still be the one I must make of myself.

Educate the children to be pious Catholics as long as it is possible. (Now, of course, one cannot expect them to understand much.) I can say from my own experience how painful life is when we live like halfway Christians, that is more like vegetating than living.

If a man were to possess all the wisdom of the world and call half the earth his own, he still could not and would not be as happy as one of those men who can still call virtually nothing in this world their own except their Catholic faith. I would not exchange my lonely cell—which is not at all bad [next word illegible] —for the most magnificent royal palace. No matter how great and how beautiful it might be, it will pass away, but God's word remains for all eternity. I can assure you that if you pray a single sincere "Our Father" for our children, you will have given them a greater gift than if you had provided them with the most lavish dowry a landholder ever dreamed of giving his daughter. Many people would laugh at these words, but they are true just the same.

Now, my dear children, when Mother reads this letter to you, your father will already be dead. He would have loved to come to you again, but the Heavenly Father willed it otherwise. Be good and obedient children and pray for me so that we may soon be reunited in heaven.

Dear wife, forgive me everything by which I have grieved or offended you. For my part, I have forgiven everything. Ask all those in Radegund whom I have ever injured or offended to forgive me too.

This could be seen as a preliminary, or draft, copy of the letter he was to write on August 9, 1943, which would be his final farewell.

102

If so, the change in tone in the latter might indicate a prudent conclusion that, since it would have to be turned over to the military authorities for mailing after his death, it would be best not to risk including anything they might consider subversive and, hence, sufficient grounds for refusing to send it on. Another and possibly more likely explanation, however, is that the immediacy of death brought a new perspective which made the obvious attempt to make one final justification of his stand seem much less important to him.

In any event, the text of this letter permits the reader to draw his own conclusions.

Greetings in God, my dearest, beloved wife and all my children: Your letters of July 13 and 25 have been received, and I am truly grateful for them. Today it is exactly four weeks since we saw each other for the last time in this world. This morning at about 5:30 we were suddenly told to dress ourselves; the auto was already waiting. Along with several other men under sentence of death, I was brought here to Brandenburg. We did not yet know what would happen to us. Not until noon was I told that my sentence was confirmed on July 14, and is to be carried out today about 4 P.M. Now I wish to write you a few words of farewell.

Dearest wife and mother! I thank you once more from my heart for everything that you have done for me in my lifetime, for all the love and sacrifice that you have borne for me: and I beg you again to forgive me if I have hurt or offended you, just as I have forgiven everything. I beg, too, that all others I have ever offended may forgive me, especially Father Fürthauer, if perhaps my words offended him when he visited me with you. I forgive everyone from my heart. May God accept my life in reparation not only for my sins but for the sins of others as well.

Dearest wife and mother! It was not possible for me to free you from the pain that you must now suffer on my account. How hard it must have been for our dear Saviour when, through His sufferings and death, He had to prepare such a great sorrow for His Mother— and they bore this all out of love for us sinners. I thank our dear Jesus, too, that I am privileged to suffer and even die for Him. I trust that, in His unending mercy, God has forgiven me everything and will not abandon me in the last hour. Dearest wife! Think again of that which Jesus has promised those who have made the nine First Friday devotions to the Sacred Heart. Even now Jesus will come to me in Holy Communion and strengthen me for the journey to eternity. In Tegel, too, I still had the grace of receiving the Blessed Sacrament four times.

My heartfelt greetings for my dear children. I will surely beg the dear God, if I am permitted to enter heaven soon, that He may set aside a little place in heaven for all of you. In the past week I have often prayed to the Blessed Mother that if it is God's will that I die soon, I may be permitted to celebrate the Feast of the Assumption in heaven.

Many greetings, too, to my in-laws, relatives and acquaintances. My greetings, too, to Brother Majer[2] and I thank him for his letter which brought me great pleasure. Also thanks to Father Karobath for writing.

And now, all my dear ones, fare thee well, and do not forget me in your prayers: keep the commandments, and through God's grace we will soon meet again in heaven! Heartfelt greetings once more to my confirmation godchild.

And now your husband, son, father, son-in-law and brother-in-law greets you once more before his final journey. The heart of Jesus, the heart of Mary, and my heart are one, united for time and eternity. Mary with Child so dear, give us all your blessings.

This letter was written on a special form provided for this grim purpose by the authorities. The form had a double address flap, one to be addressed by the writer and then turned over to the prison authorities who would forward it to the military court personnel whose address was printed on the second flap. The letter would then be mailed by them to the family when notification was received that the execution had taken place.

The concluding line—simply translated here—is actually a two-line rhyme, probably taken from one of the Marian hymns that meant so much to Jägerstätter. It served as an extraordinarily suit-

[2] Brother Majer (possibly, Maier) was a friend under whose influence Jägerstätter had entered the Third Order of St. Francis. Apparently they had met during his earlier period of military training and had kept in contact with each other. Brother Majer was himself a casualty of World War II.

able sentiment to stand as the last words he was to write: *Maria mit dem Kinde lieb uns noch allen Deinen Segen gieb!* This survey of Jägerstätter's time in prison is not quite complete. Dean Kreuzberg spoke of two other chaplains who had contact with him in Berlin. One of them, Father Bernhard Kunza, is the priest who furnished the Düsseldorf attorney with a letter of recommendation to the Occupation authorities. Since he is still living in Berlin, I wrote to him and asked if he could furnish any further information. I also offered to go to Berlin to see him if he felt such a trip would prove helpful. His reply was friendly, and he assured me that all he could tell could be put in a letter:

First, Franz Jägerstätter was a *radikaler* ["thoroughgoing"] Catholic Christian; he was a member of the Third Order of St. Francis. He often told me, "I cannot turn the responsibility [for my actions] over to the Führer." In this sense he often answered me, "I cannot reconcile my conscience with fighting for the Führer."

Kunza, like everyone else, had apparently tried to make the man change his decision; he seems to have introduced a new argument by referring to future opportunities to serve the Church.

When I told him that it was probable that he could have been inducted as a medical corpsman so that he would not have had to fight in the sense of being called upon to kill; and when, in order to save his life, I advised him to apply for a pardon—since the Church and Germany would need people like him more than ever after the war—he merely replied, "*I cannot promise you that.*" [Italics his.]

In my letter I had raised the question of Jägerstätter's mental condition in those days, pointing out that many people considered him to be a fanatic. He rejected this possibility emphatically:

Not for an instant did I ever entertain the notion that Jägerstätter was "fanatic" or even possibly mentally deranged. He did not give the slightest impression of being so. I was far more inclined to marvel at his bravery and his simple, deep, and genuine piety. In justifying his conscientious objection, he also referred to a priest who is supposed to have come to the same decision (I assume he meant the Pallotine, Franz Reinisch).

Kunza pointedly assured me that "in any case, all of our advice was directed to the goal of saving his life." He went on to suggest that "the chaplain of the Brandenburg prison could doubtless give you information covering his final hours—if he is still alive, which I do not know at the moment."

Unfortunately, Chaplain Jochmann is no longer alive. But the same news article about my research which had unearthed the chaplain of the Linz prison brought a second great contribution to this study. The day after the item was published, I received a letter from the Mother Superior of an Austrian convent. She headed the letter, "A Report on the Case of Franz Jägerstätter of St. Radegund," and explained that she was "taking this opportunity to report a few details bearing upon the heroic death of our compatriot drawn from the final hours before his death."

After explaining that she had been assigned to the Catholic Charities Hospital in Berlin from 1938 to 1946, and that she and the others frequently heard many details concerning the last days of men who had been condemned to death from the late Archpriest Rev. Jochmann, who often served as confessor to the prison, she turned to more specific matters:

On the night before Jägerstätter's execution he [Jochmann] was again on hand to help the prisoners. The executions were almost always scheduled for seven o'clock in the morning, and the priests sought out the condemned in the next line of cells who were generally in a state of complete disorganization.
About twelve o'clock he entered Jägerstätter's cell. The condemned man had already received the last sacraments that afternoon. He found him completely calm and prepared. Not a word of complaint passed his lips. On the table before him lay a document; he had only to put his signature on it and his life would be saved. When the priest called his attention to it, he smilingly

pushed it aside with the explanation: "I cannot and may not take an oath in favor of a government that is fighting an unjust war."

The priest offered to bring him a few devotional booklets. When this was declined because he wished to put the time left to good use, he next offered to read him something from the New Testament. This, too, the man refused on the grounds that "I am completely bound in inner union with the Lord, and any reading would only interrupt my communication with my God." And with that the eyes of the condemned man shone with such joy and confidence as he looked at the priest that he was never able to forget that glance.

Later he was also to witness the calm and composed manner in which he walked to the scaffold. On that very same evening, Father Jochmann was to say in the company of the sisters, "I can only congratulate you on this countryman of yours who lived as a saint and has now died a hero. I say with certainty that this simple man is the only saint that I have ever met in my lifetime."

In one sense, the Jägerstätter story comes to its natural end at this point. But Sister Georgia's letter fills another gap—and perhaps even suggests that there may be more to the story than we are now able to reach or even to understand. She tells how, once the war was over, her Mother Superior sent her to the Brandenburg crematorium to trace the urn containing Jägerstätter's ashes. Apparently this was not too difficult a task, for Kreuzberg, in a letter to the widow dated August 21, 1943, had told her that the ashes had been buried on the 17th and added, "I said some prayers today at his grave, and a few flowers have been planted there too."

After obtaining the necessary permission from Pastor Karobath, the urn was given over to Sister Georgia's care, to be returned to Franz's home parish for burial. The journey from Berlin, she recalls, was delayed by transportation difficulties, and she had the urn in her room for several days, as a result of which she said, "I can testify that I found extraordinary help in a spiritual matter through Jägerstätter's intercession." "In our eyes," she concludes her report, "Jägerstätter, whom we knew only from the chaplain's account, was one of God's special friends."

A Train to Hell

That is the whole story. And yet it is not, for the difficult task of explaining why Jägerstätter decided upon his solitary rebellion, and what impact that rebellion had upon others, remains. One explanation of his behavior which still has general currency in St. Radegund draws heavily upon his close relationship with his *Bibelforscher* cousin. Much is made of the fact that they spent hours together discussing religion and studying the Bible. Since this sect in Austria, like Jehovah's Witnesses in the United States, rejects participation in the wars of "earthly powers" in anticipation of a coming Armageddon in which they will fight to eternal victory, many of its members were put to death for their refusal to support Hitler and his wars. It is, perhaps, natural that the villagers should put two and two together and come up with the answer that Jägerstätter's refusal to serve in the army may be attributed to his cousin's influence.

It is fairly easy to dispose of this explanation, however. Those closest to Franz at the time make it quite clear that this was not the case. One close friend introduced the surprising note that Franz had never really liked his cousin. Jägerstätter's wife insisted that his cousin had no influence at all upon her husband. Perhaps the most conclusive testimony on this point was provided by Fr. Fürthauer and the woman who was married to the cousin at that time. The priest insisted that in all his discussions with Franz he had never brought up the theological position maintained by the sect. Fr. Fürthauer was aware of the close relationship between his sexton and the local *Bibelforscher*; it is true, he admitted, that they spent a great deal of time together in religious discussions. The fact of the matter was that Jägerstätter was trying to bring his cousin into the Catholic fold. Moreover, he added, the cousin had already been inducted into the Home Guard before Jägerstätter was called into service in February, 1943.

The cousin's former wife was interviewed at her home in a village some distance from St. Radegund, where she is now married to a customs official. She did not know anything about her former husband's whereabouts, beyond the fact that he was then a "bishop, or something," in the sect and traveled widely, in the Steiermark province, she believed. When she was asked to indicate how much influence her husband and his religious beliefs had had upon Jägerstätter and his stand, she answered promptly and emphatically: "None at all." As she saw it, Jägerstätter had studied the Bible on his own until he became "too one-sided" on the issue of the Fifth Commandment and its application—this led him to the independent conclusion that he could not fight in the war. Franz and her husband had discussed this issue at great length, but as for the question of influence, it was Jägerstätter who was always "working on" her husband. Her husband had taken the position that the individual believer should not permit himself to be trapped into a hopeless situation by taking the absolutist stand of refusing all military service; instead, he felt, one should try to get into some limited or noncombatant service. Jägerstätter, on the other hand, always insisted that nothing less than total refusal was required—and even after her husband had left for service—in the Signal Corps, she recalled—Franz continued to insist that his cousin had done the wrong thing. After the war, she conceded, her husband agreed that his cousin had been right, and he told her he would follow Franz's example if the occasion were ever to present itself again.

It is quite clear, then, that Jägerstätter's position cannot be traced to the influence of this fundamentalist sect. However, Pastor

Karobath did introduce one reservation. He agreed that the sect's theology had no influence upon Franz's action, but he suggested that the *example* set by the members of that sect in holding fast to their beliefs no matter what sacrifice they were called upon to make might have strengthened his commitment. As he recalled, Franz had often spoken with admiration of their faithfulness.

If the explanation given by the villagers proved wrong on this score, it nevertheless appears that the true answer lies in their identification of the "new" Jägerstätter's two principal characteristics: his intense religiosity and his equally intense political opposition to the Nazis. These two characteristics were so intimately linked to each other that it might be preferable to speak of their mutual interpenetration.

The statement written in prison at Kreuzberg's suggestion clearly supports this interpretation, but the most persuasive evidence is to be found in the commentaries Jägerstätter wrote shortly before he received his final orders to report for induction. In introducing this material at this point, a few preliminary comments must be made.

First, it should be noted that excerpts quoted here (and the complete text to be found in the appendix) approximate direct translation of Jägerstätter's own words and phrasing as closely as possible. The logical form and sequence of the argument, the imagery, and the references to Scriptures and other religious sources are his. Of course, as one might expect of a man with so limited an education, the original lacked proper punctuation, paragraphing, spelling, and other refinements of form. No attempt has been made to reproduce these failings in the translation.

But these are not too important anyway. Such stylistic shortcomings fade in importance when compared with the essential clarity of reasoning and the depth of spiritual insight and commitment found in these writings. After all, niceties of grammar and spelling and rhetorical finesse are minor considerations in the light of the message these commentaries contain, a message "prophetic" in quality which should carry the same force for us today that they should have carried for religious men in Hitler's Reich. The reader who is tempted to smile condescendingly at what may strike him as a simple crudity of thought or overly "pietistic" illustration

110

might do well to bear this in mind: the exact grammarians, the people who could spell faultlessly, the masters of dazzling syllogistic argument, somehow found it possible, in most cases, to come to terms with and give their support (or at least their acquiescence) to one of history's most inhuman and unjust regimes. This simple, untutored peasant, almost alone, with all his faults of style, was able to recognize both the evil of the day and the responsibilities it placed upon him as a believing Christian—and to accept those responsibilities though they led to the grave.

The very first commentary offers a striking illustration of what I mean in its description of a dream Jägerstätter had and the interpretation he placed upon it. I first heard of this dream from Fr. Fürthauer, who had apparently been so impressed when Franz told him about it that he was still able to describe it in detail more than twenty years afterward. The priest recalled that he had asked the peasant to write the dream down and he had then turned it over to a professor from Vienna, who happened to be in St. Radegund at the time, for an assessment of his parishioner's mental stability. The professor read the letter with care and reported that the man who had written it gave every evidence of being perfectly rational and logically consistent. Unfortunately, the priest said, he could not remember what had happened to his letter—perhaps the professor had never returned it.

In the course of my interview with Mrs. Jägerstätter, I asked if she knew anything about such a dream, and was quite pleasantly surprised by her answer that I would learn all about it in the documents she had brought with her. The first commentary is entitled "On the Question of Our Day: Catholic or Nazi?"—a question its author describes as most crucial. He goes on to explain: Once when the Social Democrats were in power in Austria, the Church had said it was impossible for a Social Democrat to be Catholic too—and now? His answer to this question starts with his dream:

Let me begin by describing an experience I had on a summer night in 1938. At first I lay awake in my bed until almost midnight, unable to sleep, although I was not sick; I must have fallen asleep anyway. All of a sudden I saw a beautiful shining railroad train that circled around a mountain. Streams of children—and adults as well—rushed toward the train and could not be held back. I would rather not say how many adults did not join the ride. Then I heard a voice say to me: "This train is going to hell." Immediately it seemed as if someone took me by the hand, and the same voice said, "Now we will go to purgatory." And oh! so frightful was the suffering I saw and felt, I could only have thought that I was in hell itself if the voice had not told me we were going to purgatory. Probably no more than a few seconds passed while I saw all this. Then I heard a sigh and saw a light—and all was gone. I woke my wife right away and told her what had happened. Until that night, I never would have believed that the suffering in purgatory could be so great.

At first this traveling train was something of a riddle to me, but the longer our situation continues, the clearer the meaning of this train becomes for me. Today it seems to me that it is a symbol of nothing but National Socialism, which was then breaking in (or, better, creeping in) upon us with all of its many different organizations—like the NSDAP, NVW, NVF, HJ, etc. In brief, the whole National Socialist Folk Community, together with all those who sacrifice and fight for it.

To illustrate his point he refers to news reports of new gains in Party membership, most of them obtained through the Hitler Youth, and to the exceedingly small numbers of adults who did not belong to some Nazi organization, or were not willing to contribute to Nazi collections. There are only two alternatives possible: participation in the National Socialist Folk Community, and contributions to the red boxes as well, must either help or hinder us Catholics in our efforts to gain salvation. If it is useful for winning salvation, then it is a blessing for the whole German people that Nazism with all its organizations is so widespread and so strong among us—for I believe the German people were never so deeply involved in the works of Christian charity or so ready to contribute as they are today to the Nazis.

This dream must have had a profound and lasting impact on him. Fürthauer did not come to St. Radegund until 1940, so it was at least two years after this experience that the peasant described the dream to him—and here, of course, we have a document pre-

112

sumably written at least two years after that. In Jägerstätter's commentaries the dream comes to symbolize in the strongest terms the standard of Christian political behavior he has decided to follow: **Thus I believe God has shown me most clearly through this dream, or revelation, and has convinced me in my heart how I must answer the question: should I be National Socialist—or Catholic?** I would like to call out to everyone who is riding on this train: "Jump out before the train reaches its destination, even if it costs you your life!"

Is it "political opposition" or is it "religious commitment" when he reads in every act of support for the Nazis an act of personal fealty to Hitler? He anticipates a controversy now raging among German Catholic historians when he notes: **In Germany, before Hitler came to power, it was once a matter of policy to refuse Holy Communion to Nazis.** He goes on to ask, **And what is the situation today in this Greater German Reich?** The answer, of course, is that many who have become Nazis and have turned their children over to the Nazis for their formation now approach the communion rail with no spiritual misgivings at all. He finds this difficult to comprehend. **Have they then—while for more than two years now a horrible human slaughter has been going on—established a new policy which sees all this as something permissible or not to be mentioned? Or has the teaching authority of the Church already made or approved the decision that men may now join a party that is opposed to the Church?** These rhetorical questions lead him to a bitter indictment: **It simply means that there is no longer any likelihood that there will be a bloody persecution of Christians here, for virtually anything the Nazis want or demand Christians will yield.**

The remark that "for more than two years now a horrible human slaughter has been going on" is the most astonishing statement in all of Jägerstätter's writings, if one takes it to indicate the extermination of Jews and other "inferior races" in Nazi concentration camps. One would not ordinarily expect a peasant in the remote village of St. Radegund to know about them. However, one of the camps, *Mauthausen*, was located in the Mühlviertel area near Linz, and it was possible that the loaded trains passing through Braunau or

Titmoning could have made this a matter of more general knowledge than many people are willing to admit today.

If his charge against Christians is valid, it seems to apply most immediately to the spiritual leaders of the Catholic faith. Without denying the truth of this fact, he makes a moving plea for charity in judging them. Let us not on this account cast stones at our bishops or priests. They, too, are men like us, made of flesh and blood, and can weaken. They are probably much more sorely tempted by the evil enemy than the rest of us. Maybe they have been too poorly prepared to take up this struggle and to make a choice between life or death. Would not our hearts, too, skip a beat if we were suddenly faced with the certain knowledge that this very day we would have to appear before the judgment seat of God?—and we ordinarily bear the responsibility for just a few of our fellow men. One cannot easily visualize for himself, therefore, the serious decision forced upon our bishops and priests in March, 1938. Perhaps, too, our bishops thought it would be only a short time before everything would come apart at the seams again and that, by their compliance, they could spare the faithful many agonies and martyrs. Unfortunately, things turned out to be quite different: years have passed and thousands of people must now die in the grip of error every year. It is not hard to imagine, then, what a heroic decision it would require for our people to repudiate all the mistakes that have been made in recent years. This is why we should not make it harder for our spiritual leaders than it already is by making accusations against them. Let us pray for them instead, that God may lighten the great tasks which still stand before them.

A more profound cast is given to the whole problem by his suggestion: If, in all earnestness, we consider the time in which we now live, we will be forced to admit that the situation in which we Christians of Germany find ourselves today is much more desperate and bewildering than that faced by the Christians of the early centuries in the time of their bloodiest persecution. But this is no reason to accuse God or to complain that we have been chosen to live at such a time. Instead, it should inspire us to new efforts to

114

rise, with God's help, out of the mire in which we are stuck and [to] win eternal happiness.

At this point his theme of religious commitment takes over completely. Of course, one may not look upon the sufferings of this world as the worst of all evils. Even the greatest saints often had to suffer frightfully before God welcomed them into His everlasting mansions. The Lord did not even spare His apostles from suffering, and most of them had to give their lives in martyrdom even though they had worked so valiantly for Christ. Yet here are we, actually expecting our sinful life to be free from pain and struggle and our death to be a gentle one—and all this to be crowned with eternal blessedness in the hereafter!

Christ Himself, most innocent of all, endured the greatest suffering ever borne by man, and through His suffering and His death purchased heaven for us. And we do not want to suffer for Him? If we look into history and study recent centuries, there is no need for us to wonder why things are as they are today. Recorded there is a steady decline in deep and pious faith along with a steady advance of the new paganism. Religious writers predicted decades ago (some of them centuries ago) the woes that would come over mankind if men did not reform. We need only glance at Russia to consider the sufferings its people have to bear—and when will they be freed from their misery?

Yet in our case everything should be as painless as many believe?

The second commentary, "Little Thoughts Concerning Our Past, Present, and Future," asks, What good things, then, will the future bring to us Austrians and Germans? Many of us are already dreaming of a better future once the war is over. His own answer begins with a discussion of free will and the effects of the original sin of Adam and Eve: And so it will continue until the end of the world: Every sin carries its own consequences.

The sin he has in mind is the political sin of accepting Nazi rule. He scoffs at the notion that if the war were to end badly for Germany, nothing much would happen to Austria and Bavaria. . . . Are Austria and Bavaria, then, free from responsibility for the fact that we have a National Socialist instead of a Christian govern-

115

ment? Did Nazism fall down upon us out of a clear blue sky? I think we need not waste many words about that, for anyone who has not been sleeping through the past ten years knows perfectly well how and why things have come to be as they are.

There are many who regret the decision of the spring of 1938, but who are not prepared to renounce it—and in this connection he suggests an interesting parallel between the Austrian people who accepted Nazism and the Russian people who accepted Bolshevism. The Holy Week figure is introduced here in a most effective way: If it is ever to come about that Christ will reign in our lovely Austria, then that Maundy Thursday will have to be followed by Good Friday, for Christ, too, had to die before he could rise from the dead. For us Austrians, our Maundy Thursday was that infamous April 10, 1938. That was the day the Austrian Church let herself be taken prisoner, and ever since she has lain in chains. Only when that vote of approval is balanced by an equally resounding act of repudiation will there be for us, too, a Good Friday. We are already being called upon to die, but not for Christ—many actually have lost their lives helping to win Nazi victories.

Such an act of repudiation need not result in immediate martyrdom, because the Nazis will do everything they can to win a rebel over to their Folk Community. They will kill him and risk making him a martyr for his faith only when they lose patience and realize that there is no longer much chance of winning this man over, and that he could become a dangerous influence upon others.

This fusion of political thought and moral imperatives becomes complete in the next few paragraphs. Furthermore, I believe that the Lord will not make it hard for us to risk our lives for our faith in such a test. Thousands of young men are being recruited in these trying days of war to risk their lives for National Socialism. Many have already had to lose their young lives so that others at home could prolong theirs for a time from the fruits of aggression (while, in the process, murdering thousands of children's souls!). With each new victory Germany wins, the sense of guilt will grow ever greater for us Germans. Why, then, should it be more difficult for a man to risk his life for a King who does not only burden us with duties, but also gives us rights; whose ultimate victory is certain, and whose Kingdom, for which we would be fighting, will last forever?

Through His bitter suffering and death, Christ freed us only from eternal death, not from temporal suffering and mortal death. But Christ, too, demands a public confession of our faith, just as the Führer, Adolf Hitler, does from his followers. The commandments of God teach us, of course, that we must also render obedience to secular rulers, even when they are not Christian. But only to the extent that they do not order us to do anything evil, for we must obey God rather than men.

And who is able to serve two masters at one time? Many will probably say or think that for the time being one can remain a Christian in secret until things have changed. And there is no chance that National Socialism will endure forever. It may even be that it has already lasted as long as it can. Even Christ's kingdom on earth would soon collapse if God were suddenly to take away all our rights and leave us only with obligations—though God has the power and the right to do so. But is it not possible that, once the German Reich is defeated, our "release" might come at the hands of another anti-Christian power? We know all too well how things stand with the Christian faith in other nations on this earth: in Russia for example. And England and America are not much better, though perhaps more civilized and at the moment not so crude as the Russians. From whence, then, is something better to be expected?

The Christians of the first centuries could have used the same reasoning: let us make sacrifices to the idols as the government demands; in secret we can still remain Christians. And some must have done so, too. Moreover, in those days many rulers did not stay on the throne very long, but their successors were often not much better—sometimes, in fact, worse. In actual fact, the first Christians would have had to live to an age of more than 300 years before they could have enjoyed the free practice of their faith.

A lengthy discourse on abortion and contraception follows as evidence of the decline of German culture which suddenly concentrates on the point that practices like these are no less reprehensible than many of the atrocities charged against the Russians in the war. Jägerstätter poses the question whether for such a people [the Germans, that is] God should still perform miracles as he once did when he permitted the Israelites to cross the Red Sea without even getting their feet wet?

Throughout the history of the Church her enemies have always tried to destroy her, but that effort cannot succeed because Christ has promised she would never be conquered. It is already something of a divine miracle to witness two opposing powers, each with the same objective, tearing each other apart instead of combining forces. For this reason, it can easily happen that there is really no need for God to take a part in stopping them. Instead, these powers will wear each other down to the point where neither will have the final victory.

If these circumstances suggest the quality of the divine plan, other aspects of the situation partake more of the diabolical. Blessed Catherine Emmerich has revealed that Lucifer himself will be set free fifty or sixty years before the year 2000 and that other devils will have been turned loose before then. This is a sign that we are not dealing with a small matter, but that the great life-and-death struggle has already begun. Yet in the midst of it, there are many who still go on living their lives just as though nothing has changed, as if this great and decisive struggle is no concern of theirs.

The complete text of these commentaries is impressive in the strength of its logical sequence and in the care Jägerstätter takes to make his case. The first two are the lengthiest, and set forth the major outlines of his argument; the others elaborate upon relevant aspects of that argument. In the third commentary, "Bolshevism —or National Socialism?" he addresses himself to the sad fact, as he sees it, that one can always hear Catholics saying that this war Germany is fighting is probably not so unjust after all because it will bring about the destruction of Bolshevism. One hears echoes of this argument today when people set out to explain, or even justify, the fact that the spiritual leaders of German Catholicism supported Hitler's wars, some even telling their faithful that it was their "Christian duty" to fight in them.

Jägerstätter did not see it that way. Noting that German forces were indeed deep inside the Soviet Union and were engaged in efforts to subdue the population, he asks, **What are we fighting in that country? Bolshevism—or the Russian people?** In an ironic view he notes that throughout history, when rulers have invaded other lands they have usually done so to take something from the conquered lands, not to give them something. He feels that the same principle applies to the war in progress: **If we were merely fighting Bolshevism, would other things like iron, oil wells, or good grain lands have become such important considerations?**

In contrast to this, **when our Catholic missionaries set out for heathen lands, did they also take planes and bombs, hoping to convert and improve the heathen by such means?** The answer is implied in the question, but it opens the way to a rather important conclusion. **Whenever anyone has taken up arms to wipe out Christianity** (as people have often thought they could in the past), **the blood of their victims has always become the new seed and shoots from which Christianity flowered anew with more vitality than before. Now, could this not happen again if one spills Bolshevist blood? Could not this, too, become new seed? Are we Christians today perhaps wiser than Christ Himself? Does anyone really think that this massive bloodletting can possibly save European Christianity from defeat—or bring it to a new flowering? Did our good Saviour whom we should always try to imitate, go forth with His apostles against the heathens as German Christians are doing today?**

The war which we Germans are already carrying on against almost all the peoples of the world [is not] something that broke upon us without warning—like a terrible hailstorm, perhaps, which one can only watch helplessly and, at most, pray that it will end soon without causing too much damage. To Jägerstätter, Hitler had made his policies and intentions abundantly clear, and war was inevitable, unless, he adds, the other nations of the world followed Austria's example of surrendering without a struggle. It would not be sinful if the Austrian people withdrew the approval they had given in 1938 and refused to go any further.

At the very least, other peoples have the right to pray to God for peace and ask that He strike the weapons from the hands of us

Germans. Is it not a sheer mockery for us to ask God for peace when we really don't want it? For if we did, we would lay down our own weapons. Or is the guilt we have taken upon ourselves still too slight? As least let us continue to beseech God that He may let us come to our senses and acknowledge at last that other peoples and nations have a right to life upon this earth. Failing this, God in His might will be obliged to call for the final reckoning lest we Catholics of Germany force all the peoples of the world to place themselves under the Nazi yoke.

The last line of this commentary—Almost all of us are quite willing to glut ourselves on the spoils of thievery, but we want to saddle the responsibility for the whole dirty business on one person alone!—leads into a more elaborate discussion of "The Crooked Game" in the next. The title refers, of course, to the widely held belief that it was all right to give every appearance of being a loyal Nazi citizen while, at the same time, remaining true to the Christian faith. Jägerstätter will have none of this, even though he makes some allowances for prudence and for obedience to legitimate demands of the civil authority.

His basic objection, as one might expect, is to the dishonesty such a position implies. The man who would later reject the military tribunal's offer of noncombatant service to save his life, because acceptance would involve a "lie," asks simply, If dishonesty were not harmful to our efforts to attain eternal blessedness, what difference would it make whether or not one has freedom of belief? Or is dishonesty wrong even if we injure no one by it? Most certainly yes—if only because we generally, in fact always, injure ourselves. For though we cannot hurt God by our falseness (we can only offend Him), we can hurt His Church. Later he specifies: By playing our crooked game, we actually bring serious scandal down upon the whole Catholic Church ...

The self-inflicted injury lies in a growing aptitude for "the crooked game"; a man is not likely to give it up even at the moment of death. He suggests that those who have openly broken with the Church and have even turned to the persecution of Christians might suffer lesser agonies in hell than those who have swindled their whole lives through, always trying to deceive their spiritual leaders and their closest associates. Even a dishonest man is entitled to honest treatment—first, because one should not repay evil with evil; second, because the evil man is just as much my brother as the man who is good; and, finally, because it is our duty to help such a man by our example as well as by our acts, even when we are rewarded for our pains with ridicule and scorn.

Getting down to cases, he asks, Is a man upright and sincere when, on the one hand, he is a member of the NVP or some other Nazi organization and makes sacrifices for it and takes up collections for it while, at the same time, he wishes the whole outfit would fade away and disappear? I think many have the idea that they can fool the others in this way, but we ought not think our opponents are so stupid. They know full well that someone who still fulfills his Sunday obligations and gives some semblance of being religious in other ways has to be cheating somebody, since no one can serve two masters at the same time. For a while, of course, they will let it ride, since they know that such people really fool nobody but themselves and, in the process, do the greatest damage to themselves and to the Church. Needless to say, they will rarely trust such double-dealers with important political appointments.

Willingness to co-operate with the Nazis to achieve or preserve some temporal advantage jeopardizes the Christian's chance to convert others. What must people of other faiths think of us and our faith if it means so little to us?

He continues in this vein: Actually, we should be ashamed of ourselves in comparison with the truly committed Party member who, even though his faith was rooted only in worldly things, fought for his ideals and for his National Socialist ideology in the face of all prohibitions and did not fear even prison or death. Would they have achieved their victory if they had been as timid and cowardly as we Catholics of Germany are today?

But we Catholics apparently entertain hopes of winning a glorious victory for our faith without any battle—and, to top it all, we expect to do this after first fighting for the enemy and helping him win his victory! Can anyone really believe this is possible? In my opinion such a thing has never happened throughout the whole history of the world. Modern man, of course, is very inventive, but if he has progressed so far as to discover a way of winning a victory without a struggle, I have not yet heard of it.

The fifth and sixth commentaries explore the range of individual responsibility. The crucial question is posed in the opening paragraph:

One often hears it said these days: "It's all right for you to do this or that with an untroubled mind: the responsibility for what happens rests with someone else." And in this way responsibility is passed on from one man to another. No one wants to accept responsibility for anything. Does this mean that when human judgment is finally passed on all the crimes and horrors being committed at this very time that one or two individuals must do penance for them all someday? He, of course, thinks this is not the case. It is unjust to load one's responsibilities upon the shoulders of others and, besides, those others may be acting from quite another set of moral principles, which, however false they may be in substance, could blind them to the real nature and consequences of their acts. It is quite possible that in the judgment of God such a person in high position might bear a lesser responsibility than perfectly ordinary individuals among the common people.

To illustrate his point he offers "a little example." Let us assume there are two men performing virtually the same service for National Socialism. The first regards what he is doing as good and just according to his viewpoint; the other considers the whole thing—its ideas, sacrifices, and struggles—to be unjust! The second, however, believes that he is much better than the other because he does not hold the same convictions, even though he sacrifices and fights the same as the first man. Whether the Party for which he is sacrificing and fighting benefits from or is hurt by his actions apparently makes no difference to him. His principal concern—or so it appears to me—is that he himself need not suffer any physical harm. In my opinion, a greater guilt rests upon the individual who is fully aware that the results of his efforts are more certain to be bad than good but who, nevertheless, co-operates simply in order to spare his pampered body from danger and privation: a greater guilt, that is, than that borne by those who regard what they do as their duty and who, furthermore, see nothing at all bad about it according to their understanding.

Naturally, the words sound sweet to our ears when we are told that others bear the responsibility for the results. But Jägerstätter did not find such sweet assurances convincing. In the commentary titled, "Is There Anything the Individual Can Still Do?" he states the case for the position summed up in the familiar lines, "This above all, to thine own self be true." He admits that to speak out would mean only imprisonment and death, and that there is not much that can be done any more to change the course of world events. And he adds, *I believe that should have begun a hundred or even more years ago. But as long as we live in this world, I believe it is never too late to save ourselves and, perhaps, some other souls for Christ.*

This last sentence may well serve as the sharpest summation of his declaration of personal rebellion, and it is followed by a pessimistic evaluation of things as they were. It was no wonder to him that confusion was abroad: *People we think we can trust, who ought to be leading the way and setting a good example, are running along with the crowd. . . . And the thoughtless race goes on, always closer to eternity. As long as conditions are half good, we don't see things quite right, or that we could or should do otherwise.*

Only when things go wrong will they stop, and then it will be too late for second thoughts, and people will become desperate. Yet whatever risks it may involve, he feels some protest should be made now, some effort should be undertaken to guide and direct: *It is not good if our spiritual leaders remain silent year after year. . . . Do we no longer want to see Christians who are able to take a stand in the darkness around us in deliberate clarity, calmness, and confidence—who, in the midst of tension, gloom, selfishness, and hate, stand fast in perfect peace and cheerfulness—who are not like the floating reed which is driven here and there by every breeze—who do not merely watch to see what their friends will do but instead ask themselves, "What does our faith teach us about this," or "can my conscience bear this so easily that I will never have to repent?"*

If road signs were ever placed so loosely in the earth that every wind could break them off or blow them about, would anyone who did not know the road be able to find his way? How much worse it is if those to whom one turns for information refuse to give him an answer or, at most, give him the wrong direction just to be rid of him as quickly as possible!

The seventh commentary moves on from this point to answer the challenge of those who point to the evils of the day as evidence that God—at least a merciful God—does not exist. Proceeding from the parable of the wheat and the tares, he focuses his argument upon the foolish expectation that God will periodically come down from heaven to straighten out the affairs and solve the problems of man. There will, of course, be a Second Coming, but it will be of quite another kind. These complaints are based upon a totally false set of expectations, which, in turn, are based on an incorrect notion of the nature of Christianity.

If God were to take away the persecutors, there would be no more crowns of victory for us to win. Besides, has God not once already been merciful to us and, through His divine power, drawn a mightly stroke to cancel our debts? Christ has done penance for our debt of sin and has made atonement, and all of us who accept His teachings and live according to them can become blessed for all eternity. What more do we want? Should Christ let Himself be crucified for us again? Or was the miracle of His resurrection, and the other miracles that He worked, too small for us, so that we still wait for a miracle that will make it possible for us to believe in His teachings? Has Christ, then, not shown us clearly enough, by word and example, the way to heaven?

These lamentations on the part of the people lead to his question: Are not most of us already, or still, Christians? Referring to one of the songs in the hymnal—"How Happy the Christians"—he asks what is wrong: Is the text of the hymn false? Or are we no longer Christians? There are few "happy" people to be found today, he suggests, but the usual explanations in terms of the war or these bad times lead him to ask, Do we believe that the first Christians had an easy time of it, just because so many of them were happy? Or has God's mercy grown smaller so that we can no longer hope for forgiveness of our sins?

The fault lies in our excessive concern for the well-being of the flesh and our failure to remember that the pain God sends us can actually be helpful toward winning eternal happiness, if we bear it with patience and out of love of God. The power hell holds over the world is far less potent than the power of God. But to win the struggle, the Christian must avail himself of the weapons of the spirit to be found in the sacraments of the Church as instituted by Christ.

The eighth commentary, "War or Revolution," is particularly important, since it relates most directly to the framework in which Jägerstätter is seen as "the rebel." It reveals, for one thing, that he and Adolf Hitler were in full agreement as to the essential meaning of the Nazi Movement and the Folk Community. It is, moreover, almost entirely devoted to the question of the war and the implications of serving in that war. For this reason, even though the full text of the other commentaries has been reserved for an appendix, an exception is made in this case:

Many, it is true, have the idea that this war which Germany started is a war pretty much like many others that have already taken place. But it is not a war like the others in which simple greed for territory played the major role: instead, it is more of a revolution which has already brought almost the entire world into its grasp. The Führer has actually said this himself: the National Socialist is the greatest revolutionary of all time. If this were really an ordinary war between nations, like so many others, and if Germany were actually to emerge the victor, then, once the war was over, one would have to be given exactly the same rights, as a Catholic, that every other German citizen would possess. But since it is more of a revolution, or war of ideology, I could fight as much as I wanted for the German Fatherland and still, if (after the victories of which they are already so certain in their hopes) I refused to acknowledge the National Socialist Folk Community, they would regard me as an enemy despite all the hardships and sacrifices such a poor soldier must bear—an enemy just like all the others who did not voluntarily capitulate to the National Socialists, as did the Austrians four years ago.

These considerations alone should certainly be enough to convince one not to fight for this State, or National Socialist Folk Community. And, further, I believe that many have not forgotten what the Holy Father said in an encyclical several years ago about National Socialism, that it is actually more of a danger than Communism.[1] Since Rome has not to this day rescinded that statement, I believe it cannot possibly be a crime or a sin for a Catholic simply to refuse the present military service even though he knows this will mean certain death. For is it not more Christian to offer oneself as a victim right away rather than first to murder others— who certainly have a right to live and who want to live—just to prolong one's own life a little while?

Of course, people today come up with every conceivable argument to put the issue and the conflict in a favorable light. For instance, one is simply fighting for the German State, inasmuch as Christ commanded that one must obey the secular rulers even when they are not religious. This last part is admittedly true, but I do not believe that Christ ever said that one must obey such rulers when they command something that is actually wicked. For

[1] This seems to be an overstatement of the papal position. However, other sources cite a statement in *Osservatore Romano* of October 11, 1930, to the effect that "belonging to the National Socialist Party of Hitler is irreconcilable with the Catholic conscience, just as belonging to Socialism of any kind is in general irreconcilable with it."

Cited in Hans Buchheim, "Wie ist in Peter Schier-Gribowskys Fernsehfilm 'Auf den Spuren des Henkers' Die Erwähnung des Anti-semitismus der Oester-reichischen Christlich-Sozialen und speziell des Hirtenbriefes des Linzer Bischofs Gföllner vom 21. 1. 1933 zu-Beurteilen?"—a mimeographed inquiry prepared in April 1962. Buchheim also quotes a January 1, 1933, pastoral of Bishop Gföllner's as including the statement: "All committed Catholics must reject and condemn it [National Socialism]; for if, according to the statement of Pope Pius XI, it is impossible to be a good Catholic and a true Socialist at the same time, then it is also impossible, at one and the same time, to be a good Catholic and a true National Socialist." One may assume with confidence that Jägerstätter was familiar with this statement by the bishop of his diocese and that it played a considerable part in the formation of his personal evaluation of the National Socialist Movement and its successes in Germany and Austria.

I believe it is as impossible to fight for the German State without at the same time fighting for the National Socialist Party as it would be to say that I am fighting only for God the Father, but not for the Son or the Holy Spirit. For at this moment the German State and the National Socialist Party constitute one inseparable entity. People today also speak of the defense of the Fatherland. Have we Austrians forgotten the year 1938 in so short a time? Can I still say that I have a Fatherland when I live in a country where I have nothing but duties and no longer possess any rights? Above all, can there be any talk of defense of the Fatherland when one invades countries that owe one nothing and robs and murders there? What more can we Catholic Austrians lose if we fight no further for the German State? Will we, perhaps, lose our religious freedom or our economic independence?

Could it be perhaps that they have told us too little about what they will do with those who do not profess National Socialism? Naturally, it would be very pleasing to the gentlemen of the Party if we first helped them on to further victories. But that we Catholics must make ourselves tools of the worst and most dangerous anti-Christian power that has ever existed is something I cannot and never will believe.

In the perspective of all the developments in armaments in the past twenty years, one may be shaken by the seemingly prophetic opening lines of Jägerstätter's final commentary, "On Dangerous Weapons." But his references to terrifying weapons that the human mind has invented and will probably continue to invent, or to the possibility that man could invent a weapon capable of smashing the entire world into ruins, serve merely to introduce what he considers the most dangerous weapons of all, those weapons of the spirit and mind with which one tears the true Catholic faith from the children and from men's hearts (or no longer permits it entry there).

In my discussion with Fr. Fürthauer, the priest mentioned a "catechism" that Jägerstätter was supposedly writing for his children in anticipation of the day when religious instruction by the Church would be forbidden. Since Mrs. Jägerstätter knew of no such "catechism," it seems most likely that these commentaries were intended for this purpose. The final commentary would certainly seem to support this assumption. Although its discussion of the spiritual means of defense against intellectual weapons has little direct bearing on the act of rebellion for which Jägerstätter was put to death, his reference to the fact that one is expected, as a matter of course, to fight for all sorts of things shows that he places the struggle for the children's souls in the context of his refusal to serve; and the concluding lines, even though they do refer to the more special concern of this commentary, have a broad enough application to deserve quotation here: are we, then, released now from our obligations . . . just because they are so much harder to fulfill than they were ten years ago? I doubt it. For the harder the battle here, the more glorious will be the victory someday.

If the letter to his godchild, written two years before the Nazis came to power in Austria, foreshadowed the ideas set forth in the commentaries written four or five years after that tragic event, the prison statement merely sets the final seal upon the step he had taken as a logical consequence of those ideas. It restates his inability to reconcile the obligation to render blind obedience with the fact that man is a creature possessing free will. Yet he does not see his decision as arising out of any superior wisdom or courage of his own. If God had not given me the grace and strength even to die for my faith if I have to, he admits, I, too, would probably be doing the same as most other Catholics. He sees his act as precisely this, dying for his faith. There are probably many Catholics who think they would be suffering and dying for the faith only if they had to suffer punishment for refusing to renounce the Catholic Church. But I believe that everyone who is ready to suffer and die rather than offend God by even the slightest venial sin also suffers for his faith. Indeed, he goes on to say that the latter may deserve a greater reward in heaven, for in the case of apostasy the issue is so much clearer that the individual has little choice but to recognize his moral obligations.

For him, the question reduces itself to a choice between two "kingdoms," and he freely grants that whoever decides to reject the Nazi rulers thereby forfeits the rights and privileges offered by that regime. But, he insists, the same is true of God and His Kingdom; anyone who is not willing to undergo sacrifice and to fight for them will lose all claim to the rights and privileges of eternal life. Under the circumstances, I definitely prefer to relinquish my rights under the Third Reich and thus make sure of deserving the rights granted under the Kingdom of God. Whatever price this may involve can never equal the values to be gained, for the sorrows of this world are short-lived and soon pass away and the rewards of heaven are such that I believe we would almost go out of our minds with joy if we could be sure of possessing them even for a limited time. And all we must do to win them forever is to keep His commandments and love Him. He borrows a scriptural comparison: Consider what great efforts and sacrifices so many of us are prepared to make to gain worldly esteem, or an athlete to win a prize. If we were to make the same efforts to gain heaven, there would then be many and great saints. For the Kingdom of Heaven, too, will not be ours without effort and sacrifice. Christ has said Himself that the Kingdom of Heaven can be won only by those who storm it and take it by force.

Jägerstätter's position, as revealed in his own writings, was clearly one of political opposition rooted in religious commitment, culminating in an act of rebellion against the political authority, which he regarded as a spiritual "storming of heaven." Perhaps Fr. Fürthauer gave the most accurate description of his parishioner's stand when he said that the man had formally offered his life in reparation for the sins of Christians and offered himself as a "victim" for the sins of the whole world; that he had decided it was better to die than to have Christianity perish, and he was prepared to demonstrate to the Nazis that the course they had chosen was unjust. Jägerstätter was absolutely convinced of the injustice of the war and, the priest added, he insisted that a Christian is never permitted to support such an unjust cause.

The question inevitably arises whether this man's conscientious objection to Hitler's wars implied or was based upon a pacifist rejection of all war as incompatible with Christian teaching and belief. Both his pastor and his widow deny that such was the case, and they both assured me that Franz undoubtedly would have taken up arms had Austria chosen to resist the Nazis. There is some support for this opinion in the sympathetic, even envious, references to those nations which had tried to repel the German aggressions against themselves. Indeed, one might go further and say that Jägerstätter's stand was in great part motivated by patriotism. Although he occasionally says "we Germans," he clearly sees himself as an Austrian unjustly deprived of his rights and his nation, at one point dismissing the argument that a man has a duty to fight for "the Fatherland" by asking if he still has a "Fatherland." He looks forward to the resurrection of "our lovely Austria"—if the people repudiate the approval they gave to the *Anschluss* in 1938. Finally we have the testimony of the Linz cellmate who stressed Jägerstätter's deep attachment to his country.

There are, however, other indications which suggest at least a predisposition to a pacifist commitment. In all of his exhortations against the Nazis, he avoids anything resembling a call for violent opposition; the actions he recommends always take the form of withdrawing support and refusing further contributions. There might be "practical" explanations of this. He may have recognized the hopelessness of any violent uprising, though, if one considers his thoroughgoing acceptance of martyrdom as a price one should be ready to pay, this should not have been a strong deterrent. Or this could reflect an acceptance of the Nazi regime as the *de facto* "legitimate authority," leading to a careful distinction on his part between a permissible recourse to passive nonco-operation and an active resistance which might have been considered a treasonous, even sinful action under the traditional theological definitions of the subject-ruler relationship.

The evidence is overwhelming that Jägerstätter did accept the basic premises upon which the pacifist alternative—that is, the theory and practice of nonviolence—is based. He told his cellmate that as a Christian he preferred to do his fighting with the word of God and not by force of arms. Similarly, his prison statement specifically declares that we need no rifles or pistols for our battle, but, instead, spiritual weapons—especially prayer, the shield which the flaming arrows of the Evil One cannot pierce. Other references to the "resistance" he would have his fellow Catholics mount against the Nazis are set in terms of the powers and strength to be obtained from the sacraments of the Church. His all but final injunction at the conclusion of the prison statement is in the same vein: Let us love our enemies, bless those who curse us, pray for those who persecute us. For love will conquer and endure for all eternity.

Although one would probably not consider Franz Jägerstätter a pacifist, strictly speaking, had he been acquainted with the works of such priests and theologians as Franziskus Stratmann, Max Josef Metzger, and Johannes Ude, he would have been quite receptive to their ideas. Stratmann, a co-founder of *Friedensbund Deutscher Katholiken*—a Catholic peace movement which gained a wide following before the Nazis came to power—had received international notice long before Jägerstätter's struggle, through his book, *Weltkirche und Weltfriede* (Augsburg, 1924). Metzger, perhaps best known for his part in the *Una Sancta* movement for Christian reunion, was a German priest who worked in Austria and wrote several pamphlets and articles supporting a pacifist position. Metzger was imprisoned by the Nazis three times and he, too, was finally beheaded by the Nazis in Brandenburg on April 17, 1944. Ude, perhaps the most controversial of the Catholic pacifists, with whose writings Jägerstätter could have—but apparently did not—come into contact, held an extreme position, arguing from the Fifth Commandment, not only for the abolishment of all forms of capital punishment and war, but also for promoting vegetarianism. Although he had authored a flood of articles over a period of more than fifty years, his best-known work, *Du sollst nicht töten*, was not published until 1948, long after Jägerstätter's death.

Did Jägerstätter formulate his fateful decision "entirely on his own"? Certainly the present review of documents must have suggested the possibility that they may have been a reflection or rewording of arguments he had encountered elsewhere. Both his knowledge of the situation and the depth of his analysis of the faults of the Nazi regime would seem to be far beyond the capacity or the experience of a peasant in an isolated rural village. The possibility at once presents itself that Jägerstätter had been somehow involved in the organized anti-Nazi resistance or, at least, had been exposed to material circulated by this movement. This seems not to have been the case. Investigation did disclose that an underground opposition group had been active in Maria Schmölln, another small community in the general area of St. Radegund, but there was nothing to suggest that its operations had extended beyond its immediate community. Mrs. Jägerstätter, who certainly should have known if such were the case, was quite definite in saying that her husband had never had contact with any organized group of Nazi opponents and that no anti-Nazi publications or communications had ever come into his hands. Pastor Karobath, too, while confessing to a vague recollection of some resistance activities in the general vicinity, which were revealed after the war, told me that he had never had an inkling of such activities before then, and that Franz most definitely was not involved. Indeed, an organized resistance group would probably have avoided any links with so outspoken or imprudent an opponent of the regime, someone who was so sure to get into trouble sooner or later. This does not mean, of course, that there were no outside political influences on Jägerstätter's thinking. His opposition to the Nazis undoubtedly reflected a continuation of the opposition that had been mounted by the *Bauernbund* and similar groups before Hitler came to power in Austria, but these influences were obviously too general and too remote to be traced in the final development of his stand against military service.

The sources of the religious content of that stand are, to some degree, easier to identify. Thus the frequent scriptural allusions and quotations fully substantiate the views of his fellow villagers who attribute his behavior to his constant (in their eyes, excessive) reading of the Bible. The religious pamphlets to which reference is made in the prison letters should also be mentioned. It is from such sources, one may assume, that such references as the one to the statement of Blessed Catherine Emmerich must have been drawn.

Aside from the Bible itself, it seems that the principal source of Jägerstätter's religious thought is to be found in the lives and teachings of the saints. The elderly woman who identified herself as his stepfather's sister recalled that he was always to be found reading a religious book. When I asked if she could tell me the name of any specific book, the best she could do was to say that she remembered one called *Beispiele* ("*Examples*") or "something like that." This is probably the book that Pastor Karobath identified as *Helden und Heiliger* ("Heroes and Saints"), by Hans Hümmeler—a compilation of brief biographies of men and women who had led exemplary Christian lives. This book was such a favorite of Jägerstätter's, the priest recalls, that he seems to have read it through more than once, and it made such a deep impression on him that "he wanted to become a saint" himself.

A review of the volume found in the parish library was not too helpful in providing direct links to Jägerstätter's writings, however. The entry dealing with Anna Catherine Emmerich, for example, stressed her peasant origins, her frequent practice of praying in the fields (alongside her father), and the fact that she had had visions —all of which suggest rather clear parallels to Jägerstätter and his religious behavior. On the other hand, neither the prediction concerning Lucifer's being freed in the 1930's or 1940's nor any other direct prophetic quotations were to be found in this brief biographical sketch. So, too, with the entry for St. Clare: the statement attributed to her in Jägerstätter's prison statement is not included. These references must have come, then, from other sources.

A more intriguing fact, however, is Jägerstätter's failure to mention two other saints whose biographies *are* included in this book and whose lives and actions would have a direct bearing upon his own position. The first is St. Martin of Tours, whose refusal to serve in the armies of Imperial Rome after his conversion to Christianity—and precisely on the grounds that this conversion made it impossible for him to do so—is described in detail. Yet Jägerstätter makes no mention of him in any of his writings.

The other omission is significant for two reasons. The first lies in the substance of the saint's behavior as described in the book. The saint in question is Jean Baptiste Vianney, the Curé of Ars, and the incident described is one in which he was ordered to serve in Napoleon's army: "An induction notice for Jean Vianney? He prepared to flee rather than jeopardize his calling in the *Rekruten-*

hölle [literally: "hell of the recruits"] of Lyon. That he did so for a year and was forced to waste that year in hiding in the woods of the Pyrenees was martyrdom and punishment enough for his ill-considered flight."

Substitute Jägerstätter" for "Jean Vianney" and "Enns" for "Lyon" and you have a good summary of the peasant's letter to Pastor Karobath. Add to this the fact that Franz apparently did give some passing thought to going into hiding "in the woods," and the parallel becomes all the more striking. But, again, no reference is found to this "draft dodger" who was also a hero and a saint. A probable explanation of both these "omissions" lies in the possibility that Jägerstätter had read an earlier edition of this work which may not have included these accounts. The volume now in the library is undated, but it appears relatively unused and bears the description, "A new one-volume special edition" on the title page. If the edition with which he was so familiar did not include these two saints, Jägerstätter was deprived of two "examples" that would have brought him much comfort and solace in his days of trial.

For one who was always so sensitive to possible supernatural meanings and implications, the second point of significance in the Vianney story would certainly have been a matter of great importance to him. Jägerstätter's "official" farewell letter tells how he had been praying that, if he had to die, he could do so in time to celebrate the Feast of the Assumption (August 15) in heaven. How much more deeply impressed would he have been had he known that the day on which he was writing his letter—the day he knew he was to die—was the feast day honoring that very saint who had refused to serve in the armies that had brought most of Europe under the mastery of an earlier tyrant.

Although there has been a revision of the official church calendar since the time of Jägerstätter's execution in 1943, so that the feast day of the Curé of Ars is now celebrated on August 8 instead, this does not disturb the relevance of the coincidence. However, another saint whose feast is still celebrated on August 9th is St. Romanus (A.D. 258). What little is known about this early martyr bears striking similarities, too, to the Jägerstätter history. He is described in Butler's *Lives of the Saints* as, "A doorkeeper of the Roman church . . . whose unreliable *acta* make of him a soldier in Rome at the time of the martyrdom of Laurence. Seeing the joy and constancy with which the holy martyr suffered persecution, he was moved to embrace the faith and was instructed and baptized by him in prison. Confessing aloud what he had done, he was arraigned, condemned, and beheaded."

Franz always wanted to be a saint; at least this is what Fr. Karobath reports. Perhaps that was the real core of Jägerstätter's stand, yet it remains a genuine act of rebellion against a temporal power he obviously viewed as being diabolical in nature and in origin. Hence his dismay over the many who still go on living their lives just as though nothing has changed, as if this great and decisive struggle is no concern of theirs. The only possible course, for him at least, was rebellion; and in his eyes this was the gravest life-and-death struggle of them all, for it was eternal life or eternal death that was at stake.

The Martyr
and His Village

A revealing coincidence marked the beginning of the critical stage of Jägerstätter's rebellion. It will be remembered that his final induction notice ordered him to report at Enns on February 25, 1943. One day before, the front page of the local regional newspaper, the Braunau *Neue Wacht am Inn*, carried the banner headline, "The Commandment of the Hour," over the text of a speech given in Berlin by Propaganda Minister Goebbels. A paragraph from this address may serve as an index to the prevailing temper of the time in which the peasant was called to make his stand:

> There must now be an end to middle-class niceties which, even in this fateful struggle, want to abide by the principle: "Wash my back, but don't get me wet!" The danger before which we stand is gigantic. Therefore, the efforts with which we set out to meet it must be gigantic. The hour has come to take off our kid gloves and bind our fists for action. We can no longer make fleeting and superficial use of the rich war potential of our own country and the regions of Europe at our disposal. We must reach to the very last drop, and this must be accomplished as speedily and in as thoroughgoing a manner as is organizationally

136

and factually conceivable. A false exercise of restraint would be completely out of place at this point. Europe's future depends on our struggle in the East. We stand ready to defend it. The German *Volk* places its most precious national blood at stake in this battle.

Other 1943 issues of that same paper carried items which revealed that this determination went beyond mere propaganda statements. They contained the names of people executed, charged with a wide range of capital crimes, including such offenses as "black market" butchering of livestock, listening to foreign broadcasts, and even—in one case where it led to a costly fire in a defense plant—smoking in a forbidden area. Such news items must have significantly impressed the populace with what pressures were available to the authorities to make sure that the people contributed as required to the war effort.

Other, less formal, social controls were in operation too. Voluntary dedication to the aim of bringing the war to a speedy and victorious conclusion played its part, and there is every reason to believe that St. Radegund and its people were not behind in this respect. Maybe they did not share the extravagant regional pride of the guidebook which held Braunau "sacred to every German" because it was Hitler's birthplace, and described the surrounding area with its "more than a million inhabitants" and "rich historical past" as standing "inspired and joyously creative in the midst of the tumultuous life of the Greater German Reich"—its people, "German to the core since earliest times." Perhaps it is true that few Radegunders were ardent supporters of the Nazi regime; certainly, none of them today admits to it. Even the man who was installed as mayor under the Nazis, as several villagers took pains to assure me, accepted that responsible post only to make certain that no more intensely committed Nazi "from the outside" would be brought in to direct local affairs.

Making such allowances, and granting even that Pastor Karobath may have been too prone to characterize one or another of the villagers as having been "a big Nazi," it is still reasonable to assume that some of the denials are exaggerated. The truth must lie somewhere in between—and, regardless of how many or how few ardent Nazis the village may have had, it is certain that the overwhelming majority of the population did support the war effort and shared the hope that the military forces in which their friends, neighbors, and relatives were risking their lives would emerge with a speedy and unambiguous victory.

After all, there *were* certain arguments which always arose, because of which Jägerstätter had stopped frequenting the local taverns; someone had to be saying "Heil Hitler" to provoke him to the "Pfui Hitler" rejoinder. He *was* the only one to make so strong a point of refusing to contribute to Nazi collections (or to accept Nazi benefits). This fact is still advanced as one of the strongest and most consistent community recollections of the man. While all the others "did their duty" by accepting without protest or hesitancy the military service demanded of them, this man—*and only he*—took an open and final stand against the regime, against the war, and even against the victory for which the rest of them were hoping.

The fateful "struggle in the East" was in its Stalingrad phase in 1943. Word was undoubtedly coming to St. Radegund, and would continue to come for months, of those who lost their lives in that German military disaster. Eighteen men from the neighborhood fell before February 25; between then and the date of Jägerstätter's execution, six more would die in battle. Of the fifty-seven names listed on the community war memorial, thirty-three died in Russian territory and seven in the Balkans. In a small, tightly knit community like this, each of these losses would have been accepted by all as a direct and personal bereavement. It would not be too much, therefore, to expect that this sorrow would be translated into an active resentment against anyone who dared to take a stand which was both a refusal to support the common effort and an adverse judgment on that effort, which cost so much in sacrifice and sorrow.

This does not seem to have been the case, at least not to the degree one might expect. Pastor Karobath does speak of the widow having to "suffer much," and she and her daughters do admit that some people were unpleasant and said unkind things, but even they agree that there had been no general pattern of rejection or ostracism and no overt reprisals directed against the family.

Other villagers reached near unanimity in denying that Franz had been condemned or resented for what he had done. One or two referred to occasional instances where there was some sign of animosity, but these were evidenced by "the few Nazis" and were not at all representative of the village, they insisted. The prevailing attitude then—as it is remembered now—was one of real sadness for Franz and concern for his family, one woman saying that it "broke my heart" every time she saw the three fatherless girls. As a result, it was unthinkable that the widow and her family would be penalized on Jägerstätter's account. Quite the contrary; people did what they could to help—in one case "everyone" pitched in to make some necessary repairs to the Leherbauer barn. It should be noted that this differs somewhat from the information obtained from the widow. Her recollections are that very few went out of their way to express their sympathy or to offer their assistance at this trying time; most of them, she felt, tended to be fearful that they might fall under suspicion or otherwise get into trouble for doing so. It is probably of some significance that this was the "breaking point" for Mrs. Jägerstätter as far as our interview was concerned. After suggesting that I did not need to record this unhappy fact (because "Franz always said such things should be forgotten"), she started to cry. During the hour or so that had preceded this, she had been able to cover much more sensitive matters—including the visit to the Berlin prison—without giving way to her emotions. Whether this breakdown was a matter of accumulated strain or an indication that there was really more unpleasantness and animosity than people are inclined to remember is difficult to say.

Two factors may have operated to mitigate or eliminate the resentment one would ordinarily have expected to find. The first is related to the nature of the community itself. The same Geschlossenheit, or mutuality of concern, that made each war casualty a loss suffered by all, operated in Jägerstätter's case too. He would be considered "one of us" and, consequently, would find protection against the forces of the world outside St. Radegund. Several people mentioned this as an explanation of the fact that there was no open rejection of the man or his family. As one woman put it, the community would never "shut out one of its own"—unless, she added, he had committed some "real" crime. It is interesting to note the implication that, for her at least, Jägerstätter's action would not fit that category. Another villager pointed out that the family strains are so interwoven that each member of the community is likely to have some blood relationship, however remote, to the others and that this would make for greater understanding of one who "went astray." Even one of the outsiders I spoke to, a man who used to make regular vacation visits to St. Radegund, stressed the fact that the St. Radegund people were so intimately linked with one another that the community would rise above such an issue and would never think of resenting the man or his family. Of course, the fact that there was a later instance of a deserter, who certainly took a more questionable stand than that taken by Jägerstätter, but who was sheltered and protected by the community, may be seen as clear validation of the influence of this *Geschlossenheit* upon community thought and action.

The other mitigating factor relates more specifically to Jägerstätter himself. It was recognized by all that the death penalty was a foregone conclusion in his case and that there could be no charge or even suspicion that he was motivated by cowardice. One veteran of the war gave the most explicit statement when he said that Franz had forfeited all the chances of surviving the war that men in the service enjoyed. This point is given more touching emphasis by another man, one of the peasant's closest friends, who recalled being greeted by Jägerstätter's mother upon his return from the war and a prisoner-of-war camp with the sad observation, "If Franz had been sensible, he might be coming home now too." Under the circumstances, no matter how strongly the others may have differed with him, they had to credit the man with displaying an exceptional degree of personal heroism in following the course he chose.

Thus, the absence of open resentment or animosity may be taken as an accurate characterization of the community's attitude at the time. On the other hand, occasional comments encountered in the interviews might suggest the presence of a *covert* resentment that may not have been suspected even by those who were subject to it. The recurring statements, for example, that "people felt that he was no better than others," that everybody had his duty to perform in wartime, and that even priests had accepted the call to service, could be interpreted in this light. In a somewhat different vein, the general agreement that he had not been sufficiently concerned about the welfare of his family—an opinion, incidentally, as widely held now as it was then—carries unmistakable overtones of a strongly adverse judgment that could hide an undercurrent of ill-feeling.

But if any such feelings were prevalent in the community at the time, they were unrecognized or have been forgotten. Even the police officer whose efforts to change the peasant's mind had failed was described by several persons as having taken his death as a great personal sorrow. An elderly woman said there had been much sadness and weeping in the village over the affair; everyone, she added, had loved "Franzl" deeply.

To say there was grief over the outcome is not to say, of course, that the action itself was looked upon with favor or even indifference. The reason for the sorrow, the evaluation of the man, and the explanation of his action all find their expression in the remembered community judgment that Jägerstätter was *g'spinnt*, that is, "touched in the head." It was generally taken as a self-evident fact that his political and religious fanaticism had finally combined to unsettle him mentally, so much so that he was no longer able to put things in their proper order of priority—which, in the villagers' eyes, places the care and protection of farm and family at the very top of the list. His overly rigorous religious upbringing in the home of his grandmother, which was later complemented and intensified by the equally "excessive" religiosity of his wife, were thought to be contributing factors. Added to this, in the minds of at least two women who had personal experience of his lineage, were the inborn characteristics of the "Huber strain" handed down to him by his mother. His mother's sister-in-law described this endowment as a stubborn unwillingness to let go of any idea, no matter how fantastic, once it was fixed in the mind.

141

Similarly, the former wife of the *Bibelforscher* cousin characterized "the whole Huber clan" as being likely to go overboard in whatever they did or felt; this would carry over into feelings of guilt, so that things that ordinary people would be able to dismiss as unfortunate mistakes or as "water over the dam" would prey upon their minds and continue to be an oppressive burden on their consciences.

Perhaps this all but unanimous agreement that the man was the victim of mental derangement is still another explanation of the lack of open hostility or resentment at the time. After all, such a condition would invite compassion and understanding, and help to weld tighter the bonds of community protectiveness. The few who did not share this evaluation of Franz's mental condition—his wife, Pastor Karobath, Fr. Fürthauer (but even he had asked the Viennese professor to give him an opinion of Jägerstätter's dream)—would have been in no position to challenge the community judgment, and would have found it difficult to do so had they made the effort. As one outsider remarked, looking back upon the community's reactions at the time, it had already been taken for granted that Franz was mentally unhinged because of his religious excesses—indeed, she added, he was quite aware that this opinion was current. His arrest and execution merely confirmed the judgment that had already been made. In her eyes, incidentally, the villagers were opportunists who changed their political colors to suit the prevailing fashion and were not at all pleased when a man like Jägerstätter came along to tell them how wrong they were and to point out their moral obligation to do otherwise.

Whether, as this woman implies, the explanation of Jägerstätter's stand in terms of mental instability reflects a conscious or unconscious defensive rationalization on the part of the villagers, or whether, on the contrary, it is a tenable hypothesis, lies outside the scope of this writer's competence and well beyond the quality of the data I was able to gather. None of the priests who served his spiritual needs during the period in question was prepared to support the suspicion I reported to them, nor was his attorney; some emphatically rejected the possibility, others pleaded inability to make a decision one way or the other. As far as they were concerned, he gave every impression of being in sound mental health.

Jägerstätter's action is still considered fanatical by his fellow Radegunders. This may seem somewhat surprising, especially when one takes into account that St. Radegund is a religiously homogeneous community. There is, I was told, only one non-Catholic resident in the whole parish territory, which includes all of St. Radegund as well as a portion of a nearby village. As Catholics, all of the people interviewed share the same system of moral and theological values—though not necessarily the same interpretation of them—which motivated this man to put his life in jeopardy. By the same token, all of them are aware of the high status their Church has always accorded martyrs for the faith. One might expect, then, that the peasant's stand would have come to be regarded more favorably—or at least less critically—than was possible at the time.

These same considerations were present and should have been taken into account at the time. If we make allowance for the controls exercised by a totalitarian regime and for the emotional impact of the overriding commitment to the national war effort, however, we could understand a tendency to overlook values which might have supported Jägerstätter's action.

One could say there has been a slight change in the community's judgment since then. Several villagers are prepared to grant the possibility that he had done something great—although the man who used this specific phrase prefaced it with the limitation, "in one sense," and added that "in another sense" his actions had been "pointless," and "inconsiderate" to his family. Occasionally someone granted that the peasant might one day be canonized; however, such remarks were often set in the context of frank disagreement with Pastor Karobath's insistence that Jägerstätter had been the only one of his flock to recognize and fulfill his true Christian duty.

The fact that Franz's ashes had been given a ceremonial burial in the presence of the whole parish in 1946 and that his name is included on the community war memorial are clearly due to the pastor's firm insistence and do not necessarily reflect the temper of his parishioners. The burial of the ashes was a purely pastoral decision; the war memorial issue was more complicated and gave rise to some controversy. In our discussions, the villagers tended to minimize the extent of this controversy and to insist that it was a closed issue, but there is some reason to believe that the currents run a little deeper than these reports would suggest. The memorial itself is a sizable structure standing in the far corner of the churchyard cemetery. Originally built to honor the dead of World War I, it has been remodeled to include the names of the victims of the Second World War. Since it is a community honor roll and is located on church property, jurisdiction in the matter was shared by the pastor and the village authorities. In keeping with his personal conviction that Jägerstätter was a martyr, the priest insisted upon including his name on the list. The veterans, understandably enough, protested that such a listing would be highly improper in view of the purpose of the memorial. The substance of the argument is not of crucial importance—although one might question whether, in view of his objection to Fürthauer's laudatory oration at a serviceman's funeral, Jägerstätter himself might not have objected. What is important is the fact that there was an argument. According to the pastor, the issue became so heated that a special village meeting had to be called, at which complaints might be heard and considered. The head of the local veterans' group also admitted to me that there had been considerable discussion, and said he had called a special meeting of the membership for a policy decision.

The affair was settled by a Solomon-like compromise. Jägerstätter would be listed, but his name would come at the end and be preceded by the phrase *seinem Gewissen folgend* ("in obedience to his conscience"). The matter appeared settled until the last moment when a woman came in to protest that her husband, who was missing in action and officially considered dead, had been overlooked in making the list. The only solution was to block out the qualifying phrase to make room for the extra name. As a result, the Jägerstätter listing is now indistinguishable from the others. Most of the villagers insist that there is now no feeling about the matter one way or the other. Some pointed out that since he must have taken the military oath in his earlier period of military training, he was actually entitled to be included as a fallen soldier. The objection that if he were to be listed, all the men who had served and returned should be listed, too, was apparently never taken seriously and is heard no more. Perhaps the pastor exaggerated the intensity of the opposition; however, I am inclined to doubt that he did. On the other hand, what one of Jägerstätter's close friends maintains is probably true: since there could be no question of his bravery, the local veterans honor him as much as they do the others listed on the memorial.

In estimating Jägerstätter's action, most villagers focused upon its political implications, stressing the imprudence or uselessness of making a stand against the regime, especially in time of war. Very few concerned themselves with the moral content of that stand. As one man put it, even if hundreds or thousands had followed the peasant's example, nothing would have changed. If, however, he had gone into service, he could have avoided killing anyone, and still would have had some chance of coming back. If he had been killed, it would have been just "one of those things." By acting as he did, he assured that his children would be deprived of a father's care and protection. A local official added another note of disfavor by suggesting that the veterans felt that Franz's refusal carried with it the implication that those who did accept military service were "dumbbells," and he added that one must remember, after all, that there *is* such a thing as duty, and these veterans believed that by obeying the law and doing their duty, they had done the right thing.

Since this was about the closest anyone came to setting the issue in terms of moral alternatives, I proceeded to ask the official if he agreed with my impression that very few people in St. Radegund would say that Jägerstätter had done the right thing. He did—and then immediately dissociated himself from this stand by adding that since Franz had acted in accordance with supernatural values as he had understood them, it was a difficult judgment to make. He apparently had no difficulty in reconciling this position with his obvious acceptance of the community opinion that Franz had been a trifle unbalanced.

To sum it up succinctly, the community continues to reject Jägerstätter's stand as a stubborn and pointless display of essentially political imprudence, or even an actual failure to fulfill a legitimate duty. It is to be explained and forgiven in terms of an unfortunate mental aberration brought about, or at least intensified, by religious excess. The question of whether his action was morally right is, for the most part, set aside. While some of the villagers were quite willing to accept the possibility that he might someday be formally acknowledged a saint, this possibility was not considered at all incompatible with the community's general disapproval of his action.

It would be wrong to infer from this that the issue is a matter of continuing concern or controversy for the people of St. Radegund. This is not true. At some point or other in the course of every interview, almost everyone explicitly stated that "nobody ever talks about these things any more." Indeed, although no one in the community raised any objections in my presence, I did learn that the wisdom of "stirring the whole business up again" was the subject of at least one rather lively barroom discussion one evening after I had left a group.

One woman told me that the only time the matter is discussed at all is when "someone has had a little too much wine to drink and the talk turns to whether or not Franz was a saint." She was probably referring to the kind of argument that occasionally seems to develop when the pastor joins the men who have gathered in the inn across from his residence. Fr. Karobath is convinced that his churchyard does contain the remains of a martyr-saint, and he is not at all reticent about expressing that conviction to his parishioners. One might expect that so strong and outspoken a commitment on the part of the spiritual leader of the community would be reflected in a more favorable community evaluation of Jägerstätter and his action.

There are perhaps two reasons why this is not the case. The first is related to the personality of the priest himself. He is not a man given to subtlety of expression—and especially not in this matter. Even though he admits that the others do not like to hear these things, he seems to take personal satisfaction in stating his position as bluntly as possible. Furthermore, the fact that he is himself a

146

wounded veteran—having lost a foot in World War I—places the others with whom he argues at something of a disadvantage. One can easily understand, then, that the forthrightness of his position, however admirable it may be as a measure of his own integrity, tends to block any development in the community of a more favorable attitude toward the man he praises so highly.

A more general reason is related to the role of the pastor in a village like St. Radegund. The peasant community expects a priest to restrict himself to "purely theological" affairs and not to meddle in more worldly matters in his sermons or other parish activities. Although Jägerstätter's rejection of military service was to him (and to the pastor) essentially a "theological" matter, the community, as we have seen, is more inclined to place it in a political context, as an action challenging the virtually unquestioned obligation of the loyal citizen to "do his duty" when the nation finds itself involved in a war. Thus, for a pastor to maintain that the man who did question that obligation and did go on to reject the "duty" it would have imposed is really the only one in the whole community who recognized and performed his true *Christian* duty is regarded by many, if not all, of the Radegunders as a clear-cut case of "meddling."

Before I came to St. Radegund to make this extended inquiry, I had anticipated that the extent to which the whole affair had been forgotten would be a focal point of the investigation. An earlier visit had given me the false impression that people no longer remembered the man at all; the young girl who drove the taxi I had hired was not familiar with the Jägerstätter name and had to obtain special directions from the pastor. Shortly after my arrival in 1961, however, I learned that her difficulty had stemmed from my use of the family name instead of the "house name" (*Leherbauer*), which was more familiar to the people in that area. My expectation that the man and his action had faded completely from the memories of those who had known him was quickly disproved. But this merely presented a new problem centering on the younger generation. What did they know about the case; from what source had they learned what they knew; and, most important perhaps, what did they think about it? In this connection, little of value could be obtained from their elders. For example, the schoolmaster said that the matter was never mentioned in school since, unlike the more intellectually aggressive students one finds in an urban setting, his charges concerned themselves only with the bare essentials of the curriculum. On the other hand, the pastor, who teaches religion as part of that school curriculum, informed me that he made a point of telling all the children about Jägerstätter, and of presenting him as a model worthy of imitation.

Such limited and conflicting information made it all the more essential that I speak with a number of residents who were too young to have known Jägerstätter personally or, if they had known him at all, would remember him only as an overly strict sexton who had kept them "in line" when they attended church services as children. It soon became obvious that this optimistic goal was not to be attained, and it was necessary to settle for three less-than-satisfactory interviews.

In part, the disappointing results can be traced to the problems of reaching these young people and communicating with them. Beyond this, however, there was a very definite lack of interest and a very limited fund of knowledge among these young people concerning Jägerstätter. Three interviews proved the futility of further inquiry. All three young people knew of the man; all ultimately admitted knowledge of his execution, but two of them required probing questions to establish that they knew of Jägerstätter's death. They insisted that they knew nothing at all about the circumstances of his case or why he acted as he did. Only one of the three young men could be pressed beyond this point. None of them, understandably enough, could tell me anything from their own recollections about Jägerstätter as a person (although one was overheard a short time later telling a visitor to the community about the "great change" that had come over the man when he married).

Only one of them could be induced to express a personal opinion, and that was the most openly unfavorable opinion of all my interviews with the villagers. After saying that Jägerstätter had "something like an idea that the war was unjust," he went on to say that he had been executed "for treason or some such charge," and cremated. When prodded into a statement of what people thought about it all today he volunteered his own opinion and took specific issue with the position taken by the local pastor. Fr. Karobath, he said, "idolizes" (*schwärmt*) the man and has even gone so far as to preach here and elsewhere that he was a saint, but as far as this young man was concerned, the action *did* constitute treason. If one's Fatherland is engaged in a war, one has no alternative but to fight for it. He was willing to grant that it was Hitler's war and not, strictly speaking, Austria's, and that this may have had some bearing on the question, but he felt that Jägerstätter was absolutely wrong to take the stand he did. This young man was not inclined to extend this opinion to others, however; he said he had no way of knowing if other boys his age felt the same way, and that this was merely his own personal opinion.

Since this young man was described as exceptionally bright, a model student with a *gymnasium* education, his opinion may be taken as a considered judgment, and not a parroting of opinions he had heard from others. He remembered Jägerstätter vaguely as sexton and also thought he might have heard something about him from his aunt, but more likely from his father. His parents, both dead, were described by one villager as among the more ardent supporters of the Nazi regime; his aunt was the only resident who found an excuse to avoid being questioned by me. Both factors may have contributed to the firmness of the young man's opinion and his willingness to state it.

The other two boys were also in a position where they might have been expected to know more about the case than they claimed, and to have more of an opinion than they were prepared to state. The first was the son of a village official and the grandson of the distinguished former mayor who had been Jägerstätter's godfather and frequent advisor. Yet all he could say was that he "guessed" he had first heard about the affair at a neighbor's house and that he knew nothing at all but the fact of Jägerstätter's execution for refusing to serve in the army. The third was the son of one of Jägerstätter's closest friends, and also a remote blood relative on his mother's side. He frankly and repeatedly stated a complete lack of interest in the matter or in what others in the community thought about it. When pressed to say how he had first learned anything about Jägerstätter,

149

he said that he assumed he must have heard his father and his uncle (who is now a lawyer in Vienna and was a close boyhood friend of Jägerstätter) discussing the matter. All three were willing to grant that neither they nor the others of their age group really knew, thought, or even cared much about the case of the local rebel. If this is true, and I am inclined to believe it is, it is possible that the disappointing results of this admittedly limited sampling actually reflect an accurate representation of the situation as it concerns the younger generation. It is certain that the parents make no effort to tell the story to their children; in fact, the elder generation admit that they seldom, if ever, think about the case or discuss it among themselves.

It would follow that the impression obtained on my first visit was not so much incorrect as premature. Unless something should happen to change the present patterns of ignorance and indifference, there is a very good chance that the Jägerstätter history, perhaps even the memory of his name, will be lost to St. Radegund in a generation or two. All that will remain will be his name on the war memorial, with nothing to indicate that he was in any way different from the others listed above him.

Within the circle of more direct familial relationships, the story will be different, at least for a time. The only possible obstacle to some effort at keeping his memory alive there would be a feeling that his action had brought shame or scandal upon the family record and should, therefore, be quietly but permanently buried. Not even the slightest hint of this attitude was uncovered in the course of the interviews which, in addition to Jägerstätter's immediate family, included visits with his godchild and his sister-in-law, who had spent considerable time in the Jägerstätter household, and with a woman relative of his natural father who remembered Franz as a very young child. Since this woman's son is now married to the youngest Jägerstätter daughter, an effort was also made to determine what he knew and thought about the father-in-law he had never known.

The young man's parents gave no impression of any sense of embarrassment associated with their memory of the man; in fact, at times it was evident that they took some pride in their relationship to him, if only because he was important enough to have excited the interest of a professor from America. His mother, the relative of Jägerstätter's natural father, said that the whole family had experienced great shock and deep sorrow. That Franz's own father had fallen in the first war did not enter into her considerations at all. She remembered being present at the burial of his ashes, and she stressed the fact that many St. Radegund people participated in the service. As another token of her family's favorable remembrance, she and her husband had saved a news clipping from the Linz *Volksblatt* (March 6, 1946) which reported the details of his sacrifice. The "fine little boy" who had been such a "good helper" on her family's farm until his mother took him to his new home in St. Radegund still has a warm place in her heart. It was a source of particular joy for her, she said, when her son brought Jägerstätter's daughter home to live with them as his wife—especially, she added, since the girl bears such a strong resemblance to her father.

The interview with the young husband revealed the same disinterest in the Jägerstätter affair that had marked the responses of the other three young men I interviewed. This may be explained in part by the fact that he has always lived in Tarsdorf, a village about four or five miles away from St. Radegund, but one would suspect that his mother's personal relationship with the man involved—to say nothing of his own marriage to Jägerstätter's daughter—should have been enough to stir his interest anyway. He laughingly dismissed any idea that Franz was regarded as "a family skeleton" and told of learning of him "about ten years" before through an article in the newspaper. Asked if he felt he would have acted as Jägerstätter had done, he replied in the negative, and amplified that reply by noting that he had already completed his own course of required military training. The question was restated: Would he have done so if he had held the same moral objections to military service? After giving the matter some thought, he answered that he would still not have done so. He did not share the opinion that his father-in-law had been guilty of treason. He pointed out that most people had been "against the war and the Nazis" but had gone on to serve anyway, a course of action he apparently considered proper. Thus there was no sense of shame or resentment in his opinion, and cer-

151

tainly no indication of pride or approval—there was nothing, in fact, to suggest that the affair meant anything to him one way or the other.

Franz Huber, the young man for whom Jägerstätter had served as confirmation sponsor and to whom the 1936 letter of spiritual counsel had been sent, lived and worked at the *Leherbauer* farm before being called into service in 1942 and again following his discharge after the war. At the time of his sponsor's arrest and imprisonment, he was either in action in the Stalingrad campaign or, more likely, in a hospital in Braunau, where he had been sent after being wounded early in that campaign. This suggests an interesting sidelight to the Jägerstätter story: while the peasant had seen to it that the boy did not get involved in Hitler Youth activities, he apparently did not attempt to keep him out of military service. Huber made no reference to such attempts, and the clarity of his recollections in other respects would indicate that he would not have forgotten them.

Most of Huber's recollections bear upon and confirm the description of Jägerstätter after the change had come over him. He had not been surprised by his sponsor's refusal to serve, because he had already made his intentions amply clear. Though aware then and since that most of the Radegunders considered the man a little unbalanced mentally, he had never doubted his sanity. To assume this was, he felt, nothing more than a convenient way for them to dismiss an affair about which they would prefer not to think.

Mrs. Jägerstätter's sister, the "Resi" of the prison letters, was interviewed at the nearby town where she was employed as a cook for a sawmill crew. It was not a particularly productive interview, however, for she proved to be exceptionally shy and most reticent about volunteering information. "Cue" questions, which were intended to open a flow of spontaneous recollections, missed their objective. She, too, dismissed the idea that there was anything mentally wrong with her brother-in-law. She could not say where he had gotten the idea of rejecting military service, but he had "thought the whole thing through" with great care. She confirmed my impression that the people of St. Radegund had not so much resented

Jägerstätter's action as that they held him to have been much too extreme in his religious commitment.

I had hoped in particular that she would be able to describe the manner in which the tragic turn of events had been regarded by her own family, the peasant's in-laws. According to her, they felt that Franz should have accepted the call to service out of consideration for his dependents. But they were not at all ill-disposed toward him nor would they regard him today as a family scandal or a source of shame. In fact, she added, he had probably risen in their estimation because of his decision and his courage in persevering in it.

These "family" interviews involved persons in a peripheral relationship to Jägerstätter. The most revealing information would be that furnished by his immediate family—his wife and three daughters. His mother is no longer living, although it is clear from the prison letters and what others have said that she objected strongly to his stand and had tried to enlist several people in the vain attempt to "bring him to his senses." She had been heard to complain that she "couldn't get through to him any more," and that he and his wife had shut her out of the whole affair. These fleeting references, however intriguing they may be, serve only to suggest that Jägerstätter was under considerable pressure at home, and that this pressure emanated from another person endowed with "the Huber strain" of stubborn persistence. In one discussion with the widow I raised the point that it was strange the mother had not written to her son. This was explained as insignificant because the mother did not like to write and left everything along that line to her daughter-in-law. When I asked if the fact that the mother had not accompanied the wife to Berlin had any special implications, Mrs. Jägerstätter was obviously surprised and explained that someone had to stay home to take care of the little ones. But, it might be noted, Resi was available for that.

I assumed that the daughters could have little information of sufficient significance to justify questioning them extensively. Jägerstätter's godson admitted that he had often wondered about their attitude, but that he had never felt right about asking them. Originally I planned to speak to each daughter separately in the rectory office made available to me by Fr. Karobath, but this was not done for what I believe are two sound reasons. First, as children they had been too young to have many personal memories of their father or to have any direct knowledge of the community's reactions at the time. Second, whatever information they would be able to give concerning later community reactions would probably not be important enough to justify exposing them to the ordeal of a direct interview. Jägerstätter's references in his prison letters to the "sacrifices" little Rosalie was making for him and to the prayers they were all saying for him offer some evidence of what the children's attitudes were. Another piece of evidence is provided by an anecdote told by a woman who had been a frequent visitor to the village in those days. She remembered coming along the path and finding the youngest Jägerstätter child playing at the top of a ladder. She called the child down and then scolded her, telling her she could have fallen down and hurt herself. She has never been able to forget the grave response to her warning: "Then I would die and be an angel and be with my daddy."

There was nothing in the manner of these young women, two of whom are married and have families of their own, to suggest that this calm acceptance of the father's eternal happiness has diminished or otherwise changed. The information that was obtained from them in visits to the *Leherbauer* home where two or all of them (and their mother, of course) were gathered around the table related mainly to their acceptance by other children in school or elsewhere. Except for one daughter's reference to some "unpleasantness" the eldest had experienced at school, which she herself dismissed as unimportant, none of them had been the object of any reprisal or ridicule on their father's account.

The second daughter, Marie, was spending the summer at home recuperating from one of the series of hip operations she has been obliged to undergo. Since she was engaged in a "home study" course in the English language, I spent a considerable amount of time coaching her. In the course of these study sessions, when the two of us were alone, I occasionally took the opportunity to raise some questions. I asked her, for example, if she and her sisters had read their father's letters. They had. And what did she personally think of her father's action? He had done the right thing. Did her two sisters feel the same way about it? Again her reply was a quiet statement of what she took to be a self-evident fact: of course they did. When an effort was made to probe more deeply into the family's experiences following the execution, she said that many people in the village had shunned the family and had not wanted to help them lest they might be implicated in the father's opposition to the regime. There was some name-calling too, she recalled. On the other hand, there were some people who went out of their way to help—and now, she assured me, everything has settled down and there is no ill-feeling on anyone's part.

Shortly before leaving St. Radegund, I took the opportunity to ask Marie to tell me frankly what she and her sisters thought of my coming and whether they might not have preferred the matter to rest. She replied that it was certainly very hard on her mother to have all the old wounds opened up again, but as far as her own feelings were concerned, it was a good thing that other people would get to know about her father. I made the comment that it was my impression that the village was not particularly inclined to discuss the matter, and that the attention I had stirred up would probably die down again as soon as I was gone. She agreed, adding that this reticence on the part of the others might be a sign of "an uneasy conscience."

The family had, of course, known of my project and its purpose even before I had obtained the grant which made it possible. Except for the pastor, no one else in the community knew the purpose of my visit until I was ready to begin my interviewing. However, none of us could have anticipated the extent of the attention it would bring to them and the village. The Linz news item which had brought the letters from Fr. Baldinger and Sr. Georgia was picked up by other papers in various parts of Austria. It caught the interest of the editor of one of the more sensational week-end papers, which sent two reporters to the village to interview the pastor and the family, as well as me. The misgivings I felt over their visit were fully justified when the result of their efforts appeared as an emotional and crudely exaggerated front-page account of the affair. I was so afraid that the tone of the article would offend Mrs. Jägerstätter that I did not show her the copy I bought at a newsstand.

However, someone else had taken care of that by sending a copy to the house.

In retrospect, the article with all its distortions may have contributed significantly to the success of my own probes. For one thing, both Franz Huber, the godson, and Mrs. Jägerstätter's sister had read the article and, as a result, had been looking forward to my coming to them for information. Huber told me he would have come to St. Radegund to seek me out if I had not called upon him soon. And there is good reason to suspect that it was partly Mrs. Jägerstätter's desire to "set the record straight" that prompted her to bring the prison letters and the commentaries to the formal interview we had scheduled for her.

Such a conclusion would be justified in terms of her personality and spiritual outlook. On other occasions, for example, she has "corrected" discrepancies in published reports about her husband's case. In a personal letter to me, she has taken the trouble to point out errors in a book by Msgr. Fried, an account of anti-Nazi Catholic resistance in Austria, including a report on Jägerstätter. For one thing, this account had Franz reporting *six* days late to the induction center; her correction, substantiated by documentary evidence, pointed out that he was only four days late. Another point made in that same letter is even more revealing. Fried had said that she and her husband had gone to Communion every day and had read the Bible together every evening. This was not true, she confessed; the tasks involved in caring for three infant daughters often made it impossible for her to join him in these spiritual activities.

Of course, this reveals something more than a passion for accuracy. It is also a clue to her own humility and her admiration for the spirituality of her husband. His story is best told, she seems to be insisting, when everything is kept in its proper balance; and it is for this reason that I could anticipate her dissatisfaction with the tone of the Sunday newspaper article, a dissatisfaction strong enough to cause her to show such intensely personal documents to me.

Privacy is important to Mrs. Jägerstätter. In a sense, she "walks alone" in the community—a spare woman, reserved and soft-spoken, even withdrawn, in manner. During my stay I observed her in her almost daily visits to the parish church for morning Mass, arriving by herself—usually on foot but sometimes on bicycle—and always sitting alone in the pew. Her greetings to the other women present at these services would be little more than a courteous, but distant, nod; seldom, if ever, was she observed to "visit" with them in the churchyard, on the path, or in the open square before the general store. This very obvious distance between her and her neighbors first led me to suspect that there was some coolness toward her on the part of the others which might reflect a kind of ostracism provoked by her husband's stand. In a letter written before I left for St. Radegund, she had told me that she was aware that many people still resented the fact that her husband had not accepted military service. However, this suspicion was not supported by any definite evidence; and certainly none of the villagers was willing to admit that such was, or ever had been, the case. Everyone, even those who in a sense "blamed" her for changing the beloved lusty youth into a "religious fanatic" and thus, in effect, for the tragic consequences of this change, spoke favorably of her as a person, as an exemplary mother to the fatherless children, as a capable operator of the *Leherbauer* farm, and as a sincerely devout (perhaps, like her husband, excessively so) Christian. When I asked others why she always seemed so much alone, the answers reflected a community assumption that she preferred it that way, that she "keeps everything inside her" and shuts others out. One can easily see how Franz's mother might be brought to complain that she could not get through to her daughter-in-law, even though they shared the same house; that even while her son was still alive and in prison she was not "let in" on all that was taking place.

There must have been some truth to the complaint, too, if one recalls the mother's open opposition to her son's stand (and, before that, to his intensified religiosity), but this would not account for the widow's "apartness" in other respects. Pressed for an opinion on this, one of her husband's closest friends granted that something of a cleft did exist between the widow and the other residents, but he, too, insisted this was not related to any community animosity toward her on Franz's account. It was nothing more, he felt, than the result of a feeling that a woman who was running a full-scale farm enterprise should not be spending so much time in church. This, of course, is the same criticism that had been directed against her husband's behavior. However, it could be sharpened in her case by the generally accepted belief that she was responsible for his failure in this respect as well. If true, the cleft would be greater than that which had separated him from the rest of the community or which would exist between the villagers and any farm operator who was regarded as a *Frömmler*, an excessively pious person.

Perhaps this is reading too much into the situation; she might have brought these documents to the interview even if the article had not appeared. However, the fact that she had never mentioned their existence before—not even when she showed me some old snapshots of her husband—gave me the distinct impression that she would not have *volunteered* them. Since I did not suspect that any such documents existed, I would never have been in a position to request that she make them available to me.

As for the substance of my interview with the widow, most of it has already been presented at appropriate points in earlier chapters: the account of her visit to Berlin; the reasons for her husband's withdrawing from much of the social life of St. Radegund; the behavior of her neighbors following his arrest. She was fully aware of the fact that they looked unfavorably upon his decision and that they were inclined to think of him as a victim of mental derangement. Her insistence, contrary to the widespread belief, upon the fact that she had tried to persuade him otherwise, suggests that she is also aware that she is held "responsible" for the whole chain of events by having produced the "great change" in his religious behavior. She confirmed that a change had taken place, but denied that it had been as extreme or as sudden as others maintained. She recalled meeting Franz at a dance at Ach, where, someone else told me, she had been working as a waitress in one of the inns. The courtship lasted six months. As she explained it, "He had to find a wife" because it was time for him to take over the operation of the farm. Even before that first meeting, she had heard of him and his reputation for being "a lively fellow" who liked the girls. She admitted that after their marriage he did become more deeply involved in religious activities and parish responsibilities and abandoned some of his former pleasures because he now saw them as temptations to vice. Strangely enough, she was most explicit in her denial that he had made pilgrimages to Altötting prior to their marriage, insisting that he had made his first visit there in 1941. However, she did confirm the fact that he had considered entering the religious life as a lay brother before he met and married her.

Different people saw the same behavior in vastly different contexts. To the family, the rebel's behavior was accepted and honored as obedience to a moral imperative imposed upon him by his religious commitment—a commitment which, in their eyes, was not excessive, although they certainly recognized it as exceptional. The rest of the village, on the other hand, saw Jägerstätter's refusal to serve in the army as a thoroughly tragic and ultimately senseless act of religious fanaticism, born of a sadly disordered mind.

Stated this crudely, the general opinion should not be taken to mean that the people who accepted it so easily are unfavorably disposed toward the man or his memory. They do not resent what he did; they regret it and disapprove of it. But their regret and disapproval are cushioned by their continuing warm regard for him as "one of us"—and, if the comments so frequently encountered are sincere, an especially well-loved "one." They simply do not understand, even now, just as they could not understand then, what he was trying to say and do in those last months before his arrest. Nor should this surprise us. The same elements of the Jägerstätter story that make it so unique—in particular the idea that a relatively uneducated man from an isolated rural village could have such profound insights into the political and spiritual implications of his time—should lead us to expect that other men from that same social milieu could never really understand him or accept the path he tried to point out to them as the only path worthy of the Christian bound for salvation.

The Martyr
and His Church

In Robert Bolt's *A Man for all Seasons*, a play about St. Thomas More, one character, speaking of More, says the following about saintliness: "From his wilful indifference to realities which were obvious to quite ordinary contemporaries, it seems all too probable that he had it." Writing about Jägerstätter after the war, Dean Kreuzberg, the prison chaplain, has seen in Mrs. Jägerstätter's visit to the prison a parallel between St. Thomas More and Jägerstätter. The most impressive parallel of all, however, lies in the personal religious commitment of both men, which led to their implacable opposition to a secular ruler who had embarked upon an immoral course of action. More's stand focused upon a restricted range of political opposition and certain acts of his king, but was set in the context of complete loyalty to that king in all other matters; Jägerstätter, on the other hand, opposed the Nazi regime *in toto* as an intrinsically immoral government which could have no claim on the loyalty of a Christian subject. The ever-recurring confrontation between Caesar and Christ applies to both situations, in which these men found themselves called to acts of personal rebellion.

What position did "the Church" take, as it was represented by the men who had been delegated the task of providing spiritual guidance and direction to the Christian flock in these two critical instances? The capitulation of the English Church to Henry's will is well known. As for the Austrian Church in the time of Hitler, an equally formal capitulation was not the question. But what Jägerstätter described as perhaps the saddest hour for **the true Christian faith in our country, and the day the Austrian Church let herself be taken prisoner** cannot be gainsaid. No adequate study has yet been made of the full measure of the support given by that spiritual leadership to Nazi rule in Austria, beginning with Cardinal Innitzer's ill-advised "Heil Hitler" greeting, extending to the official efforts to assure acceptance of the *Anschluss*, and ending with the support of the regime until its last days. There was some opposition sufficiently annoying to provoke the Nazis to reprisal actions, even against Innitzer himself. But support for the regime as "legitimate authority" was far stronger. There was no inclination at any time to call for the repudiation of the hasty acceptance of Hitler's rule in 1938, or to support those who, like Jägerstätter, did just that.

This brings us to what may be the real heart of the matter. How were this peasant and his action received by those to whom his spiritual care had been entrusted? More important, how is his action remembered today? For in these two questions we will find intimations of attitudes we may expect in the future when Caesar and Christ will once again make conflicting demands upon the loyal obedience of the Christian citizen.

The answer to the first of these questions is known from earlier chapters. Every single one in the long series of spiritual counselors to whom Jägerstätter had turned, from his pastor to the chaplain who called his attention to the paper lying before him in his death cell, regarded his action as an imprudent, foolhardy, and unnecessary sacrifice. All of them advised him that the order of priority, as far as his personal obligations and responsibilities were concerned, began with his duties as husband and father and loyal citizen; that he had neither the competence, the information, nor the right to challenge the secular ruler as to the justice or injustice of the war in which he had been ordered to serve. Undoubtedly, all of them were motivated in part by the desire to save this man's life; but it seems safe to say that none would have advised him in this fashion if they, too, had believed the war to be unjust—or agreed that as a Christian one had a moral obligation to refuse to support that war. None of the priests I spoke to or corresponded with claimed to have shared the belief that the man was mentally unbalanced or a victim of religious fanaticism. Even the one instance which might suggest doubt, Fürthauer's recourse to the opinion of a visiting "expert," was probably a case of seeking support for his personal judgment, because of other feelings in the village. Looking back on their associations with the man, the terms in which these priests chose to describe him are words like "constant," "consistent," "thoroughgoing," and so forth. Kreuzberg was impressed by the way Jägerstätter's face lighted up when he heard that a priest had taken a similar stand. Jochmann reported the way the condemned man's eyes shone with joy and confidence in a glance he was never to forget. What his friends and neighbors are willing to grant as a possibility that really does not concern them too much was accepted by these priests—at least as most of them report their attitudes across the distance of two decades—as a certainty; that is, he committed himself to martyrdom in quest of personal salvation. This was the basis upon which Kreuzberg was to congratulate the condemned prisoner for his steadfast courage; this is what causes Fr. Arthofer, a priest who wrote a postwar article about Jägerstätter in which he obviously follows Karobath's notes, to declare that the man always wanted to be a saint; this is what Bishop Fliesser of the Linz diocese apparently meant by the peasant's "thirsting for martyrdom," even as he intervened to block publication of the Arthofer article.

Yet none of them was able to give Jägerstätter the one kind of support he needed. They could congratulate him for his unswerving commitment and give him assurance that he would not be committing a sin by following his conscience to the grave—but none had been able or willing to tell him that *he was right*. He believed he had been called upon to witness for his faith. As such, he was a solitary witness. Like Reinisch the year before and Max Josef Metzger, who was to follow them both to the same scaffold less than a year later, Franz Jägerstätter had to stand alone in his moment of decision. In a very real sense his action must be described as a stand *against* his fellow Catholics and their spiritual leaders who were wholeheartedly committed to, or at least willing to acquiesce in the war effort. The challenge Carl Amery, the German-Catholic journalist, made in 1963 in his book *Die Kapitulation, oder deutscher Katholizismus heute* ("The Capitulation, or German Catholicism Today"), unpleasant though it may sound to those who seek to justify the tragic past, is nonetheless irrefutable: "If, then, the Catholic heroes upon whom so much worth is placed today were prophets, it must be said that they were prophets taking a stand against their own religious milieu fully as much as against the domination of the heathens."

The priests who had some direct and personal contact with Jägerstätter have confidence in his sincerity and admiration for his consistency; their opinions have grown to something approaching conviction that he was indeed a martyr for his faith. Pastor Karobath has reaped some measure of unpopularity among his parishioners for his open declarations to that effect. At the end of a lengthy interview, Fr. Fürthauer went to get his breviary, and displayed the memorial card announcing his former sexton's death, explaining that "he always felt" this man would be canonized someday. Dean Kreuzberg made it clear in his conversations with me that he shared this belief; he had already put himself on record to this effect in his letter of August 21, 1943, to the widow when he comforted her with the advice, ". . . be absolutely sure of one thing: he has attained his eternal goal and is now living in the indescribably blessed presence of God where he will be a good protector and helper for you and your three children."

The most recent published account by a priest who knew Jägerstätter and served his spiritual needs is the article "Er folgte seinem Gewissen" ("He Followed His Conscience"), in the August 25, 1963, issue of the official weekly paper for the Linz diocese. This article by Fr. Baldinger represents the first official notice given to Jägerstätter's case by the Linz diocesan authorities. After printing the text of Jägerstätter's farewell letter (of August 9, 1943), Baldinger declares, "When I make a careful reading of the letters written by Jägerstätter before his death and since published, I can do nothing else but agree, 'Yes, this was a saint, for he had sacrificed every-

163

thing—his possessions, his family, and his life—for his conscientious convictions.' " He goes on to conclude:

From time to time God seems to choose a man from whom something entirely out of the ordinary is demanded, something that is not to be generally imitated but which is to be for us at the given moment something like a pointing finger. Jägerstätter's behavior is for us an admonition to be true to the voice of our personal conscience; his death was, without question, an act of reparation and an offering on behalf of many.

The Baldinger article, and particularly its cautionary note that Jägerstätter's rebellion is not proposed as a model for the ordinary Christian, brings us to the consideration of the official stand taken by the most responsible leaders of the Linz diocese. Before publishing Baldinger's article, the editor of this same paper, at the personal intervention of Bishop Fliesser, then the ruling ordinary of the diocese, had turned down two articles about Jägerstätter, one by Karobath and the other by Arthofer.

The St. Radegund parish "Jägerstätter file" contains a letter written to Arthofer on February 27, 1946, and signed by the editor. After noting that an article on the same case had been rejected by the Bishop the year before, he explains that he felt it necessary to submit Arthofer's article for the Bishop's approval. The account of the Bishop's decision then takes the form of a direct restatement of his position on Jägerstätter. The Bishop believed that this case had to be presented in a framework of fundamental Catholic morality "if it is not to create confusion and disturb consciences." Arthofer's exposition, he felt, made no effort to avoid the "danger" that this case might be "wrongly understood and merely sensationalized." It was, therefore, to be rejected.

But the Bishop did not stop with this; he went on to record for us, through the editor's letter, his own recollections and evaluations of the case:

I have known Jägerstätter personally, since he spent more than an hour with me before he was to be inducted. To no avail I set before him all the moral principles defining the degree of respon-

164

sibility carried by citizens and private individuals for the actions of the civil authority and reminded him of his far greater responsibilities in his own state of life, in particular for his family. I am aware of the "consistency" of his conclusions and respect them—especially in their intention. At the time I could see that the man thirsted after martyrdom and for the expiation of sin, and I told him he was permitted to choose that path only if he knew he had been called to it through some special revelation originating from above and not in himself. He agreed with this. For this reason, Jägerstätter represents a completely exceptional case, *one more to be marveled at than copied*, and it is to be presented to the people only in a suitable and unambiguous manner. [Italics added.]

Arthofer's article was entitled "Heldenhafte Konsequenz" ("Heroic Consistency"). The Bishop, as his comments are recorded for us in the editor's letter, takes up the term *Konsequenz* ("consistency") and uses it in what appears to be a sarcastic way, keeping the term in quotation marks.

It is clear that the priest's article had not met with the Bishop's strict standards, for the letter continues to say that the Bishop would be "grateful" if Arthofer were to turn to that difficult task "as a theologian and writer and spiritual counselor" in such a way as to define whatever in Jägerstätter was more properly to be seen as "true heroism worthy of imitation." A refusal to support the German cause in World War II was definitely not what the Bishop had in mind, for the letter goes on (still with direct attribution to Fliesser),

I consider the greater heroes to be those exemplary young Catholic men, seminarians, priests, and heads of families who fought and died in heroic fulfillment of duty and in the firm conviction that they were fulfilling the will of God at their post just as the Christian soldiers in the armies of the heathen emperor had done.

Then follows a most revealing rhetorical question and answer:

165

Or are the greater heroes the *Bibelforschers* and Adventists who, in their "consistency," preferred to die in concentration camps rather than bear arms? All respect is due the innocently erroneous conscience; it will have its reward from God. For the instruction of *men*, the better models are to be found in the example set by the heroes who conducted themselves "consistently" in the light of a clear and correct conscience. [Emphasis on "men" in the original.]

The editor concludes the letter by writing, as if to emphasize once more that the decision to reject the article was not his: "Thus [spoke] the Bishop. Jägerstätter is to be treated from the standpoint that he was a martyr to his conscience."

One often encounters explanations of official Catholic support for Hitler's wars, whether in Germany or in Austria, which stress the terrors and the totality of the control exercised by the Nazis. This letter, written *after* the war, *after* the Nazis were gone from the scene, cannot be so easily dismissed. When we recall that this letter was written in the period in which evidence of any kind of resistance or opposition to the Nazi regime was exploited to the fullest to dissociate the Church and others from the evils of the Nazi regime, Bishop Fliesser's continued support for the men of the armed forces as "greater heroes" than those who preferred to die in concentration camps rather than support a cause they considered immoral is indeed remarkable.

In an effort to probe more deeply into this incident—and to discover if perhaps there was some other information relating to the Jägerstätter visit to be found in the diocesan archives, I arranged to visit the author of this revealing letter at his Linz office, where he was still serving as editor of the paper and as secretary to Bishop Fliesser's successor. As soon as I introduced myself and stated the purpose of my visit, he at once recognized Jägerstätter's name as that of "the peasant who was executed." He vaguely remembered first hearing of the case through a discussion with a priest whose name he could not recall, and he went on to say that this was the extent of his knowledge about the matter. My suggestion that the priest might have been the man's pastor was greeted with the statement that this was definitely not so. This might be taken as evidence that Arthofer was the priest he had in mind, but I decided it was best not to mention this name lest its association with a potentially sensitive incident jeopardize further discussions. Needless to say, I did not mention the letter—which I had already seen —for the same reason. Furthermore, there was a real possibility that it had been another priest, after all.

To guide the discussion, I mentioned the book of Jakob Fried, who at the suggestion of Pope Pius XII had undertaken to collect the stories of heroic acts by Catholics in Austria during the Nazi era. He had included Jägerstätter's story in his book and had mentioned Franz's visit to his bishop. Very much to my surprise, the editor met this reference with a warning that the Fried book had been produced in haste and had proved unreliable in some respects. However, he did not specifically claim that the report of such a meeting was one of these inaccuracies. Instead, he asked if the exchange between Franz and his bishop was supposed to have taken place in the form of a personal confrontation or if it had been conducted through correspondence. Told that they had met in person, he voiced his sympathetic regret that there would be no documentary evidence.

It was quite obvious that a more indirect approach was required, and I introduced the question of whether the diocesan paper edited by him had ever carried an article about Jägerstätter. He said it had not, but he seemed to remember that the local daily newspaper, not published under Church auspices, had once carried a brief item. This led me to remark that I found it rather surprising that a case which had been reported and discussed in religious papers of other Austrian dioceses, and those of other countries as well, had not given even passing attention in the paper of the central figure's home diocese. The response to this was a noncommittal recognition that this might be true. Pressing further, I noted that his paper was then in the process of publishing a series of articles dealing with the Catholic Church's teachings about the priority always to be given by the individual to his religious duties, and I suggested that the Jägerstätter story would seem to offer a significant illustration of those teachings. His response was again friendly, but completely

167

noncommittal. It became clear that I was not going to learn much about the Jägerstätter-Fliesser meeting from him and, since I obviously could not introduce the fact of the letter any more, I was obliged to postpone further inquiry until some future visit.

But this first session was not a total loss. The editor-priest made the suggestion that the local daily might wish to carry a story about my investigation; and since one of the editors of that paper happened to be in his outer office at that very moment, he invited her to join us. Though I had some misgivings, I had no good reason to reject a suggestion that was undoubtedly meant to be helpful. Indeed, it had an immediate value in that it gave me the opportunity to reiterate to the young lady my astonishment that the diocesan paper had ignored the case so completely. Although it was possible for me to be even more forceful in this restatement, freed as I was from the strictures of propriety that had restrained me in my earlier comments to him directly, it was quite obvious that the repetition in his hearing had no noticeable effect upon him. Later, his suggestion was to prove much more helpful than I expected: the article appeared the following morning, and in a matter of days I was to receive the letters from Fr. Baldinger and the Vöklabruck nun which I have already described.

The second point of value gained from this otherwise unproductive interview lay in the clues it provided to the thinking of the higher diocesan officials about Jägerstätter. For one thing, the editor suggested that a careful check be made to determine whether the peasant had had any links to the *Bibelforscher* or Adventist sects. There may be some significance in the very fact that the two groups were paired in precisely the same manner in the 1946 letters. He explained that the uniqueness of Jägerstätter's position in the light of traditional Catholic teachings suggested such a connection. While he was prepared to admit that some Catholics held pacifist positions of one kind or another, he clearly considered them of doubtful orthodoxy, worthy to be classed with the doctrinal antiwar teachings of these two non-Catholic sects. He also introduced the possibility that an individual who held so unique and inflexible a position might not have been in full possession of his mental faculties. He recommended, therefore, that some thought be given

168

to investigating the man's family history to see if there were any record of mental illness. Such a possibility was indicated, he felt, by the fact that the man's final decision had been taken and held "against his family, against his spiritual advisors, and against his bishop." Though he did use this latter phrase, perhaps he did not mean it to confirm the visit to the bishop. He had listened to me being interviewed by the editor for the local daily and may have been recapitulating the story as I had presented it to the young lady.

There is an obvious and striking parallel between these two suggestions and the "explanations" of Jägerstätter's behavior that were so generally accepted in St. Radegund. The chancery may have actually checked into the matter at some earlier point, learned about the man's close association with his cousin, and heard tales of the extremes to which his "religious fanaticism" had gone. However, in the absence of any definite evidence, it is safest to conclude that these suggestions reflected nothing more than the assumptions this man would have made about anyone who had acted as Jägerstätter did. This is significant in itself, for if Jägerstätter's action can be so easily dismissed or suspected by a religious leader holding a post of great influence, one should not be surprised to find the same opinions held by the less educated and humbler residents of the peasant's village.

My second visit to chancery headquarters—ostensibly to report back to the editor and to inform him of the valuable responses to the news item published at his suggestion—took place three weeks later. Its real purpose, of course, was to pursue further the earlier unsuccessful attempt to discover what he could tell me about the official diocesan position with respect to Jägerstätter. After some preliminary pleasantries, I told him he would be interested to know that I had found evidence to verify the fact that a meeting had taken place between the peasant and the bishop, and that the advice given by the latter had followed the lines indicated by Fried in his book. This news brought an expression of polite gratification that my research problem had been solved for me. But there was no suggestion that he could add anything.

I then mentioned that I had also uncovered a somewhat surprising, even disturbing fact: Bishop Fliesser had actually intervened

169

at least twice to block publication of articles about Jägerstätter in the diocesan weekly. I added the personal judgment that this could be construed as a grave injustice to the man who had followed his conscience to the grave. He listened quietly and merely commented that he knew nothing about this—the Bishop had never discussed the matter with him. There was nothing left to do but to confront him with the fact that he himself had written the letter in which the evidence was found—adding, of course, that I assumed the affair had escaped his memory.

This, he assured me, must have been the case: "so many papers and articles" pass across his desk that it is impossible to remember them all. The fact that the letter had been written to Arthofer led him to comment that the priest could not have known anything about what happened to Jägerstätter because he was in Dachau when it all took place. Informed that he had heard the story "secondhand," he dryly observed that Arthofer "is always writing about all sorts of things."

It is likely that the editor's memory was far more complete than he indicated, but that he preferred not to confirm the story, thereby protecting his former superior from criticism. And, of course, I could not say that I had a "right" to any information; the diocesan authorities were under no obligation to furnish me with information that could only prove a source of embarrassment to Bishop Fliesser's memory. The issue, however, resolved itself into something of a "happy ending" when the diocesan paper published the Baldinger article. Even if it is true, as I have good reason to suspect, that its appearance in print was not completely unrelated to the fact that the present book was in preparation, this publication does represent some measure of recognition, however belated, of the heroism of the man who had been a member of the Linz flock.

Twenty years is, of course, a long time to wait for such recognition. The peasant's widow and her family could have taken much comfort and spiritual strength during the intervening years had the recognition been permitted in 1946, and the pastor's urgent efforts to mold a more favorable community opinion of his executed parishioner would have had a greater measure of success if some evidence had been at hand that his diocesan superiors went at least part of the way with him. A generation has been lost in which the immediacy and the saliency of the lesson to be learned from this case have faded. There is no reason to believe that the near total disinterest on the part of the young people of St. Radegund can be overcome at this late date.

Yet, if the matter can direct fresh attention to the religious questions involved in this story and its implications, others may benefit from what the young Radegunders still continue to dismiss as "ancient history." The most immediate of all these questions would seem to be the objective moral merit of the peasant's decision. The editor's letter stated that the Bishop was willing to respect Jägerstätter's action as the product of an "inculpably erroneous conscience." But is this true? If the Nazi war effort did not meet the traditional requisite conditions of "the just war," and I have seen no serious theological effort to prove the contrary, it would seem that the opposite was true—that the Bishop, not the peasant, and all of the Catholics he regarded as "greater heroes," were acting in erroneous conscience, that only Jägerstätter acted in accordance with the *objective* fact that Hitler's wars were not the just wars in which the Christian is permitted to bear arms.

This possibility came up in my conversation with the editor and met with the immediate response that it was difficult to see how an individual living in an isolated rural village and having so limited an educational background could be competent to reach a conclusion about the justice or injustice of the war. His answer, however, misses the central point: if it is true that the wars were unjust, Jägerstätter's decision, however he may have come to it, was the morally correct one—and all the other people, still speaking in the context of *objective* validity, acted in a manner which could quite properly be described as at least a material violation of the Fifth Commandment. This is not to imply a moral condemnation of those others. In the peasant's own words, it would be enough to say that they had not been "given the grace" to see or act otherwise.

However, this does not mean that we are obliged to accept the Baldinger interpretation that Jägerstätter's behavior is "not to be copied," but is something reserved for the rare person chosen by God to point up a needed lesson. In all his writings, beginning with the letter to his young godchild, the peasant made it clear that he believed suffering, even martyrdom, was an essential and expected part of the Christian's heritage. Here, too, his stand departed from the pattern prevailing within Christianity in general. An even more important question posed by the Jägerstätter story, then, is the extent to which the Christian is, or may be, "called" to social and civil dissent or disobedience when conformity would involve behavior he considers morally questionable.

There are areas, of course, where the issue has been recognized and resolved. Sex and family morality is one such area. No matter what degree of social and civil approval may be given actions that have been traditionally defined as immoral in this sphere (divorce, contraception, sterilization, concubinage, etc.), the spiritual leadership is most insistent upon Catholic refusal to accept these new standards. So, too, with literature or with styles of clothing which are held to violate traditional moral norms. If the inability to conform should bring with it the social penalties of ridicule, ostracism, or, even worse, then the faithful are reminded of the eternal rewards to be gained by bearing such sufferings for their faith.

Moving from these areas of predominantly personal behavior to those involving behavior held to involve the welfare or the continued existence of the political community, the emphasis shifts abruptly. Now "legitimate authority" becomes decisive, and the individual is expected to suppress or silence personal doubts concerning public decisions that go contrary to his moral inclinations (unless, one must add, those public decisions seek to intrude upon the institutional prerogatives of the religious community itself). In issues related to the maintenance of public order and to the prosecution of, or preparation for, a national war effort, the Catholic citizen suddenly seems to lose both his competence and his right to make an independent moral judgment of the behavior required of him. In case of doubt, the "presumption of justice" is granted to the civil authority.

Thus it was that this peasant, who had somehow come to recognize the inherent immorality of the Nazi regime and the injustice of its wars, found himself facing the opposition of those placed in spiritual authority over him and was forced to stand in total isolation because he could not conform to the behavior expected of him by his fellow Catholics. It must be granted that the priests and others who counseled him were motivated by the desire to save his life, but they must also have believed he was wrong in his insistence that to do as they suggested would have placed his soul in jeopardy. All of the appeals to patriotism, the repeated references to the priests and seminarians who had accepted military service, the assurances that the individual had no business concerning himself about the high-level policy decisions made by his civil superiors—all of these testify to a willingness to accept theologoical formulations which, in fact, surrender all judgment in this area to Caesar. Even the argument Baldinger felt had the strongest appeal for the peasant would have restricted the moral implications of the soldier's behavior to the level of person-to-person relations. He writes:

> I tried to make it clear to him that the individual soldier can do much good through his good example, and especially through works of charity toward his comrades. How many had already conducted themselves in an heroic manner by helping wounded or dying comrades, or protecting the civilian population in the land of the so-called enemy when cruel or inhuman comrades threatened them with violent or unjust treatment. A good soldier could practice a Christian apostolate at the same time.

It is not difficult to imagine how contradictory the notions of a "Christian apostolate" and military service in the Hitler forces must have seemed to Jägerstätter.

The harsh truth is that Jägerstätter had chosen to take his stand at a time and in a place where the religious community itself had abandoned all pretensions to the traditions of protest and prophecy that had marked its earlier history. Shepherds and flock alike had succumbed so thoroughly to the temptations of conformism and accommodation—albeit in the guise of "prudence" exaggerated to a point where the virtue of fortitude was all but forgotten—that they had lost all sense of identity and purpose. The religious community with which this peasant linked his heroic act of rebellion

173

proved to be unable and unwilling to give him the support he might have sought from it.

Nor has the situation changed. Baldinger's cautious implication is proof enough of this. But there is other evidence to show that this failing is not limited to one diocese. It is endemic to the situation in which the Christian today finds himself. Not only has his religious community foresworn the role of prophecy, but it seems at times to deny the legitimacy and efficacy of martyrdom as well. A prominent Catholic editor of a German intellectual journal was quite unwilling, for example, to accept my suggestion that the peasant deserved to be held up as a model of the behavior that should be expected of any Catholic ordered to fight in a war he believed to be unjust. According to him, the Church may never make demands of its members that would prove to be "too great a burden" and "drive them away." Furthermore, he went on to say, bishops should never take a stand which would certainly curtail or endanger the continued operation of the Church as an institution by risking or provoking retaliatory actions by secular authorities.

On the surface this might appear to be little more than a disagreement on tactics and approach, but it hides a much more profound difference in principle and philosophy. The self-proclaimed "realist" with the "practical" approach is almost always an advocate of a "situation ethics" that tends to reduce itself to a kind of moral relativism. It is entirely proper, of course, to insist that circumstances and setting must always be taken into account when one seeks to convert moral imperatives into a specific act. But it is quite another matter to permit these essentially extraneous considerations to negate or overrule basic obligations, so that the individual finds himself compromising with evil or, what can be just as bad, justifying the compromises made by others. It is so very easy to forget that prudence, in terms of which most such compromises are made, has been defined (in a 1958 statement of the American hierarchy) as "something quite different than inclination toward 'how much or how little' and mediocrity generally; it is a virtue—that is, an energy—of commitment and effectiveness arising from a conviction about ends in view."

All of the heated controversy centering upon the failure of the

Christian churches to mount an effective protest and opposition to the Nazi evil really calls into question this new morality of situation ethics. Whether in Rolf Hochhuth's exaggerated and somewhat irresponsible indictment of Pope Pius XII in his play *Der Stellvertreter* (*The Deputy*), or in my own past work dealing with German Catholic support for the Hitler war effort, or in Guenter Lewy's recent study, *The Catholic Church and Nazi Germany*, the same pattern of acquiescence or silence whenever the *institutional* "good of the Church" seemed to be involved emerges. The shocking evidence that theological loopholes were sought by which confessors could spare doctors and nurses the potentially dangerous necessity of refusing to co-operate with Hitler's involuntary sterilization program is all of a piece with the objection I have encountered that bishops should not have been expected to "trouble the consciences" of the Catholic faithful with respect to the justice or injustice of Hitler's wars.

There are two highly significant components to such a point of view. The first is a clear unwillingness to come into open conflict with political authority on matters not specifically and directly involving the institutional prerogatives of the Church. Partly, this may reflect too eager a readiness to surrender all such areas of public policy and concern to the state under the "presumption of justice" favoring legitimate secular authority; this certainly was involved in the official Church support for the Nazi war effort, though it does not totally explain it. In addition, there was a fear of the reprisals that might have to be borne by religious leaders personally or by the institution of the Church committed to their charge: church services, already curtailed, could have been forbidden altogether; the priests in Dachau (one bishop was reportedly callous enough to dismiss them as "martyrs to their own stupidity") might have been joined by many others—and even, one would have to assume, by some bishops as well.

It follows, then, that there was little disposition on the part of the German and Austrian spiritual leaders to consider, much less suggest to their faithful, the possibility that the "Christian duty" to which they were being called might actually be a violation of the Fifth Commandment, a form of murder—as knowing and willful partici-

175

pation in an unjust war would have to be. If we add to this consideration that these same leaders would be understandably hesitant about demanding of their followers possible martyrdom—especially when they had every reason to suspect that such a call would almost certainly have gone unheeded—one can more easily see how the record of German Catholicism could have become such that it could be characterized by Carl Amery as an outright "capitulation" to the milieu. What makes this charge particularly telling, however, is his conclusion that this continues to be the prevailing pattern.

Jägerstätter's action constitutes an outright rejection of the whole concept of "situation ethics," in that he insisted upon total commitment to a set of unchanging moral obligations which made it impossible for him to play "the crooked game" that the new morality permits and even seems to recommend. It should not come as a surprise, then, that those who did, and still do, accept that new morality would find it difficult to see the true meaning of his action. They are simply unable and unwilling to recognize or accept the broad scope of individual moral competence and personal moral responsibility he demanded of himself and others. What Bishop Fliesser would interpret as a "thirst for martyrdom" and, therefore, exceptional—if not excessive—and quite out of keeping with the "prudent" course of action he preferred, was undoubtedly present in Jägerstätter's case. But a careful reading of Jägerstätter's prison letters should make it obvious that he did not go out of his way to assume that martyrdom. Instead, he expressed the hope, almost to the very end, that events might still develop in such a way as to permit him to return to his home and family. His increasingly frequent references to the possibility of an early peace might be read as a source of such "last-minute" hopes. Nevertheless, it is true that he did not have much faith in such faint possibilities, that he was resigned to the realistic expectation that he would, in fact, be killed for the stand he had chosen to take. Thus, while he did not seek martyrdom, he willingly accepted it—*gratefully* accepted it as a means of attaining his salvation.

This is far removed from the statement attributed by a syndicated American columnist to a "council expert" at the Second Vatican Council. According to this expert, "We [the Church] don't encourage vocations for martyrdom. To prevent this the Church will make almost any adjustment." He was not speaking in the particular context with which we are concerned here, but this brief citation would serve admirably as a retroactive summary of the history of the Catholic Church in Hitler's Germany, including of course, Jägerstätter's Austria.

The Linz diocesan editor and the expert, along with many others who have expressed similar sentiments, have caught the true spirit of what seems to pass as Christianity in the modern conformist world. Jägerstätter did not, but this was because he did not choose to identify himself with the religious community as he knew it but, rather, as he had found it in the lives of the saints he had studied so thoroughly. This "community of the saints" is what he had chosen in preference to the "Nazi Folk Community," for to him it represented the true spirit of Christianity.

Again, the parallel between Jägerstätter's story and Thomas More's comes to mind. None of the peasant's writings refer to this member of the "community" with which he had so fixedly identified his interests and intentions. We can only assume that this story was also missing from the edition of *Heroes and Saints* in Jägerstätter's possession. Or, perhaps, he may have been so awed by More's exalted position that he was unable to see any similarity between the witness to which they both were called.

The parallel does break down on many points. More was one of the great and influential men of his day, a fact which explains why a king was so anxious to win his support. It was a matter of real importance that More maintain his silence, for, were he to give his support to his ruler, it would be widely noticed and would serve to convince others of the legitimacy of that cause. And were he to decide to speak out in open opposition to the king, his words could prove to be the spark to ignite the fires of rebellion.

Not so with the simple peasant from St. Radegund. Outside of his immediate circle of friends, relatives, and neighbors, there was no one to note whether he complied with his induction orders or not. Nor was it a matter of any real importance as far as the nation's cause was concerned. A hundred or a thousand Jägerstätters marching heroically to the executioner's block in preference to serving in the tyrant's armies would not have weakened those forces enough to cause or even hasten his downfall. With millions of German and Austrian Catholics loyally answering Hitler's call to arms, one stubborn peasant who refused would certainly not have been missed. As for the few who would know or care about what he did, there was not much danger that his acceptance of service would have "given scandal" in the sense that others would have followed his lead. Their decisions had already been reached, and they were not altered by this peasant's action and its consequences. Even today they view his sacrifice as nothing more than a tragic and meaningless show of religious fanaticism—a judgment toward which even the diocesan authorities at Linz seem to incline.

More and Jägerstätter: a "great" man and a "little" man. Yet the difference is one that may enhance rather than diminish the significance of the latter's sacrifice. For the very fact that none would notice or be likely to be affected by what he did serves to reduce the issue to the individual and his conscience in silent and inner confrontation with God. Certainly that is what it meant to Jägerstätter himself. That same confrontation existed for Thomas More, but, to the extent to which he knew others would take account of what he did, he was not alone. As far as the St. Radegund peasant knew, the choice he made would pass unnoticed by the world and would completely fade from human memory with the passing of the handful of people who had known him personally.

Perhaps he was amazed when so many people tried to persuade him to change his mind, or when the dignitaries of the military court offered to exempt him from the bearing of arms if he would only agree to take the oath. Perhaps he came to feel that he had become important, not as a person, but as a symbol to the military of what was possible if one refused to offer the kind of acknowledgment and acquiescence upon which its authority rested. But even so, he would not have deluded himself into believing that he was anything more to them than such a symbol. He had no great ambitions to change the world or singlehandedly bring about the fatal weakening of Hitler's armies and the consequent collapse of the regime he recognized as evil. Nor did he give any sign that he expected (or even wanted) others to notice and follow his example.

He stood alone—and he knew there was nothing else for him to do but bear his solitary witness. As long as we live in this world, he had written, I believe it is never too late to save ourselves and perhaps some other soul for Christ. This much, it seems safe to say, he did. For him, that would have been enough.

The words of Reinhold Schneider, the great German Catholic poet and historian, would have won Jägerstätter's complete assent: "When it becomes the 'sacred duty' of a man to commit sin," he wrote, "the Christian no longer knows how he should live. There remains nothing else for him to do but bear individual witness—alone. And where such witness is, there is the Kingdom of God."

The Martyr as Rebel:
A Sociological Summary

To this point, I have deemed it appropriate to separate the historical "reconstruction" of the singular story of Jägerstätter's life and death and the presentation of his writings from any more technical analysis that would focus upon the implications of his behavior or the responses to that behavior which might interest the specialist primarily. But I came to Franz Jägerstätter's history as a student of sociology, and some attention must now be given to these special implications and dimensions, even at the expense of burdening the reader with a marked change in style. The task of discovering what broader lessons can be found in Jägerstätter's story for the behavior of man in society is essential. There will be no attempt to drown the reader in a flood of "sociological jargon." The new emphasis, however, may determine the use of certain—perhaps "unusual"—terms.

By choosing to render Jägerstätter's history as a tale of rebellion, a structure has been imposed upon it from the start. It has been placed in a framework, enclosed on the one hand by a concept of "social control" and, on the other, by one of "social deviance." This setting is not arbitrary, however, but would have suited Jägerstätter's conception of his own actions. He recognized that he stood apart

180

from his fellows, both Catholic and Austrian, and he accepted the fact that there would be penalties to pay. Certainly, too, those who were aware of the actions he proposed recognized that the man and his activities deviated from the norms determining their own behavior.

A sociologist who insists upon a voluntarist approach to human behavior must, nevertheless, address himself to the indisputable facts of consistent, and to a degree, predictable, regularities in the behavior of members of a given society. To a large extent, these regularities can be attributed to an array of agencies and influences that he calls "social controls." Social controls operate in instances where an individual, because he is acting within a specific social context, does something he would otherwise not have done, or refrains from doing something he otherwise would have done. Some of these controls are "formal"; that is, they are explicit, they have been initiated by an "authority," and they carry clearly stated and supposedly impartial sanctions. Others are "informal"; these are not clearly defined, the promulgators or ministers of these controls have no recognized mandate, and the sanctions may vary from offender to offender.

When one turns from the kinds of controls to the manner in which they take effect, one may make another distinction: between "external" and "internal" controls. External controls are attributed to the presence of an outside cue or agent, such as a police car at the side of a road which inspires passing motorists to reduce their speed. Internal controls operate when behavior can be explained in terms of some value, emotion, belief, etc., which acts as an inner imperative, as when a driver maintains a moderate rate of speed because he believes it is "wrong" to endanger others by reckless driving. The distinction between "external" and "internal" controls becomes somewhat more complicated when we remember that these "inner" values, emotions, etc., were learned and therefore ultimately come from an "outside" source. However, these distinctions still retain some value when, in a specific situation, an attempt is made to locate the critical or deciding influence.

This brief, and perhaps superficial, explanation of the concept of social control can serve as an introduction to the concept of "social deviance." For while, in general, the behavior of most members of a society is governed by regularities, almost always there are those who do not conform to the regular patterns, who manage to escape or reject the social controls that produce conformity. Howard S. Becker has called these people "outsiders"; their actions can be described as "publicly labelled wrongdoing."[1] Unfortunately, the literature dealing with deviance has centered its attention on the "problems" of society: crime, delinquency, sexual deviation, alcoholism, drug addiction, etc. The notion of deviation begins to presuppose some kind of personal weakness or stigma. But this need not be the case. The rebel, the martyr, the saint, *as social types*, represent forms of social deviance that should be perhaps even more challenging to the student of social behavior. Peter Viereck has proposed a new national hero: "the unadjusted man"; his description might serve as a model for the social deviant: "a new liberator . . . a bad mixer . . . scandalously devoid of 'education for citizenship' . . . the final irreducible pebble that sabotages the omnipotence of even the smoothest-running machine."[2] Viereck identifies St. Thomas More as the kind of man he had in mind, but his characterization might also fit Franz Jägerstätter.

When a sociologist uses the term "social deviant" it refers to nothing more than an individual's failure to conform to behavioral patterns approved or prescribed within a given society at a given time, as in Jägerstätter's intentional substitution of behavior in open contradiction to expected patterns. Whether or not the social deviant is objectively justified in his choice of principles which explain his behavior, or whether his application of these principles can meet the test of logical consistency, is not within the sphere of sociological determination in the strictest sense. It may not be a matter of much concern in the case of behavior generally considered asocial or antisocial in motivation—those comonly associated with the "beatnik," the "hobo," the delinquent, for example, although even these types of deviance may present a more complex problem than is generally recognized. It is possible to believe, for instance, that juvenile delinquency is a form of "over-conformity" to

[1] See Howard S. Becker, *The Outsiders* (Glencoe, Ill.: The Free Press, 1963).
[2] Peter Viereck, *The Unadjusted Man* (New York: Putnam, 1962), p. 4.

the actual but unacknowledged values of the society with which delinquents appear to be in conflict.[3] Deviance becomes more complex in character, however, when it takes the form of a refusal to violate what the individual holds to be the significant or underlying *real* norms and values of human society.

Conscientious objection, especially in time of war, is such a form of social deviance. As Dahlke puts it, "For purposes of analysis the conscientious objector may be one whose behavior is set on a *wertrational* [i.e., based on inner values, value-directed] basis. He follows either a prescribed role or one developed in his own life history. In either case the conscientious objector is a deviant from the prevailing norms of society at war."[4] Jägerstätter's refusal to serve in the Nazi army on the grounds that to do so would involve the betrayal of his most cherished values fits the Dahlke description; furthermore, since he knew and accepted the fact that this refusal brought with it the all but certain sanction of death, we have been dealing here with what may properly be treated as a case of extreme social deviance.

Robert K. Merton, in his now classic theoretical analysis of deviance, introduces what might be taken as a sociological definition of the martyr and sees him as "the historically significant nonconformist" who is, "in terms of social structure, culture and personality, a distinct type of social deviant." And he continues:

Following the ancient adage that "the nature of anything is best known from the examination of extreme cases," we should take note of the extreme non-conformist who enters upon his public course of non-conformity with full knowledge that he runs the risk, so high a risk as to be almost a certainty, of severe punishment for his behavior by the group. This kind of man is, in the fairly strict sense, a martyr—that is, one who sacrifices self for principle. Adhering to the norms and values of some reference group other than the group to whose expectations he will not

[3] See Gordon C. Zahn, "In our Image," *The Commonweal*, Vol. LXX, No. 12 (December 13, 1963), pp. 302–304.
[4] H. Otto Dahlke, "Values and Group Behavior in Two Camps for Conscientious Objectors," *American Journal of Sociology*, LI (1945), p. 22.

conform, he is prepared to accept, if not to welcome, the almost certain and painful consequences of dissent.[5]

Jägerstätter's refusal to serve fits this pattern, and, as we have seen, he did accept *and even welcome* the severe sanctions that refusal carried. In the first instance, his action was a violation of the formal controls established and maintained by the Nazi regime. Indeed the law was so explicit that his trial was a "cut-and-dried" affair, with the death sentence a mandatory terminus, once the officers of the court had failed in their effort to persuade the man to modify his refusal. As for the informal controls, all the interviews and Jägerstätter's writings revealed the continuous, and unquestionably well-intentioned, efforts made both in the community and in prison to induce him to conform to the demands of the war effort.

So, too, with the external control. In a way, the totalitarian social and political order of the time was able to see to it that everything "outside" of the individual person would serve to spur the behavior it considered essential. One suspects that the *Geschlossenheit*—the feeling of enclosedness and mutuality of the isolated rural community—constituted something of a barrier to the controls the more remote state authority sought to impose, but this would be more than counterbalanced by the fact that the same ties would reinforce the community's support for a war effort in which its members would be risking their lives. It is the combination of these two contrary tendencies which probably accounts for the manner in which St. Radegund reacted to the army deserter: since he was "one of theirs," there never was the slightest chance that he would be "turned in" to the Nazi or military authorities; yet his action, then and now, was held in extremely low regard by the very people who gave him shelter and protection. Something of the same holds true for Jägerstätter: He was not "resented"; there was no, or at most very little, animosity expressed toward him or his family—at the same time this willingness to tolerate his act of deviance directed against the outside government does not alter the fact that he is

<hr>

[5] Robert K. Merton, *Social Theory and Social Structure* (Glencoe, Ill.: The Free Press, 1957), pp. 364–365.

still judged to have failed to meet the responsibilities which were rightfully his in the eyes of the community. Thus one can safely conclude that, even in his closed and protective community, he was continually surrounded by reminders of the total commitment to the war effort that was expected of him and everyone else.

If Jägerstätter's behavior was, in the Dahlke term (which follows Weber's usage), *wertrational*, this would mean that it is perhaps best explained in terms of internal social controls. Jägerstätter believed so strongly that his conscience, representing for him the voice of his God, demanded that he refuse to serve in unjust wars of an immoral regime that there was never any real doubt as to how he would act. This is not to say, however, that this was a simple act of conformity to an univocal inner imperative. All other controls were absolutely unanimous in requiring that he serve in the military forces; in the case of his internal controls, it was a matter of balancing conflicting pressures one against another. Patriotic inclinations to support the nation's cause were probably not very strong in him, if they were present at all, for he had persisted in maintaining a distinction between "Austrian" and "German" even after the *Anschluss* he so strongly condemned. One must assume, however, that he had "identified" somewhat with the national cause, if only to the degree that he participated in the community concern for its members on the battlefield; in this respect his refusal to serve in the army was "letting the others down" and could be viewed as actually increasing the dangers they had to face. This would have been a powerful inner control, and Fr. Baldinger's impression that his appeals along this line had been particularly effective may have been an accurate one. Another complex of internal controls would have centered upon his love and concern for his family and the fears, so clearly indicated in his prison writings, that they would have to pay a heavy price for his action. Nor need we discount the very probable and thoroughly natural reaction of fear for himself. His frequent statements of confidence that he would continue to receive enough spiritual strength to carry him through to the end must be interpreted as a sign that he was troubled by the ever-present awareness that the temptation to save himself would also be with him until the last moment.

But, of course, the final balance was struck in favor of the values calling for a refusal to serve in the military. Whether these values were indeed reinforced by the emotional dimension suggested by Bishop Fliesser, that the peasant "thirsted after martyrdom," it is obvious from his final writings, and from his whole course of action, that all the internal controls favoring conformity had to give way. Perhaps there were other dimensions to this final value disposition that are not amenable to sociological formulation or identification. For instance, if he had been given some special "grace" or a super-natural revelation, as he obviously believed he had, this, too, would have to be viewed as a behavior mechanism working through him and "within" him and carrying a kind of power that would explain its ability to outweigh the natural inclinations or other influences that might have counseled conformity. There is a danger, of course, that such an explanation could be used to make his rebellion some-what irrelevant to its social implications for his day or ours—a danger that is best illustrated, perhaps, by the tendency on the part of Baldinger and others to treat him as a special case, someone "selected" by God to prove a point and, therefore, not to be taken as a model for the behavior of ordinary Christians.

The present study, while not at all antagonistic to the possibility that the wellsprings of Jägerstätter's actions did lie in other and higher realms, must still restrict itself to those dimensions of behavior which set him apart from his fellows as a social deviant and which can be traced, however inadequately, to the situation in which he lived and to his personal definition of that situation. It is as a rebel, not as a possible saint, that we are concerned with him here—though, like Thomas More, he may have been both rebel and saint.

Albert Camus' formulation of what a rebel is loses some of its relevance in regard to Jägerstätter's case because Camus forces a separation between what he calls the "world of the sacred" in the human mind and the "world of rebellion." For him:

The rebel is a man who is on the point of accepting or re-jecting the sacred and determined on laying claim to a human situation in which all the answers are human—in other words, formulated in reasonable terms. From this moment every question, every word, is an act of grace. It would be possible to demonstrate in this manner that only two possible worlds can exist for the human mind: the sacred (or, to speak in Christian terms, the world of grace) and the world of rebellion. The disappearance of one is equivalent to the appearance of the other, despite the fact that this appearance can take place in disconcerting forms. There again we discover the *All or Nothing*. The present interest of the problem of rebellion only springs from the fact that nowadays whole societies have wanted to discard the sacred. We live in an unsacrosanct moment in history. Insurrection is certainly not the sum total of human experience. But history today, with all its storm and strife, compels us to say that rebellion is one of the essential dimensions of man. It is our historic reality. Unless we choose to ignore reality, we must find our values in it. Is it possible to find a rule of conduct outside the realm of religion and its absolute values? That is the question raised by rebellion.[6]

Jägerstätter's answer to that question would probably be No; and this would seem to exclude him from Camus' description of a rebel. Yet one must ask whether in a social order totally committed to the effective suppression or neutralization of religious values, the man who stakes his life upon this affirmation does not challenge the assumptions and authority of the world of the secular.

Another interesting description of what he terms "the positively rebellious individual" is provided by Robert Lindner.[7] Five of the six signs by which the mature and constructive rebel can be identified—awareness, identity, skepticism, responsibility, employment, and tension—were clearly exhibited by Jägerstätter. However, to the extent that Lindner sees "skepticism" as a "refusal to accept anything on the basis of faith or authority," he, like Camus, seems to exclude the possibility of a rebellious act originating in a full

[6] Albert Camus, *The Rebel: An Essay on Man in Revolt* (New York: Knopf, 1954), p. 21.

[7] Robert Lindner, *Must You Conform?* (New York: Holt, Rinehart and Winston, 1956), pp. 191–209.

and voluntary commitment to a religious faith and its requirements. Nevertheless, Jägerstätter's refusal to countenance uncritical
obedience would seem to illustrate a form of that "skepticism"
Lindner considers one of the marks of the positive rebel.
If the term "deviant" is not to be so restricted in its use that
it applies only to the weak and the morally misfit, one might
insist that the term "rebel" have a meaning broad enough to
include a man who went to his death precisely because he saw
God as a very important part of the world of "reality" which we
may not choose to ignore and in which we must find the values
by which to live. The mutually exclusive separation of the world
of the sacred and the world of a reality in which rebellion becomes
possible would be a separation our simple peasant would find difficult, if not impossible, to understand. He keyed his behavior to its
meaning for the world of the sacred; that much is true. But he
never lost sight of the fact that he was acting *in history*, and that
his actions were responsive to the imperatives of history almost as
much as to the imperatives of his faith.
The point that must not be overlooked in this connection is
that he was a "rebel" in the eyes of his religious community, too.
All of the categories of control mentioned earlier in relation to
the secular authority apply with only slightly diminished force to
the religious authority to which he was subject. In formal public
declarations, the ruling episcopacy of Hitler's Germany had called
upon the Catholic faithful to perform the military service required
of them in the name of "*Volk* and Fatherland." In Jägerstätter's
case, this was reinforced by the personal discussion he had with
Bishop Fliesser and by the advice received from all the priests to
whom he had turned in their "official" capacity as spiritual counselors. His informal religious contacts would probably be co-ex-
tensive with the friends, neighbors, and family contacts described
in the earlier identification of controls, but in this context they
would have special importance because they would be taking issue
with his stand on *religious* and not merely on patriotic or prudential
grounds. Perhaps as sexton he would be in a position to control
the extent to which parish services and facilities would be used
as external pressures in support of the war (just as he had tried

188

to tone down Fr. Fürthauer's sermons in praise of the glories of military sacrifice), but there would still be some reminders, again of a religious nature, that those who were "doing their duty" as defined by the Nazi regime were receiving greater honor and encouragement from the spiritual community than he could ever hope to get. Finally, though internal controls of religious beliefs and aspirations were the forces that ultimately did account for his refusal to serve, there is evidence enough that other religious considerations argued for a contrary course of action. His frequent statements of his inability to believe that what he was doing was a "sin"—whether of disobedience to legitimate authority or of violating the norms forbidding any form of "suicide"—are at the same time clear testimony that such a possibility was troubling him. That this continued almost to the very end may be seen in the joy with which he welcomed Kreuzberg's news that a priest had taken the same path before him. His commitment, then, was a complete commitment to values associated with the "world of the sacred." But it was, nonetheless, a solitary witness.

In an earlier study of American conscientious objection to World War II,[8] it was deemed convenient to introduce a distinction between objectors who were "encouraged" in their deviance because they were following doctrinal directives or traditions of their religious community and those who were "resisters," since they were obliged to take a stand against that taken by their fellow communicants and spiritual leaders. The first group may perhaps hold the greater significance for a theoretical approach to social deviance, since it suggests that overt deviance may, in certain instances, be the product of conformity. The so-called "peace churches" (Mennonites, Brethren, and Friends) may have succeeded in inducing some of their young men to become conscientious objectors, even though they might have preferred to enter military service. And even if this extreme example did not apply in many cases, it could still be true that many men sought alternative service be-

[8] Gordon C. Zahn, "A Descriptive Study of the Social Backgrounds of Conscientious Objectors in Civilian Public Service During World War II" (unpublished Doctoral dissertation, Department of Sociology, The Catholic University of America, Washington, D. C., 1953).

cause their religious formation had effectively excluded from their minds all consideration of ever bearing arms.

Deviance produced by conformity to deviant groups or communities—religious or otherwise—involves, of course, a shift of focus that relates most directly to reference group theory. The "reference group" has been defined as one "whose outlook is used by the actor as the frame of reference in the organization of his perceptual field."[9] Stripped of its forbidding terminology, this means the specific group with which an individual identifies himself and whose expectations or requirements influence or determine his behavior in a given instance. The boy who refuses to "do his duty" in military service (an act defined as deviant in the eyes of the society at war) because "I am a Mennonite and we are forbidden to bear arms" has referred to his religious community as the proper guide for his behavior—regardless of whether his personal inclination was to follow the same pattern or not. Such deviant "reference groups," strange to say, are not given due recognition in analyses of deviant behavior.

This criticism does not apply to the work of Robert K. Merton. Indeed, the stress he gives to the reference-group dimension of deviance is one of the more important contributions he has made. He speaks in particular of the "non-conformist with his appeal to a higher morality" who can "draw upon the latent store of moral indignation" to support and even win some degree of tolerance for his stand (as was so clearly the case with Jägerstätter). Merton declares, "In some measure, his non-conformity appeals either to the moral values of an earlier day which have been lost to view or to moral values of a time which will come to pass. He appeals, in short, to a past or future reference group. He re-activates a forgotten set of values, standards, and practices, or activates a set which is not blemished by existing concessions and expedient compromises with current realities."[10]

The issue is complicated in the case of the "resister" deviant category into which the Jägerstätter case falls. Reverting again to

[9] Francis E. Merrill, *Society and Culture* (2nd ed.; Englewood Cliffs, N.J.: Prentice-Hall, 1961), p. 84.

[10] Merton, *op. cit.*, pp. 362–63.

the study of American conscientious objectors, these were the men who took their stand without the support—in some cases, despite the opposition and disapproval—of their religious communities. Prominent among these were the one hundred thirty-five Roman Catholics in the Civilian Public Service program. These did not, it should be noted, constitute all of the Catholic conscientious objection in America. Some Catholics were unsuccessful in their efforts to obtain the conscientious objector classification and were ultimately sent to prison when they persisted in their refusal to serve in the war. Many others, undoubtedly the overwhelming majority of Catholic objectors, accepted the limited service classification (I-A-O) and served as medical corpsmen, chaplains' assistants, or in some similar noncombatant capacity. In this country, too, the "official" Church position, certainly the position taken by virtually all Catholics eligible for service, was one of all-out support for the war effort. As a result, the small minority of Catholics who did choose to register conscientious objection were viewed with varying degrees of disapproval. Sometimes the mode of disapproval was that of a regretful tolerance; sometimes, if the commitment to the national cause was more intense, open hostility. Usually, however, it took the form of silently ignoring the dissident minority altogether.

We are concerned here with the phenomenon of conscientious objection as a form of social deviance. There is no implication that the content or substance of the positions taken by Jägerstätter and American Catholic objectors are equivalent, or, for that matter, that such equivalence applies to the individuals in the latter group. In the last analysis, each man developed and maintained his own position. The cases are similar, however, in that they all involve an open and explicit refusal to conform to the demands of the secular community and its war effort, and in that all made such a refusal without the support—indeed, in most cases, in the face of the evident disapproval—of their religious community and its leaders.

This does not necessarily mean, of course, that the reference group explanation would not apply in the case of these Catholic objectors. Other groups—ethnic or political associations, for example—may have replaced or superseded both the national and the religious identifications in the cases of these individuals. In Jägerstätter's case it is possible that his refusal to accept the *Anschluss* decision means that he continued to regard himself as an "Austrian" in contradistinction to the "Germans," who were prosecuting the war. However, this is a highly tenuous conclusion, for it must have been evident to him that all Austrians were accepting the war as "their" war to the extent that the welfare of the Austrian homeland was dependent upon the success of the Axis Powers. Only if he had been in contact with one of the Resistance groups could we say that his deviance was definitely a product of a reference group attachment to an anti-Nazi "other Austria," and this was not the case.

There is no need to explore these other possibilities, because the key to Jägerstätter's deviance should be obvious to anyone who has noted the content of his writings. His "reference group" was the Church, the same Church which failed to give him encouragement in the stand he had taken. The manner in which the apparent inconsistency between his status as a "resister" deviant and the fact that he was referring to the Church whose influence he was "resisting" holds one of the more fascinating theoretical implications of this case study. The Church with which he linked his refusal to serve was the Church of prophets and martyrs that had been abandoned and rejected by those who constituted the acting Church in Nazi Germany and Austria. These terms may be too harsh if one takes them to mean a conscious or intentional abandonment or rejection; but to the extent that the recommended behavior did *in effect* involve an explicit avoidance of steps which might bring reprisal upon the Catholic community and was justified on the grounds that it was the responsibility of the religious leadership to protect the flock against such an unhappy prospect, they do fit the circumstances.

To say this is not, as Jägerstätter put it, to "cast stones" at the priests and bishops who held the posts of responsibility. All of the pressures of the situation, for which he made allowance, would have to be taken into account in any assessment of their moral culpability. But moral culpability is not a question that concerns us here; sociologically speaking, the point of immediate significance

192

is the peasant's choice of a reference group out of the time-place context in which he was called upon to act. In Merton's term, he was appealing to a past reference group and "reactivating" a forgotten set of values, standards, and practices—or, in another sense, one might hold that his action was keyed to a *future* reference group in that he framed his aspirations in terms of enjoying eternal blessedness in the life of the hereafter. As far as this world was concerned his was "the Church" of the first three centuries, the Church of the "saints and heroes" who had kept alive a continuing tradition of self-sacrificing witness. This becomes most explicit in his prison statement when he wrote: I can easily see that anyone who refuses to acknowledge the Nazi Folk Community and also is unwilling to comply with all the demands of its leaders will thereby forfeit the rights and privileges offered by that nation. But it is not much different with God: he who does not wish to acknowledge the community of saints or who does not obey all the commandments set forth by Him and His Church and who is not ready to undergo sacrifices and to fight for His Kingdom either—such one also loses every claim and every right under that Kingdom. . . .

Now anyone who is able to fight for both kingdoms and stay in good standing in both communities (that is, the community of saints and the Nazi Folk Community) and who is able to obey every command of the Third Reich—such a man, in my opinion, would have to be a great magician. I for one cannot do so. And I definitely prefer to relinquish my rights under the Third Reich and thus make sure of deserving the rights granted under the Kingdom of God.

Whether such a choice had in fact been forced upon him (and, by extension, on every other Austrian Catholic as well) by the situation in which he found himself is a matter for the moral theologian to decide. At the very least it should inspire some new consideration of the adequacy of the traditional theory of the just war which proved so flexible that it could permit a bishop to decide *after the war* that this man was in "erroneous" conscience and the others who fought and died (and killed) did so "in the light of a clear and correct conscience." But this is not our problem. All that concerns us here is the fact that he *believed* himself to be

193

acting in full compliance with the norms and expectations of the *real* Catholic Church. To this extent Jägerstätter, too, though properly described as a "resister" deviant in the objective context, may be said to have acted in conformity with the reference group which claimed priority in his eyes.

This fact serves as a transition from the social control-social deviance frame of reference to the consideration of somewhat broader implications for the sociology of religion. Jägerstätter's action represents not only a minority interpretation of the moral calculation forced upon the individual member of the religious community, it also reflects a judgment concerning the spirit in which such a calculation must be made. We now approach the very sensitive problem of the *quality* of religious commitment, or the nature of the bonds of "belongingness." This depends in great part upon the image the individual has of his Church: is it, for instance, a body of the faithful, with each living to some extent in and for the others; or is it an institution which one joins and in which one is engaged in something of an exchange of mutual services or obligations? In the first case—and Jägerstätter could serve to typify this—one is likely to be a maximalist, never feeling quite content until he is as deeply involved in the life of the supernatural community as possible. The latter view tends more to a minimalist approach, meeting one's basic obligations but not feeling particularly engaged or obliged to look for new or deeper involvement. The former literally would be willing to walk a hundred kilometers or more to attend a single Mass; the latter would know (and be satisfied) that there is nothing wrong with missing Mass for reasons beyond his control. Jägerstätter's bitter criticism of those who brought scandal upon the Church by playing "the crooked game" of trying to co-operate with the Nazis while still meeting the formal requirements for membership in good standing was balanced on the other side by the judgment of those who believed and still believe that he had gone so far overboard in his religious fanaticism that his mind had become unhinged.

This difference in the quality of *l'appartenance religieuse*[11] has significant implications for the sociological analysis of religion as

11 The term is taken from H. Carrier, S.J., *Psycho-sociologie de l'appartenance religieuse* (Rome, 1960).

194

an institution and as a factor influencing social behavior. For one thing it should recommend caution to the researchers who are content to set their problem in terms of a verbalized statement of "religious preference" by their respondents and then proceed to develop elaborate conclusions concerning attitude patterns, status aspirations, behavioral expectations, and the like as being substantively related to that religious identification. These studies may be interesting, even highly suggestive in many instances, but unless some effort can be made to control for differences in quality or intensity of religious commitment, they are likely to remain quite superficial and often lead to serious misinterpretations or spurious projections. Religion as a factor in human behavior should be viewed as operative at the level of commitment; at the level of "preference," or mere membership identification, whatever influence it has is likely to prove merely incidental.

It should follow, then, that the religious community would be interested in developing the kind of "sense of belongingness" which would inspire the individual believer to the all-or-nothing level of commitment evidenced by a Jägerstätter, a Thomas More, and by the vast array of saints and martyrs it honors in the liturgical calendar—since, at times, this would mean that the religious community would have to become a source of dissent and civil disobedience. For, let us remember, the "Church of Martyrs" with which Jägerstätter chose to identify himself was a Church that did not flinch from taking a stand that *required* open civil dissent on the part of its members when the secular community made demands that could not be reconciled with the values for which it claimed precedence over all other values. That Church did "encourage the vocation of martyrdom," for it believed it had one overriding function and purpose: to produce saints.

This case of extreme social deviance, this solitary witness of a simple peasant, might serve the religious community as a standard by which to measure the distance and the direction in which it has moved—and is still moving. If it still believes the world was placed under its stewardship, there is a great deal for which it must answer in connection with its open support of the unjust wars of recent (and not-so-recent) history. Even more challenging is the role it has already assumed with respect to the preparations for possible future wars with the patently immoral weapons and strategies by which they will be fought. Producing saints in Hitler's Third Reich called for more than protest against confiscation of Church properties and other interferences with the institutional functions of the religious organization. So, too, one may insist that producing saints in contemporary America calls for more than new crusades against indecent literature or condemned movies or new theological elaborations of rigid demands for deviance from the secular mores governing sex and family behavior. The kind of dissent and deviance most needed today relate to the prevailing norms which perpetuate racial injustice or, an even more sensitive area, the whole complex of issues related to international authority and nuclear war. It would call upon the faithful to form their consciences and to strengthen their resolution to the point where they would be ready, like Jägerstätter, to stand apart from any and all community and national practices which fail to meet the test of their religious values and obligations. Instead of rising in horrified protest when the suggestion is made that religion is (or threatens to become) a divisive force in a pluralistic society, the religious community might better recognize that there are likely to be many occasions when it *must* be such a divisive force, as it has been in ages past when prophets came forth to denounce an erring or sinful social order and to inspire martyrs to refuse to conform to the demands of that social order.

Like all social institutions, the religious institution will normally perform a supporting function for the society of which it is a part—this will, and must, continue to be so. It is permissible to ask, however, what might have been the outcome had the religious communities in Germany and Austria taken a different stand toward the Nazi regime and its war of aggression. There would have been many more, like Jägerstätter, sent to their death by the executioner's axe—but his death, and theirs, would have been easier, with the victims knowing that they had the support of their spiritual leaders and fellow communicants. Certainly, the tragic history of that era would have been quite different had all the Christian communions served as sources of dissent and disobedience in a matter that should have obliged them to "separate" themselves, to be "a divisive force" in a society totally committed to a war effort that would have been at least of suspect justice in terms of the traditional morality of war. There is an obvious parallel here to the thesis presented in Rolf Hochhuth's controversial drama, *Der Stellvertreter*. The author "indicts" Pope Pius XII for his failure to protest publicly the infamous "final solution" and, by so doing, to call the Roman Catholic faithful of Germany to some manner of dissent and even disobedience. Although the play weakens its impact by a generally distorted and unfair portrait of the Pope, the issue it raises deserves the fullest consideration and most serious discussion.[12]

To require, or even suggest, that the Catholic Church could have assumed such a posture vis-à-vis the Nazi State may be a sociological impossibility. At the very least, it calls into question the qualitative differences between the *ecclesia* and the *sect* as defined in the Troeltsch-Becker typology. The former, a large, at least society-wide, institutional organization with a bureaucratically defined status structure, usually finds its best example in the Catholic Church. The sect, on the other hand, is usually a relatively small, localized gathering of believers which, if it has any recognized structure at all, must essentially take its form and maintain itself according to the personalities and dispositions of its membership at any given time. More pertinent to this discussion, however, is the relationship of each to the greater society and its institutions, particularly the institutions of public order. The ecclesia will see itself as an important part of that society, and to a great degree responsible for the assurance and preservation of public order. It will undertake the formation of its own members in such a manner as to make sure they will assume and perform whatever "duties" may be required of them by the government which is to be accepted as the "legitimate authority" over their civil behavior; indeed, if the ecclesia is an "established church," it will provide for the "consecration" of the individuals in whom legitimate authority is to re-

12 Hochhuth's play appears in English as *The Deputy* (New York: Grove, 1964). This point is developed in greater detail in Gordon C. Zahn, "The Vicar: A Controversy and a Lesson," *The Critic*, Vol. XII, No. 2 (October–November, 1963), pp. 42–46. A summary collection of adverse and favorable responses to the German production of the play is *Summa iniuria oder Durfte der Papst schweigen?* (Reinbek, 1963)

side. The sect, in contrast, is a grouping of individuals who accept the fact that they are "called" to "stand apart" from the general society of "this world." In their fringe position they might totally repudiate "this world" and following that, completely reject all authority (especially that of civil rulers) which would seek to win their support for, or participation in, sinful activities. On the other hand, the same type of religious association might so orient its members to a heavenly future that their "standing apart" would take the form of total compliance with the commands of a secular ruler—a meek submission to the powers of evil in this world—in expectation of the joys to be gained from that future world as a reward for the sufferings and sacrifices this willingness to bear so horrible a burden might entail. Thus, for some of the more fundamentalist Christian sects, the call for nonresistance to the evildoer might imply "going the second mile" with a warring regime—after having given voice to their protest, of course, before doing so.

These typological extremes are necessarily over-simplifications; this is consistent with their use as analytical devices. Nevertheless, this does lead to the very practical conclusion that the ecclesia will almost always perform as a control agency over its members in such a way that it will serve as an instrument of adjustment and accommodation to the demands of that greater society and its governmental institutions, whereas the sect will usually erect barriers to keep its members from being seduced by the world and led into a position where their obedience to God would be superseded by their obedience to man. The patterns are not perfect. As we have seen, there may be instances where the sect will counsel a submissive acceptance of "the double yoke." The ecclesia, too, will sometimes rise in protest when it feels some decision of the government or some practice of the greater society infringes upon its institutional domain and threatens to interfere with the performance of its own specialized functions.

All of these points are directly related to the issues raised by the Jägerstätter case. A member of an ecclesia—still in the sociological sense of the word—he did, in his writings and by his example, call upon his fellow communicants and his religious leaders to take a stand apart from and in opposition to the "Nazi Folk

Community," to refuse its demands, and to key their efforts toward the attainment of the "Eternal Kingdom" of heaven in doing so. He was, in effect, calling upon the ecclesia and its members to act in the manner of the sect. And he was making this call on the basis of its own proclaimed principles and its own definition of its nature.

Can "the Church"—the ecclesia as well as the sect—rightly be viewed, as he viewed it, as a source of social dissent and deviance? In the context of a totalitarian social order in which the full array of secular controls is organized to produce the most complete degree of conformity and consensus possible, the question is perhaps more crucial than it may at first appear to be in relation to a democratic order which prides itself on its pluralist structure. But the question is relevant to all sociopolitical orders because it concerns the quality and operation of the social ties which make possible the maintenance of social stability and, to some extent, the very existence of society itself.

A conformity that is a manifestation of consensus—that is, an agreement with the "rightness" of the behavior required by the controlling agency—is qualitatively different from an unthinking, even unconscious, adoption of behavior patterns exhibited by or encouraged by others. The latter may indeed make for efficiency and a high level of stability in social relations, but it is questionable whether human society could long exist if it were the only basis for such relations. There are, of course, advocates of "social engineering" who envision the creation of new utopias through the manipulation and application of psychological and other controls now being discovered and developed by the social scientist; but if these ambitions are ever realized, the result will no longer be a kind of "human" society but, instead, a rather complex arrangement of scientifically programmed automatons. Totalitarian regimes, as we have known them until now, have sought to evoke some level of consensus from their members, despite their ultimate reliance, if need should arise, upon unquestioning and automatic obedience. Certainly the health of a democratic order will be found to lie in the mixture of these two kinds of conformity at any given time. The difference between the totalitarian and democratic orders can be described in terms of this mixture and it, in

199

turn, will be indicated by the extent to which nonconformity (deviance) is viewed as a permissible option (for others) or as a conceivable option (for oneself).

If conformity is, in a sense, "functional," is it not, therefore, "good" for society and, indirectly, for the individuals who constitute that society? The complaint voiced by C. Wright Mills and others that the contemporary emphasis on society as a functioning system has introduced a conservative bias into the work of social scientists is, of course, immediately related to this question. The answer which springs to mind is that it depends upon what the conformist is conforming to. It may be said that it is ethically good and socially functional that everyone drive on the same side of the road, to the right here, to the left elsewhere; it would be ethically bad and socially dysfunctional for individuals to endanger the lives of others by driving on whichever side of the road might catch their fancy at any given time. On the other hand, some would hold it to be ethically bad—however socially functional it might be—to reduce budget expenditures for public welfare by resorting to euthanasia as a means of solving the problem of the criminally insane or mentally incompetent. Conformity to some practices—ritual disfigurement or dismemberment, for example— may actually be regarded as both ethically bad and socially dysfunctional.

If the judgment can be made that conformity to behavior patterns that are ethically good and socially functional *may* be approved, and that conformity to behavior patterns that are ethically bad and socially dysfunctional is to be opposed, we are still left with the problem of the other possibilities. These possibilities should be expanded to include the ethically indifferent and functionally irrelevant patterns of behavior; however, these are omitted here because they do not pertain to this particular analysis. Most of us, it seems safe to say, would hold that any combination of the ethically good with the socially dysfunctional or the socially functional with the ethically bad should be resolved in such a way that the ethical dimension be given priority. It is equally safe to say, however, that such agreement usually tends to remain fixed at the level of verbalization.

Not so, of course, with Jägerstätter, with More, with Viereck's "unadjusted man," or with Camus' rebel. But these exceptions merely serve to point out what is needed, how they differ from the others. At one point, the simplest perhaps, the difference lies in the contents of the value system by which one acts. The phrase "some would hold" in the earlier reference to euthanasia suggests this aspect of the problem: Hitler and others obviously did not so hold; Galen and other spokesmen of the Catholic Church did. In this situation, which these religious leaders recognized, in their terms, to be a grave crisis for human society and the individual conscience, they did voice a strong protest. By so doing, they showed that their Church, although an ecclesia, could counsel a position of dissent and even disobedience. Even here, as has been shown by Guenter Lewy in his book *The Catholic Church and Nazi Germany*, interpretations were applied which defined the culpability of various degrees of co-operation with the sterilization program in such a way that the "deviance" required of individual doctors or nurses affected by the requirements of that program was reduced or cushioned.

In almost every instance, the emphasis of formal and official Catholic opposition to Nazi policies was on institutional forms of protest and only incidentally and consequentially did it relate to the individual level of behavior. The fact that these leaders did not feel free to take a more condemnatory or "antiestablishment" posture in other areas not quite as clearly alien to the Catholic value-system suggests that this religious community did face a peculiar challenge to recognize and develop its potential as a source of dissent and deviance at that more significant level of the individual and his actions.

The most immediate need, if the attempt is to be made, is to *reaffirm* and *develop* the individual's capacity for making a deliberate and responsible choice. Thoreau, another "unadjusted man," asked the crucial questions and gave his answer at the same time.

Must the citizen ever for a moment, or in the least degree, resign his conscience to the legislator? Why has every man a conscience then? I think we should be men first and subject

201

afterward. It is not desirable to cultivate a respect for the law, so much as for the right.[13]

Jägerstätter probably never heard of Thoreau and certainly never read his essay. Yet note the similarity between this and the following quotation from his commentaries: **For what purpose, then, did God endow all men with reason and free will if, as so many also say, the individual is not qualified to judge whether this war started by Germany is just or unjust? What purpose is served by the ability to distinguish between good and evil?** Few Catholics in Hitler's Third Reich troubled to ask themselves these questions; fewer still displayed the clarity of moral principle and the strength of moral commitment that marked this peasant's answer and ultimately brought him to the executioner's block.

There are those, and this writer is among them, who believe that the same must be said of Catholics in other nations as well—and certainly in America today. Let me set a contemporary moral problem in terms that might provide a parallel to the Jägerstätter act of rebellion. An admittedly small body of current Catholic opinion would hold that all who are ready to accept nuclear war and nuclear preparedness in any of its forms—whether they are proposed in terms of "deterrence" or "counterforce" or what-have-you—are necessarily committing themselves in principle, if not in actual fact, to the planned extermination of untold numbers of innocents. No matter how brilliantly the moral-theologians-cum-strategists may perform in charting the course of hypothetical fleets at sea or armies locked in combat in remote and uninhabited desert reaches, the weapons they so studiously avoid condemning *in toto* are being built and designed for the same criminal use that once earned a Herod the ignominy that has not diminished in the course of two millennia. It is well to remember, too, that one of the doctrines proclaimed by Hitler which helped to excite the opposition of more enlightened and "liberal" minds was the "total war" which the Nazis proposed as theory and then executed in practice. It was unfortunate enough that the forces opposed to

[13] Henry D. Thoreau, "Civil Disobedience," in *The Works of Thoreau*, edited by H. S. Canby (Boston: Houghton Mifflin. 1937), p. 790.

the "Thousand Year Reich" were led into an acceptance and application of that theory in the process of destroying Hitler and "all he stood for"—far more significant is the unchallengeable fact that this same doctrine is now taken for granted by virtually all who pride themselves on being "realistic" and "practical" in their approach to the conduct of foreign affairs and diplomacy. In this sense, and to this degree, Hitler, and not his enemies, emerged as the ultimate victor in the ideological confrontation that supposedly justified all the horrors of World War II.

If this statement of the case has any merit at all, it would follow that there is perhaps no greater need for dissent and deviance than in this area of public policy and decision. Applying the Jägerstätter formula, it is not simply or even primarily a matter of saving one's skin; instead, it is more likely to be a matter of saving one's soul. For what is being done is being done in our name; the more democratic we claim to be in our governmental structure, the greater the share of moral culpability to be assigned to each citizen for his conformity (even his silent conformity) to any morally questionable demands of that government. It follows, then, that anyone committed to a value system that rejects these programs would be called to some measure of rebellion. At least he would be expected to do what he could to voice an effective dissent in order to bring about some crucial changes in the military policies or programs now being contemplated, or already in effect. Failing in this, there should be a readiness to evince the deviance characterized by a refusal to comply with whatever demands may be made upon one to assure his active participation in these unacceptable policies or programs.

Should it develop that this is a valid application of the traditional moral teachings on war, we would have an instance where the Church, an ecclesia, would bear the responsibility of becoming a source of such dissent and deviance. For among all the institutions of society charged with the formulation, maintenance, and transmission of values, the religious institution alone has the potential to counteract the direct and indirect pressures of the secular authority upon the individual who is both a citizen and a member of the faithful.

Certainly one could not look to the family to perform this task of producing rebels effectively. There has been a progressive attrition during the past two generations, as a result of which the family's contribution to the value formation of its members has been significantly reduced—or, it might be better to say, surrendered to the point where it now channels the values imposed upon it from without. So, too, with the school, although it certainly has not reduced itself to a comparable state of impotence. If anything, those same recent generations have witnessed a tremendous expansion of the sphere of influence of the educational institution over the moral formation of the individuals coming under its control. The spread of universal education and new advances in educational techniques have multiplied the effectiveness of the school within this widely expanded range of influence. In fact, to a great extent it is the educational institution which has fashioned the "overadjusted" man of whom Viereck writes. And this is entirely in keeping with the role ordinarily considered proper for it. The school is the mirror, not the free molder of the society of which it is a part; the responsive agent, not the creative principle. As agent, it is bound to the task of being a channel for the demanding conformity. It depends upon the social structure for whatever power it can wield; and, under the circumstances, it is not likely to undertake the task of undoing the source of its own power— assuming, of course, that it were even possible for it to do so.

The religious institution is in a stronger position to oppose or change a prevailing value system and thereby constitute the "different culture" which could offer behavior patterns to which the deviant can "conform." This is not to deny that the church, too, ordinarily serves as a set of controls supporting the established social order; but to the extent to which it claims to be something apart from *and above* the "world," to the extent to which it depends on the direction of a supernatural order, it can never be reduced to the status of a mere channel of secular authority. Sometimes— and the situation faced by Jägerstätter might have been one such time—the religious community does fail to hold its own in the manner one might expect; but it will always give at least verbal assent to the principle so urgently cited by the peasant in his writings and much more recently reaffirmed by John XXIII in his encyclical, *Pacem in Terris:*

> ... if civil authorities legislate for or allow anything contrary to that order and therefore contrary to the will of God, neither the laws made nor the authorizations granted can be binding on the consciences of the citizens, since God has more right to be obeyed than man.[14]

This declaration seems to imply at the very least that there are times and circumstances when the Church is to be a source of dissent and deviance, when this particular ecclesia is "called" to act like a sect.

There are, of course, some areas of social life in which this is recognized and where the attempt is even made to bring it into effectual application. Family and sex morality is one such area. As Thomas states it:

> In fact, to Catholics, many contemporary practices such as civil divorce and the use of contraceptives appear as culturally patterned defects. Their widespread acceptance in the dominant culture merely raises the problem of the pathology of normalcy, since what is thus considered normal contradicts the purpose of man as Catholics conceive it.
>
> Nevertheless, though the doctrinal divergence of these socially patterned defects are clear to every Catholic, the impulse to conform and the security which comes from doing as others do is bound to place a strain upon the individual Catholic. *It seems likely that minority survival under these conditions will depend to a great extent on the strengthening of solidarity among Catholics. Then the force of conformity will operate to support group ideals, and the security of the individual will be rooted in the group.*[15]
> [Emphasis added.]

[14] Pope John XXIII, *Pacem in Terris* (Glen Rock, N.J.: Paulist Press, 1963), p. 21.
[15] John L. Thomas, S.J., *The American Catholic Family* (Englewood Cliffs, N.J.: Prentice-Hall, 1956), pp. 28–29.

Not only is the Catholic urged to behave as a "sectarian" in these areas, he is also placed under direct orders to avoid seeing "condemned" movies, reading "prurient or obscene" books, and even—in some dioceses—wearing "immodest" bathing attire or, if "he" is a girl, appearing in beauty contests. It has been late in coming, but Catholics in America are finally being encouraged to "stand apart" from and speak out against community practices which violate interracial justice, and to seek out opportunities to manifest their charity toward others.

As yet, however, very little attention has been paid to the special problem posed by Jägerstätter: the need to take a stand against a government that would lead its Christian citizens into committing murder.

Perhaps it is too big an issue, too dangerous a course, for the religious community to adopt. For it certainly would carry with it the implications of martyrdom. If the Church is "in the world" though "not of the world," a secular-spiritual parallel should be manifested in any analysis of the behavior of Christians. And if this is sometimes forgotten, if the spiritual connotations of what the Christian does are separated too completely from its secular connotations, it is well that an occasional Jägerstätter makes his appearance to force a restatement and reconsideration of these essential problems.

To the sociologist, this peasant, in his solitary witness, is a case of deviance, of rebellion directed against a totalitarian social order. On another level, he exemplifies the relationship between the institutions of church and state in a crisis situation involving a conflict of values. Theologically his story may be seen as that of a believer called to witness in fulfilling the demands of his conscience, or again, on a higher level, as a renewal of the confrontation between Caesar and Christ which began with Pilate and has been repeated whenever a Thomas More or a Franz Jägerstätter received orders from a secular ruler contrary to the commandments of his God or his Church. The reader is free to choose which he considers the more meaningful statement of Franz Jägerstätter's act of rebellion retold in these pages—but he should remember that to the believer they will be the same.

Appendices

Appendix I
The Jägerstätter Documents

It had been my understanding originally that Jägerstätter's own writings were limited to the items collected by Pastor Karobath of St. Radegund, which I have referred to as the St. Radegund Jägerstätter files. These items include: (1) a letter written to the pastor himself at the time Jägerstätter received his final induction notice; (2) the farewell letter written immediately before his execution; and (3) the prison statement of position written at the request of Chaplain Kreuzberg. Pastor Karobath, too, believed that these were the only writings left by the condemned man, and he had preserved them in testimony of what he regards as an act of martyrdom that will someday be given official recognition by the Catholic Church.

In the course of my research I came across occasional references to other writings. One close friend had received two letters from Franz during the war, but had destroyed them out of prudence because of the anti-Nazi sentiments they contained. Similarly, the vicar, Fr. Fürthauer, who took over Karobath's pastorate when he was exiled from St. Radegund by the authorities, referred to a "catechism" Jägerstätter was writing for the instruction of his children in anticipation of the day, which he believed would come soon, when the Church would no longer be permitted to give such instruction. The priest could tell me nothing more about the "catechism."

Shortly before I was to leave St. Radegund, Mrs. Jägerstätter produced a packet of letters and asked if I would be interested in seeing them. Among the material she had brought were seventeen letters written from prison, a "farewell message" written on a large card, and an ordinary composition book in which her husband had written a series of commentaries on the conditions of the times and the responsibilities of the Christian living at such a time. It is, of course, extremely likely that this last item was the "catechism" which the vicar had described—in any event, the widow said she did not know of any such catechism and that these were all the writings of her husband in her possession. These documents provide a means of correcting or verifying some of the "myths" about the man which have developed since his death.

Since the commentaries are most crucial, some further remarks concerning them are in order. From time to time, individuals being interviewed would make the point that Franz was very much given —in their eyes, too much given—to reading and writing. Sometimes, it was said, he would interrupt or take time out from his work to write things down in a book he had with him. Though there is no sure evidence to support the assumption, it is quite possible that these notebook commentaries are the product of these sporadic jottings. They are not dated, but internal evidence clearly indicates that they were set down during the weeks immediately preceding his refusal and arrest. Thus, in the second of the nine commentaries, he refers to "the past decade" as the period during which "things came to be as they are." The third commentary notes that "at this moment most of our soldiers find themselves deep in Bolshevist territory"—and its somewhat pessimistic context suggests that all was not going well for these soldiers. This, together with another reference in the second commentary to "the tide" being "stemmed" in Russia would seem to date these writings tentatively as late 1942 or early 1943, about ten years after the Nazi rise to power in Germany and about the time of the Battle of Stalingrad. Another specific indication of date is found in the eighth commentary, in the description of the Austrian capitulation (in the 1938 plebiscite) as having taken place "four years ago."

The nine separate essays reveal a continuity from one to another which suggests that the entire group was conceived as a unit and most probably set down with no great lapse of time between them. In manner of style, some failings must be noted. First of all, the man who wrote these commentaries was the product of the usual rural *Volksschule* education. This made for certain limitations in grammar, spelling, and rhetorical technique. Reading the complete text, one will note the reliance upon series of argumentative questions to make a point—an approach that will strike someone accustomed to more balanced displays of sophisticated reasoning as being somewhat primitive and much too superficial. Sometimes, too, a certain carelessness is revealed in quoting Scriptures or attributing statements to saints or to papal authority. Finally, the argument will often seem to ramble, to make unexpected jumps or even double back on itself, in violation of all canons of effective argumentation.

Included in this Appendix will be (1) the complete texts of the nine Jägerstätter commentaries—except for the eighth, which is presented complete in the body of the study on pp. 125–127; (2) the prison statement written in July, 1943, at Dean Kreuzberg's request; and (3) the letter to Franz Huber, to whom Jägerstätter bore the spiritual relationship of confirmation sponsor, presumably written early in 1936. Each of these has a particularly important bearing upon this study in that, taken together, they show a continuity of thought and intention that testifies to the depth of the rebel's commitment—and to its consistency over the period beginning when the Nazis constituted little more than a potential threat to Austria's independence, and ending after Jägerstätter had apparently been condemned to death by the military tribunal.

In these translations I have sought to preserve the original sequence of thoughts and, so far as possible, the exact words and imagery used by their author. No attempt was made to reproduce the shortcomings in the original spelling and grammar in the English version. The following segment of the original German, taken from the second paragraph of the first commentary might serve to give some illustration of how the original and the translation compare:

Will nun gleich zu beginn ein kurzes Erlebnis schildern was ich in einer Sommernacht 1938 erlebte. Erst lag ich fast bins Mitternacht im Bett ohne zu schlafen obwohl ich nicht krank war, muss aber dan doch ein wenig eingeschlafen sein, auf einmal wurde mir ein schöner Eisenbahnzug gezeigt der um einen Berg fuhr, abgesehen von den Erwachsenen strömmten sogar die Kinder diesem Zuge zu und waren fast nicht zurückzuhalten, wie wenige Erwachsenen es waren welche in selbiger Umgebung nicht mitfuhren will ich am liebsten nicht sagen oder schreiben dann sagte mir auf einmal eine Stimme dieser Zug fährt in die Hölle. . . .

I THE COMMENTARIES

1 On the Question of Our Day: Catholic or Nazi?

A most crucial question today: can one be both at the same time? Once when the Social Democrats were in power in Austria, the Church said it was impossible for a Social Democrat to be Catholic too—and now?

Let me begin by describing an experience I had on a summer night in 1938. At first I lay awake in my bed until almost midnight, unable to sleep, although I was not sick; I must have fallen asleep anyway. All of a sudden I saw a beautiful shining railroad train that circled around a mountain. Streams of children—and adults as well—rushed toward the train and could not be held back. I would rather not say how many adults did not join the ride. Then I heard a voice say to me: "This train is going to hell." Immediately it seemed as if someone took me by the hand, and the same voice said, "Now we will go into purgatory." And oh! so frightful was the suffering I saw and felt, I could only have thought that I was in hell itself if the voice had not told me we were going into purgatory. Probably no more than a few seconds passed while I saw all this. Then I heard a sigh and saw a light—and all was gone. I woke my wife right away and told her what had happened. Until that night, I never would have believed that the suffering in purgatory could be so great.

At first this traveling train was something of a riddle to me, but the longer our situation continues, the clearer the meaning of this train becomes for me. Today it seems to me that it is a symbol of nothing but National Socialism, which was then breaking in (or, better, creeping in) upon us with all of its many different organizations—like the NSDAP, NVW, NVF, HJ, etc. In brief, simply the whole National Socialist Folk Community, together with all those who sacrifice and fight for it.

Not long ago one could read again in the newspaper that the Party had gained 150,000 more new members and this, of course, through induction into the Hitler Youth. Let us consider only the adults (especially those who have property or hold civil service jobs or run a business—or even those who are merely apprentices and craftsmen) and count those who do not belong to some Nazi organization or do not make contributions to the familiar red collection boxes. There are only two alternatives possible: participation in the National Socialist Folk Community, and contributions to the red boxes as well, must either help or hinder us Catholics in our efforts to gain salvation. If it is useful for winning salvation, then it is a blessing for the whole German people that Nazism with all its organizations is so widespread and so strong among us—for I believe the German people were never so deeply involved in the works of Christian charity or so ready to contribute as they are today to the Nazis. And this even though it should already be clear enough to everyone that money is no problem for the German State: it can print as much as it pleases for internal needs and, as far as the countries not yet conquered are concerned, such contributed funds would have no value anyway. Besides, the Nazis are perfectly frank in their statements as to what the *Winterhilfswerk*[1] really is. I once saw a poster in a town on which it could be read in so many words: "Your contribution to the WHW is your act of personal fealty to the Führer." The Führer, it seems, is always asking his people to prove who is for him and who is against him.

[1] Winter Relief Collection. [Translator.]

In Germany, before Hitler came to power, it was once a matter of policy to refuse Holy Communion to Nazis. And what is the situation today in this Greater German Reich? Many approach the communion rail with apparently no spiritual misgivings even though they are members of the Nazi Party and, in addition, permit their children to join the Party or even turn them over to Nazi educators for formation. Have they then—while for more than two years now a horrible human slaughter has been going on—established a new policy today which sees all this as something permissible or not to be mentioned? Or has the teaching authority of the Church already made or approved the decision that men may now join a party that is opposed to the Church?

Actually, if one gives a little thought to this, there are times when he will want to cry out. One has to marvel that in such a land even the most just can become confused. It simply means that there is no longer any likelihood that there will be a bloody persecution of Christians here—for virtually anything the Nazis want or demand Christians will yield.

True, there would not be many good priests left in Austria enjoying freedom or performing their spiritual functions if the Austrian Catholic clergy, from the very beginning at the time of the April 10 plebiscite, had set themselves firmly in opposition, instead of actually praising the Party for its many good works in order to help it win an almost unanimous victory at the polls. I believe there could scarcely be a sadder hour for the true Christian faith in our country—not even if there were no longer a single Catholic church remaining open and if thousands had already offered their blood and lives for Christ and the faith—than this hour when one watches in silence while this error spreads its ever-widening influence.

Many are already impatiently waiting to be freed from this tragic situation, and it would be a good thing for them to take a lesson from the words of the Führer: "Man, help yourself—then God will help you too." I would like to call out to everyone who is riding in this train: "Jump out before this train reaches its destination, even if it costs you your life!"

Thus I believe God has shown me most clearly through this

dream, or revelation, and has convinced me in my heart how I must answer the question: should I be a National Socialist—or a Catholic?

However, let us not on this account cast stones at our bishops or priests. They, too, are men like us, made of flesh and blood, and can weaken. They are probably much more sorely tempted by the evil enemy than the rest of us. Maybe they have been too poorly prepared to take up this struggle and to make a choice between life or death. Would not our hearts, too, skip a beat if we were suddenly faced with the certain knowledge that this very day we would have to appear before the judgment seat of God?—and we ordinarily bear the responsibility for just a few of our fellow men. One cannot easily visualize for himself, therefore, the serious decision forced upon our bishops and priests in March, 1938. Perhaps, too, our bishops thought it would be only a short time before everything would come apart at the seams again and that, by their compliance, they could spare the faithful many agonies and martyrs. Unfortunately, things turned out to be quite different: years have passed and thousands of people must now die in the grip of error every year. It is not hard to imagine, then, what a heroic decision it would require for our people to repudiate all the mistakes that have been made in recent years. This is why we should not make it harder for our spiritual leaders than it already is by making accusations against them. Let us pray for them, instead, that God may lighten the great tasks which still stand before them.

If, in all earnestness, we consider the time in which we now live, we will be forced to admit that the situation in which we Christians of Germany find ourselves today is much more desperate and bewildering than that faced by the Christians of the early centuries in the time of their bloodiest persecution. Many will perhaps ask themselves why God had to make us live in such a time as this. But we may not accuse God on this account, nor should we put the blame on others. There is an old saying, "He who makes his bed must lie in it." And it is still possible for us, even today, with God's help, to lift ourselves out of the mire in which we are stuck and win eternal happiness—if only we make a sincere effort and bring all our strength to the task.

Of course, one may not look upon the sufferings of this world as the worst of all evils. Even the greatest saints often had to suffer frightfully before God welcomed them into His everlasting mansions. The Lord did not even spare His apostles from suffering, and most of them had to give their lives in martyrdom even though they had worked so valiantly for Christ. Yet here are we, actually expecting our sinful life to be free from pain and struggle and our death to be a gentle one—and this all to be crowned with eternal blessedness in the hereafter!

Christ Himself, the most innocent of all, endured the greatest suffering ever borne by man, and through His suffering and His death purchased heaven for us. And we do not want to suffer for Him? If we look into history and study recent centuries, there is no need for us to wonder why things are as they are today. Recorded there is a steady decline in deep and pious faith along with a steady advance of the new paganism. Religious writers predicted decades ago (some of them centuries ago) the woes that would come over mankind if men did not reform. We need only glance at Russia to consider the sufferings its people have to bear—and when will they be freed again from their misery?

Yet in our case everything should be as painless as many believe?

2 Little Thoughts Concerning Our Past, Present, and Future

In spite of prophecy and soothsaying, the future remains dark to us, for it usually takes more than the mere wisdom of man to solve its riddle. What good things, then, will the future bring us Austrians and Germans? Many of us are already dreaming of a better future once the war is over.

We are all in God's hand, who directs and guides our fate, at whose words even the wildest torrents are stilled. But experience teaches us that as long as there have been men upon this earth, God has allowed them freedom of will and only seldom has He interfered in the destinies of men and peoples. And, except at the end of the world, there is little likelihood that this will change in the future. Adam and Eve ruined their life's destiny completely by their disobedience toward God. God had given them free will, and they would never have had to suffer had they listened to God instead of to the Tempter. God could have directed their thoughts differently too—and how much suffering would have been spared all humanity through the avoidance of that first sin, if God had acted to ward it off. Even His own beloved Son would have been spared this unending sorrow. And so will it continue until the end of the world: Every sin carries with it its consequences.

Yet woe unto us if we keep trying to shunt these consequences off on others and avoid doing penance for the sins and errors we have committed. If this very day God were to strike the weapons from the hands of all the peoples of the earth, would most of mankind be converted? True, there are many who hold the opinion that, if the war were to end badly for Germany, nothing much would happen to Austria and Bavaria. But let us once ask ourselves: Are Austria and Bavaria, then, free from responsibility for the fact that we have a National Socialist instead of a Christian government? Did Nazism simply fall down upon us out of a clear blue sky? I think we need not waste many words about that, for anyone who has not been sleeping through the past ten years knows perfectly well how and why things have come to be as they are.

I believe that what took place in the spring of 1938 was not much different from that Maundy Thursday nineteen hundred years ago when the Jewish crowd was given a free choice between the innocent Saviour and the criminal Barabbas. Then, too, the Pharisees had distributed money among the people to get them to cry out so as to confuse and divide those who still held to Christ. Among us, too, in March 1938, what kind of dreadful fantasies were not spoken and written against the still religiously-minded Chancellor Schuschnigg and against the clergy? The few who were not misled and who could not be persuaded to cast the disaster-bringing *Ja*-vote[2] were simply dismissed as fools or Communists. But the struggle over these "fools" has continued, even till now, in the hope of perhaps still winning them over to the Nazi Folk

2 That is, in favor of *Anschluss* with Nazi Germany. [Translator.]

Community or, at least, of getting them to make some sacrifice for this ideology.

To be sure, many could not preserve their joy over that victory very long and have come to realize that everything has turned out differently from what had been promised. And how they have scolded and muttered among themselves since then! But still they do not have the courage to openly divorce themselves from this anti-Christian Folk Community.

This does not seem to me to be much different from the case of a still halfway decent girl who has fallen under the spell of an adventurer who is interested only in seduction and the satisfaction of his sexual desires. True, for a time things may even go better for her than before and, as long as she has no pangs of conscience over it, she will not feel unhappy at all at first—until she finally comes to her senses and recognizes the real intentions of the fellow (or, possibly, when signs of the consequences begin to show). Then, no matter how much she may complain and denounce the seducer, the consequences are still hers to bear. And if she does not have the courage to end this sinful relationship, she will not find herself any the happier when, instead of loving the young man, she actually begins to hate. She will probably try to break off the relationship, but such a shameless cad is not likely to let his victim off so easily. In the first place, he will know how to keep her in line with threats, or he will demand that she return the gifts he gave her (and which she will not be too happy to give up). Such a girl can pray day and night and still not have her prayers heard until she ends the relationship; and she may not shrink back from any hardship even if he should threaten to kill her or ruin her reputation.

And now let us take a look at Russia—has the Lord perhaps stemmed the tide because of the just who were still to be found there? Many hoped this would be the year to bring release from their tragic situation, but what are their prospects now? It could well be that the Russian people joined the Bolshevist community just as willingly and in equally large numbers as the Austrians joined the National Socialist Folk Community (which is not one bit better and, at best, just a trifle less of a fraud) in March, 1938.

Or should we maybe emerge unpunished from our situation because we Austrians were almost solidly Catholic? Woe unto us if the words spoken by Christ at Capharnaum were applied to us too: I have lifted you up to heaven; nevertheless, you will have to descend to hell.[3]

If it is ever to come about that Christ will reign in our lovely Austria, then that Maundy Thursday will have to be followed by Good Friday, for Christ, too, had to die before He could rise from the dead. For us Austrians, our Maundy Thursday was that infamous April 10, 1938. That was the day the Austrian Church let herself be taken prisoner, and ever since, she has lain in chains. And not before this *Ja* (which even then was given very hesitantly and anxiously by many Catholics) is balanced by a resounding *Nein* will there be for us, too, a Good Friday. We are already being called upon to die, but not for Christ—many actually have lost their lives helping to win Nazi victories.

But I scarcely expect that this *Nein* will be given with the same decisiveness or in the same great numbers as was the *Ja* of that day. If not, how can this *Nein* succeed? Can it be of much good if it is not given in equally great numbers? There is no question but that it is pointless for each person to ask the next what he thinks or what he will do; instead I believe that there is value enough for each individual if he but free his own soul from this dangerous burden. Carrying out this decision admittedly involves being ready at all times, should it prove necessary, even to put one's life at stake for Christ and His faith. One who is ready for this decision will immediately dissociate himself from the Nazi Folk Community and make no further contributions to it. Anyone who wishes to practice Christian charity in his deeds can manage to provide the poor with something for their sustenance without the WHW[4] or VWF.[5] When this happens, they will be free to do what they wish with such a person. They will surely not chop him

[3] This probably refers to Matt. 8:1–13 and its warning: "But the children of the kingdom will be put forth into the darkness outside; there will be the weeping, and the gnashing of teeth." [Translator.]

[4] Winter Relief Collection. [Translator.]

[5] People's Welfare Fund. [Translator.]

down right away. Instead, they will make every effort to win him away from his decision, for the Powers below know perfectly well that they can do such a person much more harm by keeping or winning him as a member of the Folk Community than by killing him and making him a martyr for his faith. This step will only be taken when they lose patience and realize that there is no longer much chance of winning this man over, and that he could become a dangerous influence upon others.

Furthermore, I believe that the Lord will not make it hard for us to risk our lives for our faith in such a test. Thousands of young men are being recruited in these trying days of war to risk their lives for National Socialism. Many have already had to lose their young lives so that others at home could prolong theirs for a time from the fruits of aggression (while, in the process, murdering thousands of children's souls!). With each new victory Germany wins, the sense of guilt will grow ever greater for us Germans. Why, then, should it be more difficult for a man to risk his life for a King who does not only burden us with duties, but also gives us rights; whose ultimate victory is certain, and whose Kingdom, for which we would be fighting, will last forever?

Through His bitter suffering and death, Christ freed us only from eternal death, not from temporal suffering and mortal death. But Christ, too, demands a public confession of our faith, just as the Führer, Adolf Hitler, does from his followers. The commandments of God teach us, of course, that we must also render obedience to secular rulers, even when they are not Christian. But only to the extent that they do not order us to do anything evil, for we must obey God rather than men.

And who is able to serve two masters at one time? Many will probably say or think that for the time being one can remain a Christian in secret until things have changed. And there is no chance that National Socialism will endure forever. It may even be that it has already lasted as long as it can. Even Christ's kingdom on earth would soon collapse if God were suddenly to take away all our rights and leave us only with obligations—though God has the power and the right to do so. But is it not possible that, once the German Reich is defeated, our "release" might come at the hands of another anti-Christian power? We know all too well how things stand with the Christian faith in other nations on this earth: in Russia, for example. And England and America are not much better, though perhaps more civilized and at the moment not so crude as the Russians. From whence, then, is something better to be expected?

The Christians of the first centuries could have used the same reasoning: let us make sacrifices to the idols as the government demands; in secret we can still remain Christians. And some must have done so, too. Moreover, in those days many rulers did not stay on the throne very long, but their successors were often not much better—sometimes, in fact, worse. In actual fact, the first Christians would have had to live to an age of more than 300 years before they could have enjoyed the free practice of their faith.

And even should this great struggle for existence still have a halfway favorable outcome, can we hope that the Christianization of a people which has already sunk so low would take effect soon enough for our children to experience it? The descent downhill is usually easier and faster than the upward climb. We cannot claim that the whole blame in our case lies with the government or the ruling classes. Is it not shocking and heart-rending to think of the murder of children once carried out by King Herod? According to Blessed Catherine Emmerich, their number can be estimated at 700. And consider how the Lord punished that horrible king already during his lifetime. Yet what has one had to hear in recent years about the German and Austrian people? One no longer needs a Herod to order such a thing; the children's parents themselves take care of it, often with the help of their poorly paid underlings. The learned Professor Hermann Muckermann has reported the statistical fact that the entire four years of World War I did not account for as many deaths among the German people as did the number of children murdered every year by abortion. According to his figures, in one year in Germany there have been as many as two million children who have lost their lives through these Herod-type acts. And has the record been much better in this regard in our still nominally Christian Austria? This slaughter is not restricted to the

221

large cities; it has already spread into even the smallest rural village.

Can one, then, still speak of a German culture? We sometimes shudder when we hear of the horrible deeds perpetrated by the Russians in this war. Is the horror any less when it is possible for one to deliberately murder his own child who has never done anyone harm and who is still in a state of perfect innocence? And for such a people God should still perform miracles as he once did when he permitted the Israelites to cross the Red Sea without even getting their feet wet?

We know, of course, that the Church of Christ, the Rock of Peter, can never be conquered, because Christ Himself has told us so. We know, however, that once it was established, this Rock was very soon surrounded on all sides that it might be brought low. But this effort will never succeed! It is already something of a divine miracle to witness two opposing powers, each with the same objective, tearing each other apart instead of combining forces. For this reason, it can easily happen that there is really no need for God to take a part in stopping them. Instead, these powers will wear each other down to the point where neither will have the final victory.

Blessed Catherine Emmerich has revealed that Lucifer himself will be set free fifty or sixty years before the year 2000 and that other devils will have been turned loose before then. This is a sign that we are not dealing with a small matter, that the great life-and-death struggle has already begun. Yet in the midst of it, there are many who still go on living their lives just as though nothing has changed, as if this great and decisive struggle is no concern of theirs.

3   Bolshevism—or National Socialism?

It is really very sad to always hear Catholics saying that this war Germany is fighting is probably not so unjust after all because it will bring about the destruction of Bolshevism. It is true that at this moment most of our soldiers find themselves deep in Russian territory and are trying to render harmless and defenseless all those who live in the land and have taken to arms. And now let me ask a little question: What are we fighting in that country? Bolshevism—or the Russian people?

When our Catholic missionaries set out for heathen lands, did they also take planes and bombs, hoping to convert and improve the heathen by such means? Most of these dedicated fighters for Christianity write back to the homeland that if they only had enough goods to distribute, much faster progress could be made. And, of course, they also beg very much for prayers, for the greatest gains and conversions recorded in their work are still due to continuing prayers.

When one looks back a bit into history, he will always find just about the same story; whenever rulers have declared war against other countries, they usually have not broken into their lands in order to improve them or perhaps give them something. Thus, if one is fighting against the Russian people, he will also take as much out of that country as can be put to use here. If we were merely fighting Bolshevism, would other things like iron, oil wells, or good grainlands have become such important considerations?

Whenever anyone has taken up arms to wipe out Christianity (as people have often thought they could in the past), the blood of their victims has always become the new seed and shoots from which Christianity flowered anew with more vitality than before. Now, could this not happen again if one spills Bolshevist blood? Could not this, too, become new seed? Are we Christians today perhaps wiser than Christ Himself? Does anyone really think that this massive bloodletting can possibly save European Christianity from defeat—or bring it to a new flowering? Did our good Saviour, whom we should always try to imitate, go forth with His apostles against the heathens as German Christians are doing today?

Alas, our poor people blinded by a great insanity! Will it ever return to its senses? As the saying goes, "Nothing comes about by chance: all that comes, comes from above."[6]

But then is this war, which we Germans are already carrying on against almost all the peoples of the world, something that broke upon us without warning—like a terrible hailstorm, perhaps, which one can only watch helplessly and, at most, pray that it will end

---

[6] Nichts kommt von Ungefähr; alles kommt von oben her.

223

soon without causing too much damage? Through radio, press, mass rallies, and so forth, almost all of us knew what Hitler planned to accomplish with his program and that the financial policies relating to the national debt and the *Reichsmark* could bring no other results than those which have now become the fact, that is, unless God had chosen to take away the free will of the other peoples of the world and so direct their thoughts that they had immediately thrown themselves down before German National Socialism without a struggle. But God does permit freedom of the will to every man, and we Austrians had it too on April 10, 1938; even though the Germans had already taken possession of our country, the free will choice between the *Ja* or *Nein* had not been taken from us either by God or the Germans. And today we still have this free will. I scarcely believe that God would consider it sinful on our part if we would finally exchange this fateful *Ja*, which a good many of us probably regret already, for a *Nein*.

At the very least, other peoples have the right to pray to God for peace and ask that He strike the weapons from the hands of us Germans. Is it not sheer mockery for us to ask God for peace when we really don't want it? For if we did, we would lay down our weapons. Or is the guilt we have taken upon ourselves still too slight? At least let us continue to beseech God that He may let us come to our senses and acknowledge at last that other peoples and nations have a right to life upon this earth. Failing this, God in His might will be obliged to call for the final reckoning lest we Catholics of Germany force all the peoples of the world to place themselves under the Nazi yoke. Almost all of us are quite willing to glut ourselves on the spoils of thievery, but we want to saddle the responsibility for the whole dirty business on one person alone!

4 The Crooked Game

Are not almost all of us playing a more or less crooked game these days? Do we not know that all of us must prove ourselves to be good and precious fruit if we wish to enter the Kingdom of

Heaven? In this regard it is impossible for dishonesty to lead to perfection.

When and how is one dishonest? First, when one presents himself to his fellow men as being something other than what he really is; second, when one constantly acts in a manner different from what he really thinks, says, or writes. But is it at all possible today to speak or act as one thinks? Granted, there are times when one acts differently from the way he thinks for reasons of obedience, but this obedience should never go so far as to oblige one to perform acts that are actually evil. We know God does not demand the impossible of us, even considering the times in which we live today. We need not always act, then, exactly as we think. We need not always speak our mind; one can and may keep silent—up to a certain point. For it would certainly lead to trouble if one always told his neighbor just what he thought of him, so it is sometimes better to hold one's tongue and maintain silence. One need not always speak out—indeed, many find it unpleasant to listen when someone talks too much while they themselves have to keep silent for the time being.

True, it is doubly hard not to be dishonest when one lives in a country where freedom of belief is restricted. If dishonesty were not harmful to our efforts to attain eternal blessedness, what difference would it make whether or not one has freedom of belief? Or is dishonesty wrong even if we injure no one by it? Most certainly yes—if only because we generally, in fact always, injure ourselves. For though we cannot hurt God by our falseness (we can only offend Him), we can hurt His Church.

An old saying goes: "As one lives, so shall he die." And thus it can often happen that many are not able to give up this crooked game even at the moment of death. How harshly will they be judged who no longer go to church or receive Holy Communion—or finally leave the Church and even persecute other Christians? It is certain that they will never possess the Kingdom of Heaven unless they reform their ways. But such people who have shown so clearly where they stand have at least partially abandoned their crooked game; and I would wager that they will not have to suffer anywhere near as great an agony in hell as those who have swindled

225

their whole lives through, always trying to deceive their spiritual leaders and their closest associates. Did not Christ Himself say, "Had you been hot or cold, I would have kept you near Me; but because you are only lukewarm, I will spit you out of My mouth"?

There will also be some who think, why should I be honest with men who are without doubt bad characters and not honest with me either? The first answer is that we should never repay evil with evil. Secondly, we have no more right to be dishonest with such a person, just because he is probably no good, than we would with someone who is good; for, in the eyes of God, the bad man is just as much my brother as the man who is good. Or if we have a mission to help such a person better himself so that we may deserve to be considered good Christians and, by so doing, prove ourselves to be even slightly better than those we look down upon—then we must also show ourselves to be honest and upright with others, even when we are rewarded for our pains with ridicule and scorn.

So, we should not be surprised if one can often hear it said, "That's the way they are." By playing our crooked game, we actually bring serious scandal down upon the whole Catholic Church, since all of us are usually spoken of as a single entity. And how do we rate at this moment in this matter of integrity? Is a man upright and sincere when, on the one hand, he is a member of the NVP or some other Nazi organization and makes sacrifices for it and takes up collections for it while, at the same time, he wishes the whole outfit would fade away and disappear? I think many have the idea that they can fool the others in this way, but we ought not to think our opponents are so stupid. They know full well that someone who still fulfills his Sunday obligations and gives some semblance of being religious in other ways has to be cheating somebody, since no one can serve two masters at the same time. For a while, of course, they will let it ride, since they know that such people really fool nobody but themselves and, in the process, do the greatest damage to themselves and to the Church. Needless to say, they will rarely trust such double-dealers with important political appointments.

Does there remain even the possibility for us to convert others

226

when we so generally co-operate with everything the Party wishes or commands of us—just so we can hold on to some temporal advantage? What must people of other faiths think of us and our faith if it means so little to us?

Actually, we should be ashamed of ourselves in comparison with the truly committed Party member who, for his part, even though his faith was rooted only in worldly things, fought for his ideals and for his National Socialist ideology in the face of all prohibitions and did not even fear prison or death. Would they have achieved their victory if they had been as timid and cowardly as we Catholics of Germany are today?

But we Catholics apparently entertain hopes of winning a glorious victory for our faith without any battle—and, to top it all, we expect to do this after first fighting for the enemy and helping him win his victory! Can anyone really believe such a thing is possible? In my opinion such a thing has never happened throughout the whole history of the world. Modern man, of course, is very inventive, but if he has progressed so far as to discover a way of winning a victory without a struggle, I have not yet heard of it.

5 On Irresponsibility

One often hears it said these days that "it's all right for you to do this or that with an untroubled mind: the responsibility for what happens rests with someone else." And in this way responsibility is passed on from one man to another. No one wants to accept responsibility for anything. Does this mean that when human judgment is finally passed on all the crimes and horrors being committed at this very time, one or two individuals must do penance for them all someday?

Am I showing Christian charity when I commit an act that I consider bad and grossly unjust (but which I commit anyway because otherwise I would have to suffer injury to my body or to my business)—and then say that someone else bears the responsibility for that act? It may well be that some prominent leaders, whether

227

in the spiritual or political life, do have to bear a great measure of responsibility. Yet instead of helping to lighten that responsibility, everyone tries to load his own burdens (which he could easily bear himself) upon them so that they are dragged down deeper than ever.

Do these leaders really carry as great a responsibility before God as we sometimes believe? Or, put another way, are we always as free from responsibility as people often say (or, perhaps, as we often like to imagine for ourselves)? At some point, will God not judge more in terms of each individual's understanding than of the [direction he received] during his life? For how can we tell whether the person on whom we wish to shove the responsibility might not have a totally different outlook on the whole situation from ours and regard as a probable good something that we consider evil? Often we do not have the slightest awareness of how we humans do differ in our points of view. I am sure that each of us could speak from his own experience of how often it happens that one holds something to be wholly good, only to be faced suddenly with a completely contrary opinion. It is quite possible that in the judgment of God such a person in high position might bear a lesser responsibility than perfectly ordinary individuals among the common people.

Let us consider a little example. Let us assume there are two men performing virtually the same service for National Socialism. The first regards what he is doing as good and just according to his viewpoint; the other considers the whole thing—its ideas, sacrifices, and struggles—to be unjust! The second, however, believes that he is much better than the other because he does not hold the same convictions, even though he sacrifices and fights the same as the first man. Whether the Party for which he is sacrificing and fighting benefits from or is hurt by his actions apparently makes no difference to him. His principal concern—or so it appears to me— is that he himself need not suffer any physical harm. In my opinion, a greater guilt rests upon the individual who is fully aware that the results of his efforts are more certain to be bad than good but who, nevertheless, co-operates simply in order to spare his pampered body from danger and privation: a greater guilt, that is, than that borne by those who regard what they do as their duty and who, furthermore, see nothing at all bad about it according to their understanding.

Naturally, the words sound sweet to our ears when we are told that others bear the responsibility for the results.

6 Is There Anything the Individual Can Still Do?

Today one can hear it said repeatedly that there is nothing any more that an individual can do. If someone were to speak out, it would mean only imprisonment and death. True, there is not much that can be done any more to change the course of world events. I believe that should have begun a hundred or even more years ago. But as long as we live in this world, I believe it is never too late to save ourselves and perhaps some other soul for Christ. One really has no cause to be astonished that there are those who can no longer find their way in the great confusion of our day. People we think we can trust, who ought to be leading the way and setting a good example, are running along with the crowd. No one gives enlightenment, whether in word or in writing. Or, to be more exact, it may not be given. And the thoughtless race goes on, always closer to eternity. As long as conditions are still half good, we don't see things quite right, or that we could or should do otherwise.

But, alas, once hardship and misery break over us, then it will come to us as with the light of day whether everything the crowd does is so right and good, and then for many the end will pass over into despair.

I realize, too, that today many words would accomplish little more than make one highly eligible for prison. Yet, in spite of this, it is not good if our spiritual leaders remain silent year after year. By "words" I mean, of course, instruction; but example gives direction. Do we no longer want to see Christians who are able to take a stand in the darkness around us in deliberate clarity, calmness, and confidence—who, in the midst of tension, gloom, selfishness,

229

and hate, stand fast in perfect peace and cheerfulness—who are not like the floating reed which is driven here and there by every breeze—who do not merely watch to see what their friends will do but, instead, ask themselves, "What does our faith teach us about this," or "can my conscience bear this so easily that I will never have to repent?"

If road signs were ever stuck so loosely in the earth that every wind could break them off or blow them about, would anyone who did not know the road be able to find his way? And how much worse it is if those to whom one turns for information refuse to give him an answer or, at most, give him the wrong direction just to be rid of him as quickly as possible!

7 Is There Still a God?

How often can one also hear it asked, "Is there, then, still a God that He could look upon all that is now taking place in the world?" In one Gospel we are told how Christ once said to the Scribes, "Let them both grow together, the weeds with the grain, until it is time for the harvest." Christ did not say either that they should probably tear them out just because the grain might already be clearly outnumbered by the weeds. This Gospel actually teaches us quite explicitly that it will not be (as many think) that God will once and for all come down and wipe out evil or the evil ones so that everything can once again resume its mediocre course. True, God will come once again, but it will be with great power and majesty. And we should know, too, how far wide of the mark we are in that expectation.

If God were to take away the persecutors, there would be no more crowns of victory for us to win. Besides, has God not once already been merciful to us and, through His divine power, drawn a mighty stroke to cancel our debts? Christ has done penance for our debt of sin and has made atonement, and all of us who accept His teachings and live according to them can become blessed for all eternity. What more do we want? Should Christ let Himself be crucified for us again? Or was the miracle of His resurrection, and the other miracles that He worked, too small for us so that we still wait for a miracle that will make it possible for us to believe in His teachings? Has Christ, then, not shown us clearly enough, by word and example, the way to heaven? Even the miracles Christ performed through His apostles after His ascension were not meant solely for the Christian communities already existing at the time but, rather, were mainly intended for those who did not yet know of His omnipotence so that they might believe more easily in His teachings.

Then why these lamentations on the part of our people? Are not most of us already, or still, Christians? Does not one of our Mass hymns read "How happy the Christian"? What is wrong then? Is the text of the hymn false? Or are we no longer Christians? I believe it would not take very long to count the happy people today. Many will answer, I suppose, "Yes, it is the war," or "these bad times." Do we believe that the first Christians had an easy time of it, just because so many of them were happy? Or has God's mercy grown smaller so that we can no longer hope for forgiveness of our sins?

All of these can hardly be taken as the basis for our present discontent (if only because we can take it for granted that all of these things are really given very little thought!). But this great anxiety over the well-being of the body! Why should this mean so much if we are really Christians? Did Christ not say, "Be first solicitous for the Kingdom of God and everything else will be given to you"? The first Christians, too, knew many sufferings. Are we Christians of today, then, no longer aware that the pain God sends us can actually be helpful toward winning eternal happiness, if we bear it with patience and out of love of God?

It may well be that hell holds great power over this world at the present time, but even this need not cause us Christians to fear. May the power of hell be ever so great, God's power is still greater. Naturally, though, anyone who does not arm himself strongly against the diabolical power with the weapons for fighting and defense that Christ left behind for us as His supreme legacy when

He instituted the Most Blessed Sacrament of the Altar will scarcely be able to hold out very long against these mighty enemies.

8 War or Revolution?

This commentary has been included in its entirety in the text of this book (pp. 125–127).

9 On Dangerous Weapons

People talk today of terrifying weapons that the human mind has invented and will probably go on inventing. If man could invent a weapon capable of smashing the entire world into ruins, it would still be nowhere as dangerous as those before which mankind of today has shown practically no fear at all. These are the intellectual weapons with which one tears the true Catholic faith from the children and from the hearts (or no longer permits it entry there).

Since for almost every weapon there is also a means of defense, there are naturally means of defense against these intellectual weapons too. But unfortunately, they are seldom used.

We know that if these means of defense were put to practical and courageous use, there would be dead and wounded to be counted in this defensive struggle; for a large number of people would end up in prison.

One is expected, as a matter of course, to fight for all sorts of things and to risk his life doing so—and yet one does not dare to defend these children's souls but, instead, is obliged to watch helplessly and keep silent year after year? I believe that someday there will be bitter repentance, and perhaps eternal misery, on this account. Or are we, then, released now from our obligations to lead the children to God just because they are so much harder to fulfill than they were ten years ago? I doubt it. For the harder the battle here, the more glorious the victory will someday be.

II THE PRISON STATEMENT

These few words are being set down here as they come from my mind and my heart. And if I must write them with my hands in chains, I find that much better than if my will were in chains. Neither prison nor chains nor sentence of death can rob a man of the Faith and his free will. God gives so much strength that it is possible to bear any suffering, a strength far stronger than all the might of the world. The power of God cannot be overcome. If people took as much trouble to warn men against the serious sins which bring eternal death, and thus keep them from such sins, as they are taking to warn me against a dishonorable death, I think Satan could count on no more than a meager harvest in the last days. Again and again, people stress the obligations of conscience as they concern my wife and children. But I can not believe that, just because one has a wife and children, he is free to offend God by lying (not to mention all the other things he would be called upon to do). Did not Christ Himself say: "He who loves father, mother, or children more than Me is not deserving of My love"? Or, "Fear not those who can kill the body but not the soul; rather fear much more those who seek to destroy body and soul in hell."

For what purpose, then, did God endow all men with reason and free will if, despite this, we have to render blind obedience; or if, as so many also say, the individual is not qualified to judge whether this war started by Germany is just or unjust? What purpose is served by the ability to distinguish between good and evil? I would be ready to show blind obedience, but only in such a case where one would not injure others in the process. If God had not given me the grace and strength even to die for my faith if I have to, I, too, would probably be doing the same as most other Catholics. There are probably many Catholics who think they would be suffering and dying for the faith only if they had to suffer punishment for refusing to renounce the Catholic Church. But I believe that everyone who is ready to suffer and die rather than offend God by even the slightest venial sin also suffers for his faith. And by so doing, I believe such a one can earn even a far greater reward in heaven than does one faced with the command to renounce the Catholic Church—for, in the latter situation, one is obliged under pain of mortal sin to choose death in preference to apostasy even when the apostasy would be one of mere external appearance. A saint once said, "If one were able to extinguish the fires of hell by telling only one 'white lie' he should not tell it; for that 'white lie' would itself be an offense against God." Such an idea seems utterly ridiculous in the 19th [sic] century if one judges by the thoughts and speech of so many. It is true, we humans have certainly changed a great deal in our faith as compared with the early Christians; but God has not on this account removed even one iota from his Commandments—even though we will soon be able to date our writings in the year 2000.

I can easily see that anyone who refuses to acknowledge the Nazi Folk Community and also is unwilling to comply with all the demands of its leaders will thereby forfeit the rights and privileges offered by that nation. But it is not much different with God: he who does not wish to acknowledge the community of saints or who does not obey all the commandments set forth by Him and His Church and who is not ready to undergo sacrifices and to fight for His Kingdom either—such a one also loses every claim and every right under that Kingdom. Of course, God often grants a long reprieve before He exacts the death penalty. As soon as a man commits a mortal sin, he is condemned to eternal death, at least until he confesses that sin or, if he has no opportunity to do this, erases it by an act of perfect contrition. But if a sinner does not amend his life and reform, then finally one fine day the death sentence will be executed without any advance warning. But there remains this great difference: not only does such a sinner die the earthly death to which we are all condemned but, more than this, he is condemned to eternity in hell as well.

Now anyone who is able to fight for both kingdoms and stay in good standing in both communities (that is, the community of saints and the Nazi Folk Community) and who is able to obey every command of the Third Reich—such a man, in my opinion, would have to be a great magician. I for one cannot do so. And I definitely prefer to relinquish my rights under the Third Reich and thus make sure of deserving the rights granted under the Kingdom of God. It is certainly unfortunate that one cannot spare his family this sorrow. But the sorrows of this world are short-lived and soon pass away. And this sorrow is not at all comparable to those that Jesus was not able to spare His dear Mother in His sufferings and death.

Is, then, the Kingdom of God of such slight value that it is not worth some sacrifice, that we place every little thing of this world ahead of the eternal treasures? Did not the Apostle Paul say, "No eye has seen and no ear has heard and the heart of man has no hint of what God has prepared for those who love Him"? And once when St. Augustine wanted to write a book about the joys of heaven, St. Jerome (who, it was later learned, had died that very day) appeared and said to him: "Just as certainly as you cannot grasp the entire world in one hand, so can you never contain the joys of heaven in one book." So unimaginably great are these joys that God has prepared for us in His Kingdom—and the greatest of all is that these joys will last forever. I believe we would almost go out of our minds with joy if someone were to tell us that we could be sure that in a few days all these joys of heaven would be ours on earth and would last for a billion years. Yet what are a billion years in comparison with eternity? Not as much as a half second compared with an entire day. If the whole world consisted of nothing but grains of sand, and once every thousand years one bird would come and each time carry away a single grain of sand, one could scarcely imagine how many years would have to pass before the whole world would disappear in this slow process— still one day it would disappear; but in comparison with eternity this would still be nothing. It is absolutely impossible for man to think of any example which would even come close to a comparison with eternity. But not only the joys of heaven are eternal; this holds, too, for the terrible tortures of hell. As the Saviour once said, "Cast them out into the exterior darkness; there will be wailing and the gnashing of teeth." In the same way, the pains of hell will be so great that one simply cannot compare them at all with earthly sufferings—and, moreover, they, too, will last for all eternity.

Should it be too much for us, then, to submit ourselves completely, in our short lifetime on earth, to the commandments of God and His Church (which, besides, can serve to bring men temporal blessings and prosperity as well, if one brings God sacrifices and self-denial)? Ask the nonbeliever if he has no sorrows on this earth or if he has everything his heart desires or can do what and how he pleases. Would it have been at all possible, even once in our lifetime, to offend God by a serious sin if we had considered and believed more firmly in eternity and the bitter sufferings of Jesus Christ? If Christ had not come into this world and had not died for us, heaven would have remained closed to us, no matter how virtuous and chaste we might have been in our lives. Even though Jesus saw our meanness and ingratitude already before His passion and knew, too, that for many His bitter sufferings and death would be wasted, still He took this heavy sorrow upon Himself. The love God has for us men is so great that we can never hope to comprehend it with our human reason. And, yet, it is possible for us in our hearts—often for considerations of the slightest earthly advantages and prestige—to offend so good a dear Lord and God who suffered so for us and who promises such an unimaginably great reward if only we keep His commandments and love Him!

What, then, can an earthly master offer us in this world? And, yet, there are immediate and severe penalties for anyone who does not follow his regulations or who seriously offends such a high personage. Is it too much, then, if the Lord of heaven and earth, Who has borne so much for us and in addition promised so great a reward, should banish us to hell if we offend Him seriously— especially when He is always ready to forgive if we but ask for forgiveness and make a good resolution to reform? Consider what great efforts and sacrifices so many of us men are prepared to make to gain worldly esteem, or an athlete to win a prize. If we were to make the same efforts to gain heaven, there would be many and great saints. For the Kingdom of Heaven, too, will not be ours without effort and sacrifice. Christ has said Himself that the Kingdom of Heaven can be won only by those who storm it and take it by force. Or, again, "Enter by the narrow gate, for wide

236

is the gate and broad the road that leads to ruin and many are those who go therein. How small is the gate and how narrow the way which leads to life, and how few are they who find it."

Why do we give so little thought to eternity? Why is it so hard for us to make sacrifices for Heaven? Yes, even though we cannot see it, we are sometimes clearly aware of the presence of an invisible power which makes every conceivable effort to lead man along the path to ruin. And that is the power of hell. Lucifer knows full well what joys and glories there are in heaven, but since he himself can never return to them, he cannot bear man to know such joy. For this reason, he and his companions use every means to bind all our thoughts and desires to this world. The less we think of eternity and of God's love and mercy, the more likely Satan is to win his game. For us men there are only two possibilities in this world: either we become ever better or ever worse; there is simply no such thing as standing still. Yes, even for those who have worked hard to come ever closer to God, there can be many reverses, just as an army advancing toward its victory does not win all its battles but must endure many defeats. Nevertheless, this does not mean that the struggle should be given up as hopeless; instead, one must pick himself up with renewed strength and strive on again toward the desired goals.

Therefore, just as the man who thinks only of this world does everything possible to make life here easier and better, so must we, too, who believe in the eternal Kingdom, risk everything in order to receive a great reward there. Just as those who believe in National Socialism tell themselves that their struggle is for survival, so must we, too, convince ourselves that our struggle is for the eternal Kingdom. But with this difference: we need no rifles or pistols for our battle, but, instead, spiritual weapons—and the foremost among these is prayer. For prayer, as St. Clare says, is the shield which the flaming arrows of the Evil One connot pierce. Through prayer we constantly implore new grace from God, since without God's help and grace it would be impossible for us to preserve the Faith and be true to His commandments.

The true Christian is to be recognized more in his works and deeds than in his speech. The surest mark of all is found in deeds showing love of neighbor. To do unto one's neighbor what one would desire for himself is more than merely not doing to others what one would not want done to himself. Let us love our enemies, bless those who curse us, pray for those who persecute us. For love will conquer and will endure for all eternity. And happy are they who live and die in God's love.

III   LETTER TO FRANZ HUBER

Dear Franz,

Since you no longer have a father in this world, it becomes the spiritual duty of the sponsor to assume the father's role in the education of his godchild and therefore I would like to give you in these few lines some good guidance for the stormy time of youth. One often reads in the papers about 15- or 16-year-olds who have taken their own lives—the usual explanation being disappointment in love or difficulties with their studies. It would be more accurate if these reports were to say that these acts were also rooted in [lack of] faith; for if it were true that disappointment in love is a prime cause of suicide, few people would reach the age of thirty.

We have already learned in school that man possesses reason and free will—and our free will is especially important in determining whether we will find eternal happiness or be eternally unhappy. You know, too, that a man who wants to bring a young seedling to full growth as a beautiful and strong tree will surround it with good support to make sure that every passing wind will not be able to bend it or tear it up by its roots. And so it is with a young man; he needs a good support so that he will not be torn loose from the Catholic faith. In the very first place are the parents; they must provide this good support. And that is why I am happy to take over the responsibility of your departed father in this respect, for a mother by herself is often too weak.

Soon you, too, will be experiencing the storms of youth. But in this respect we humans are not all the same. To some they come sooner, to others later; to some they burst forth in full fury, while to others the onset is weak. Should it be that temptation is ever so strong that you feel you must give in to sin, give some thought then to eternity. For it often happens that a man risks his temporal and eternal happiness for a few seconds of pleasure. No one can know whether he will ever again have an opportunity to confess or if God will give him the grace to repent of his sin. Death can surprise us at any minute, and in an accident one very seldom has time enough to awaken repentance and sorrow. This much I can tell you from my own experience.

You will surely want to grow into a fine strong fellow, and so you can. Many people think that only athletes and champion boxers are the strongest men, but this is not necessarily true, since these often are unable to master themselves in the face of the slightest passions and temptations. For this reason those who are able to overcome even great temptation really belong among the strongest. Almost every one of us has a hidden tendency to all kinds of vice—among them, for instance, unchastity, cursing, drinking, gambling, etc. And in order to fight against all these enemies, we must start training in our youth. For if one wants to be a winner, he may not fear any battle.

It is often said that there will always be time enough for goodness, that "youth must sow its wild oats." But I believe that those who hold such an opinion will very often overlook "becoming good" altogether. One who sets out to overcome a dangerous enemy and fails to do so in his best years is certainly not likely to succeed, once age has taken over and physical and spiritual strength have vanished. It is not true, as so many charge, that our faith forbids us to enjoy our youth. I believe a young person with a clear conscience has absolutely no reason to be "down in the dumps"—for it is just such a one who can really be gay in his heart since he has no cause to fear, even were he to be surprised by death. On the other hand, there are many who can be gay only when they are a little tipsy (if not actually blind drunk) because only in this way are they able to quiet their bad consciences once again.

Why are so many corrupted so early? First, Satan uses every possible trick to get us humans on the downward path as soon as possible. Second, very few young people read good books and literature. Third, in most cases, great mistakes are also made by parents and teachers. And why should the young person read only good books and literature? In the first place because a person does not need merely physical but also spiritual nourishment. We do not always have the opportunity to listen to good and effective sermons, since not every priest has the talent for preaching.

But one often hears from many people that all this reading only makes the individual more confused than he already is. And this can often be true. There are many youngsters who read very much —but for the most part only romantic novels and crime stories which, while they often make very fine and exciting reading, hold no value at all for spiritual and religious formation. Should one happen upon a bad book, it can often do more harm than the good gained from ten worthwhile books. For this reason young people should ask priests or good teachers what books they should read. Of course, not everyone has the same passion for reading, but some amount [of reading] is to be encouraged for the long winter evenings. Those who do not read are seldom able to stand independently on their own two feet—instead, they often end up being exploited by others.

Next, how can we expect parents to be able to raise their children properly when they themselves are not entirely clear on what is good and bad? In this way it often happens that grown children are called to account by parents who have learned that their boy or girl has already fallen in love (and, still worse, that this love is no longer entirely pure). When this happens, they are usually called before the parent and given a real scolding: "You'll soon have your fill of biting your nose to spite your face, but heaven help you if you get yourself into a real fix as a result—then you can get out of here and go where you please but not come around here any more." Fine, then. Many a boy or girl will get the idea from that it's all right as long as nothing happens; and should things go badly, steps can always be taken to get rid of the child before it comes into the world. Often by giving such guidance, the parents only convince their sons and daughters to "play it safe" by practicing contraception. For this reason, if parents have no better guidance to offer their children, it would be better to leave them completely free to go their way, since these children could scarcely end up being much more stupid than parents like that.

Certainly the love which God has planted in the hearts of young people is something beautiful and holy and, therefore, it is not right that, through sin, we trample it down in dirt and filth. If it were true, as many say and believe, that this premarital sex behavior is not really so sinful, then God would not have imposed such temporal punishment upon those who violate the Sixth Commandment. Not everyone is called by God to enter the married state. Nor did he create it (as many think) to furnish the opportunity for the unhindered use of one's powers; but rather, to assure the perpetuation of the human race—and he who is unable to control himself in the days of his youth will find that things will not go any better in the married state. For in the married state, too, not everything is permitted.

Once I had a chance at a folk fair to visit a hygiene display which included wax replicas of sex organs to show how a sexually diseased person actually looks. There one could see what evil effects unchastity can have for people. There are also young men who, already in their early years, rob themselves of their whole strength through secret or "sodomic" sin (that is, where the young man is unchaste by himself). Those who are strongly tormented by this vice often find it very hard to lift themselves up again, for they are more likely to fall under Satan's domination by reducing themselves to such weaklings that they reach the point where their personal will is often surrendered completely.

What and who else share the responsibility for the tragic corruption of youth? What about the loose tongues of lukewarm or sham Christians? Yes, there are often various people who are usually regarded as wholly good Christians. They go regularly to Church every Sunday (because, for the most part, this is the custom among us?); they are thoroughly respectable (because they fear prison?)—and, as a result, one is often led to believe that they are wholly good people in whom one can place his full trust. Yet should one approach closer to speak with them about this or that— and, perhaps, even about the Sixth Commandment—would he

241

not soon discover with whom he is really dealing and how deep their faith really is? "Oh," they say, "if everything were as much against the Sixth Commandment as the priests like to say or as one reads in the catechism, who would ever be able to get into heaven? What nature demands of people can certainly not be sinful. Most doctors will tell you the same thing and, besides, it is not advisable to be too strict." One can hear this and other talk like it from people who are often taken to be perfectly good Catholics. We ought to ask ourselves once, how many people do more than nature demands of them—such as the "easy" girls or even prostitutes who are actually paid for such behavior—since it would be quite easy for most people to obey the Sixth Commandment. Then, too, there are many others who only sneer at those who do try to take the Commandment a little more seriously than they, saying such things as, "This guy doesn't trust himself," or "He can't get anyone," or even "He is probably impotent." Yet let these scoffers find out that one of those at whose morality they had sneered has fallen and they will be the first to have their mouths wide open, saying, "Just look at those bed partners; one piece of dirt is no better than another to those alley cats, those hypocrites."

In the same way those who merely laugh at the Sixth Commandment also commit a serious offense and a very grave sin. Oh, those devils in human form! They often offer things that one believes to be nothing short of sugar and honey, but which, once he bites into them, prove to be nothing less than poison. For this reason one must be much more on his guard against such lukewarm Christians than against those of other religions or, for that matter, freethinkers. Anyone who has had a chance to get around in the world and who takes even the slightest interest in how things are going in most family circles will have his eyes opened when he sees how things stand in those families which take the Faith so lightly (or have already thrown it overboard altogether): they may have money and property, but they often lead such a life that one could not imagine hell to be any more miserable, a life where, in place of love, one finds only hate, bickering, and fighting. Then many will say, "If there were a God, He could not look on for long and see how so many carry on today." I believe God has seen and will attend to them; maybe the punishing hand of God is already far nearer to us than we expect.

Therefore, we must do everything in our power to strive toward the Eternal Homeland and to preserve a good conscience. Then, even if our enemies attack us and even if they are armed, they will not be able to tear us away from this Homeland. Though we must bear our daily sorrows and reap little reward in this world for doing so, we can still become richer than millionaires—for those who need not fear death are the richest and happiest of all. And these riches are there for the asking.

We can never use the excuse before God that we did not know what was sinful, for we have had the benefit of good religious instruction, and, should one have forgotten much of it in his older years, it would not be a disgrace to take his catechism in his hands and look into it from time to time. For the catechism should always be our best comrade and guide throughout our entire life.

Should you ever be troubled by those religious doubts from which almost no one is spared completely as to whether our faith is the true faith or not, reflect upon the miracles and on our saints who have been produced by none other than the Catholic faith. Since the death of Christ, almost every century has seen the persecution of Christians; there have always been heroes and martyrs who gave their lives—often in horrible ways—for Christ and their faith. If we hope to reach our goal someday, then we, too, must become heroes of the faith. For as long as we fear men more than God, we will never make the grade. O this cowardly fear of men! Because of a few jeering words spoken by our neighbor, all of our good intentions are thrown overboard. Of course, even the most courageous and best Christians can and will fall, but they will not lie for long in the filth of sin. Instead they will pull themselves together and draw strength from the sacraments of Penance and Holy Communion and strive on to their goal. And should anxious days come upon us when we feel we are being crushed under the weight of our troubles, let us remember that God burdens none of us with a heavier cross than he can bear.

Consider two things: from where, to where
Then your life will have its true meaning.[7]

Who goes on a journey without a goal
Will wander till he is tired and poor
Who lives his life without a goal
He has matured in vain.[8]

Your sponsor,
Franz

[7] *Zwei Dinge bedenke, woher, wohin*
Dan hat dein Leben den rechten Sinn.

[8] *Wer ohne Ziel auf Reisen geht*
Der wandert sich arm und müd
Wer ohne Ziel sein Leben lebt
Der hat umsonst geblüht.

244

Appendix II

1 A METHODOLOGICAL NOTE

When research for this book was being planned, and the study was organized, I fully expected that it would only include "talking to as many people as possible and then collating and comparing their information." For this reason the proposal made in connection with the application for a grant from The American Philosophical Society specified that "research methodology will rest almost entirely upon personal interviews—beginning with the widow and relatives and the local pastor (who is quite favorably disposed to Jägerstätter and his memory) and then extending into more general community circles."

As it turned out, the extension went considerably beyond the limits of the community to include interviews in Germany (with Dean Kreuzberg and Attorney Feldmann), Vienna (with *Prälat* Fried and two regular visitors to the community), Linz (diocesan officials and a onetime prison chaplain), and other villages in the area surrounding St. Radegund (the godchild, the sister-in-law, the former wife of the *Bibelforscher* cousin). Other information was obtained through written correspondence—from the Linz cellmates and the Berlin chaplain, for instance. At the same time, for reasons to be indicated later, a smaller portion of the community itself was interviewed than had originally been planned. However, even allowing for these *ad hoc* changes, the general pattern of research activities proceeded pretty much according to the original proposal.

The Community Interviews

Several obstacles presented themselves at once to any such study by an "outsider"—and, especially, by a foreigner. The most immediate problem concerned verbal communication itself. The adequate mastery of written and spoken German gained from a previous year's study and research in Würzburg could be expected to have a somewhat diminished value in an isolated rural village of Upper Austria. My earlier travels had already introduced me to the extreme variations of the German spoken in Bavaria, Vienna, the Rhineland, and other areas as well. In particular, my first visit to St. Radegund in 1957 was remembered as an uncomfortable effort to pierce the language barrier of the provincial dialect prevailing there. The outlook was not improved by the memory that I had had special difficulty in understanding the pastor who had offered to serve as "guide" and "interpreter" on that occasion. It was clear, therefore, that a more extended research stay would require that I plan on a preliminary period of residence in the village, during which little more would be attempted than concentrated listening to the conversations and discussions of the local people in an effort to develop an adequate familiarity with their dialect. Failing this, I knew it would have become necessary to employ someone as interpreter in the interview sessions, something I hoped to avoid if it were at all possible. As it turned out, two weeks of such listening proved to be enough to develop a "hearing" facility in the idiom. I made no serious effort to speak the dialect, but this was not necessary; there appeared to be no problem for the residents of the community in understanding me when I used *Schriftdeutsch* ("formal German") in speaking to them— all my many comical mistakes in grammar and pronunciation notwithstanding. Actually, once the word got around that the foreign visitor was trying to learn to understand their *Dialekt*, the residents went out of their way to help him and to make sure that the meaning of what they were saying was clear to him. In only five or six of the interviews conducted during the period of actual research did I encounter a level of communication difficulty that might be said to have seriously jeopardized the value of the interview; none of these, it should be added, were what might be termed "crucial" interviews. Before going to St. Radegund, I had spent a week or so in Vienna studying at the *Hofbibliothek* in an effort to learn as much about the area and its people as I could. At that time I encountered some of the *Mundart* (regional literature—poetry, plays, etc., written in the vernacular) of the region. One invaluable source proved to be *Am Quell der Muttersprache* (Verlag Stiasny, Graz-Wien, 1955) edited by Johannes Hauer. This preparatory visual experience with the vagaries of the *Oberoesterreichischen Dialekt* furnished many clues that made it possible to recognize certain key differences between it and *Schriftdeutsch*. For example, the "ei" combination in the latter becomes "oa" in the dialect form: thus, familiar words like *klein* and *Stein* become *kloan* and *Stoan* in the local speech; verb forms *wir sind* and *wir haben* become *mir san* and *mir han*. It is difficult enough to catch these patterned linguistic variants in the reading; without the advance familiarity gained through such reading, however, it might well have proved impossible to catch them in conversation within the limited time available for the research effort.

Although I assumed that the language barrier could be overcome, even more serious problems seemed likely to arise. It seemed possible that a complex of obstacles relating to the question of rapport and nonverbal blocks to communication might be presented by community reluctance to discuss the matter. I assumed —an assumption that later proved unsubstantiated—that the residents might be ashamed of the Jägerstätter affair or even resentful of the man's actions and its implications for the rest of the community. I was, of course, already aware that the peasant's ashes had been ceremoniously buried in a place of honor next to the village church in 1946 and that his name was listed on the war memorial; but I was also aware that these facts could be explained almost entirely in terms of the pastor's energetic and enthusiastic insistence upon these honors for the executed man. Comments made by the pastor and the man's widow in correspondence preliminary to my actual visit had given some indication that there had been opposition to the listing on the community honor roll and that there was still some dissatisfaction that Jägerstätter had not "done his duty." There was a danger, then, that if such attitudes actually proved to be widespread, any effort to probe more deeply into community recollections and evaluations of the affair could develop into an extremely touchy matter.

For this reason I deemed it necessary to maintain secrecy concerning the purpose of my visit until such time as I felt competent to begin with the actual interviewing. Pastor Karobath and the Jägerstätter family had already been informed, of course, since the preliminary planning depended upon their willingness to cooperate with the research, but they were specifically requested not to reveal the purpose of my visit to anyone else. That they complied with this request was amply proved by the manner in which I was received in the community. My arrival was clearly not anticipated, and the early days of my stay were marked by the frank, though friendly, curiosity shown by the people I met when I joined them in the tavern of the inn where I had chosen to stay.

To satisfy this curiosity, a variety of "covers" was employed (none of which, it should be added, was totally devoid of some element of truth). Thus, it was confessed that the tired professor was there for *Erholung*, a period of rest and relaxation in a quiet atmosphere; that he was interested in learning the *Dialekt* and something about the local *Mundart*; that he even hoped to make "some kind" of a sociological investigation of the impact of war on a rural village like St. Radegund. And, indeed, until I could be convinced that my language competence and community rapport justified making a start, there was always the real possibility that I might be obliged to shift to some less sensitive subject for my study.

Another and, at least at first, somewhat confusing explanation was developed by some of the residents on their own. During the period of the postwar military occupation of this area, Pastor

Karobath had struck up a friendship with an American soldier who had continued to maintain some contact with him and the village. Since he had been particularly generous in helping to alleviate postwar shortages and other hardships, many of the people of St. Radegund remembered this man—and all thought highly of him. There was, therefore, a tendency on their part to take it for granted that this new American visitor was somehow associated with him. This mistaken assumption was undoubtedly helpful in that it made for a more receptive attitude on the part of the villagers; at the same time, it may have hampered the final results somewhat by suggesting from the very onset a more intimate relationship between me and the pastor than, for reasons to be developed later, was to be desired.

The "covers" apparently worked. Either that, or I was soon accepted at face value, whatever my purpose in coming there may have been. The first "interview" was a highly informal affair, but it was enough to show that my interest in St. Radegund had not been prematurely revealed. It took place in the guest room of the inn on an evening when the host and his wife had gone to a movie in another town, leaving the researcher and the host's mother alone. The fact that she had been the mistress of the leading *Gasthaus* (inn) at the time Jägerstätter had taken his stand made her a most valuable potential source of information. The absence of even the customary patrons on this particular evening provided an occasion for a friendly discussion that ranged over many subjects: a teacher's need for *Erholung*, the admirable qualities of the pastor, the quiet and relatively unchanging pattern of life in St. Radegund. This latter subject opened the way to a more focused observation that "many things must have been different during the war," and this was met with the response that such was indeed the case. She recalled particularly the extra work load that had to be borne by the women, with the men away in service, and the sadness caused by the many casualties among the men who had gone off to war. This gave me the opportunity to remark that I had "heard something about this man named Jägerstätter," a cue which served its purpose in eliciting a rather full discussion of the man, his stand, and the general community reaction to it. This discussion was important not only because of the information it provided but, even more, for the evidence it gave that the community was not prepared for any set line of investigation on my part.

This encouraging beginning was soon to be threatened by a development which, I feared for a time, could have destroyed all hope of achieving and maintaining even the minimal level of rapport required for a successful inquiry. The event deserves a somewhat detailed recapitulation at this point—if only to enable the reader to judge for himself its effect upon the outcome of the study. Now that I felt I was ready to begin the actual research effort, I decided to start by interviewing the officials of the Linz diocese. In the course of the interview session with one of these officials, he volunteered the suggestion that a reporter for the local daily newspaper, a young lady who happened to be in his outer office at the time, might be interested in writing an article for her paper about my research project; in fact, he added, she could even incorporate a general request that anyone having further information about Jägerstätter might send it to me at my St. Radegund address. Having no convenient basis for rejecting his effort to be helpful (indeed, my position was weakened in this by the fact that I had been stressing my inability to understand why the diocesan paper, edited by this man, had ignored the Jägerstätter story), I agreed—with some unspoken misgivings about the adverse effect such publicity might have on the project. I was able to quiet these misgivings by assuring myself that the article would not appear for several days and would probably not be too prominent when it did appear. Both expectations proved wrong. The next morning's paper carried an account of my research interest; and this, of course, meant that any reader in St. Radegund would get his first inkling of my real reason for being in their midst by reading that I had come all the way from America for the specific purpose of studying the history of a man who, as the newspaper account put it, was scarcely known to people in his own homeland. Even more disturbing, the account was given considerable prominence, covering half of page 3 and a headline—"St. Radegund: Beheaded for

Following His Conscience"—running along the top of the first page.

Upon my return to the village that afternoon, I was somewhat fearful that I might encounter an unfriendly or resentful reaction from the villagers, who might have concluded that I had been "spying" on the community during the preliminary two weeks of my stay. Fortunately, my fears were apparently groundless; there was no noticeable difference in the tone of my relationships with the villagers, and certainly no unpleasantness was encountered. If anything, the innkeeper may have been somewhat pleased at the publicity given his guest—to say nothing of the mention of his *Gasthaus* as the address to which information was to be sent. In the course of later interviews, occasional comments indicated that the individual being questioned had seen the article, but no hostility was ever encountered on that score. One or two of the villagers mentioned their surprise over the manner of Jägerstätter's execution, the general community impression having been that Jägerstätter had met death by firing squad. On a more positive side, the published news item did uncover two extremely valuable sources of information: the priest who had served as chaplain at the Linz prison and had known Jägerstätter there and the nun who had discussed the case with the chaplain at Berlin-Brandenburg the night following Jägerstätter's execution.[1]

A second obstacle to rapport was the expected tendency of a closely knit rural community of this kind to "protect" its members. Thus, if there was any tendency for the residents to be ashamed

[1] The article was published in the *Linzer Volksblatt*, Vol. XCIII, No. 154 (July 6, 1961), p. 3, and was apparently picked up by other Austrian newspapers, including *Neues Oesterreich* (July 8, 1961). *Nachrichten für den Sonntag*, one of the genre of weekend "sensation sheets," sent reporters to St. Radegund to interview the pastor, the researcher, and Mrs. Jägerstätter. The resulting front-page spread (July 15, 1961) was a rather atrocious piece of sensationalist journalism—so much so that I hoped it would not be seen by the widow. However, someone did send a copy to one of the daughters; and this may have prompted Mrs. Jägerstätter to decide to furnish the prison letters and commentaries and in this way to help to "set the record straight." If true, this would have to be regarded as another incidental, but major, gain from this publicity.

for Jägerstätter and his action, or if they considered that he had been justly punished as a "criminal," the traditional *Geschlossenheit* of the rural community might be expected to make them somewhat reticent about discussing such a potentially "scandalous" matter with an outsider. In this, they would be following the rule of "not speaking ill of the dead," a rule especially binding when the "dead" was a member of the village group. Several people, in rejecting the notion that there had been or remained any resentment of Jägerstätter and his refusal to "do his duty," made this very point by saying that the tightness of the community bonds made it certain that a member would be forgiven almost anything but some "really criminal" behavior. It is difficult to estimate to what extent this *Geschlossenheit* may have affected the information obtained through the interviews conducted with the residents. No one openly refused to discuss the case, though one woman who reportedly had known Jägerstätter as a schoolmate made herself "unavailable." On the other hand, the almost total absence of even implied antagonism toward the man could suggest that the interview responses were governed by considerable reserve and are perhaps not to be taken entirely at their face value.

Two remaining obstacles to full rapport must be mentioned, and these relate to the community reaction to the researcher himself. The first is perhaps most obvious. A few weeks' residence in their midst could not be expected to wipe away the "strangeness" arising from the fact that I was a visitor from a foreign land, especially since that country was so far removed from them both in distance and in manner of life. As a result, there would always have to be some consciousness of an imposed relationship which would tend to limit the free flow of any informational give-and-take. This hazard was intensified further by the status difference between *Professor* and *Bauer* ("peasant"), an element that could not help but introduce a certain awkwardness of association between me and most, if not all, of the people I interviewed. It would be too much to say that these obstacles presented by the differences in nationality and status were eliminated completely; however, it is my sincere conviction that a threshold of genuine friendship and mutual interest was reached which operated to keep the impact of such differences at an absolute minimum.

The other aspect of this personal obstacle to rapport relates to my actual and presumed relationship with Pastor Karobath. For obvious reasons, the pastor had to be a primary contact and source, since he could best advise me as to which residents were most likely to be able to furnish the information desired and, even more important, provide the initial leads and introductions that made it possible to arrange for the actual interviews. Respected as a leading "authority figure" in the community, he would be able to open doors that might have remained shut because of the considerations already noted and generally reduce whatever suspicion there might be of the "outsider" and his motives for probing into community affairs. But this very advantage seems to have brought with it its own disadvantage. If only for reasons of personality and temperament, this particular priest is not the most popular figure in St. Radegund—indeed, there is some reason to believe that the role of pastor in a rural community of this kind may have many general and "built-in" unpopularity factors, irrespective of the specific personalities involved.

Be that as it may, Fr. Karobath may be described as a strongly opinionated and outspoken man; and these characteristics are not always favorably regarded by his parishioners. His rigid policy of refusing to schedule weddings on Saturdays because he fears (apparently with very good reason) that the lateness of the following celebration would interfere with attendance at Sunday Mass is strongly criticized in some quarters and regarded by many as an excessively arbitrary attitude on his part. An issue bearing directly upon the research project is the pastor's firm belief that Jägerstätter was the only man in the whole community to recognize and fulfill his true moral obligations with respect to the war. This opinion, and the frequency with which he expresses it, has not increased the pastor's popularity with his flock. There was a danger, then, that too close an identification with the pastor on this particular issue might have an adverse effect upon the degree of rapport I could achieve with the villagers. People would be even more hesitant about expressing a possibly adverse judgment concerning

Jägerstätter and his stand if they suspected that this might get back to the pastor or if they assumed that the researcher personally shared the pastor's evaluation. In the first instance, therefore, explicit assurances were always given that sources of specific information would not be revealed, even to the pastor; but there is no way, of course, of estimating the extent to which these assurances were accepted. Secondly, an effort was made to convince each person I interviewed that I was primarily interested in getting the full story, the bad as well as the good. There was no effort to deny that I held a favorable evaluation (this could have been inferred from the tone of the Linz news item and my frequent visits to the Jägerstätter family), but at no time during the research period did I permit myself to get involved in a pro-or-con discussion of the specifics in the Jägerstätter case. Early in the research period—as the result of an unguarded statement made by the pastor—it became known that I had refused to serve in the American armed forces on grounds of conscientious objection; however, there was never any indication that this fact affected either the scope or the quality of the interview responses.

In over-all summary, then, I feel that whatever linguistic blocks to communication might have remained were so slight as to have no seriously limiting effect upon the research product. The question of rapport cannot be answered as easily. There was no evidence that my research interest was resented and I encountered no outright refusals to co-operate. On the contrary, the people who were interviewed were always most hospitable and generously allowed as much time as I felt was necessary for my purposes. Indeed, in some cases it was difficult to terminate the research "visit" even after this point was reached. It may be true, however, that the information obtained was not full-dimensional, since seriously adverse judgments concerning Jägerstätter and his stand might have been withheld either out of a desire to "protect" his reputation or a reluctance to take a position known to be contradictory to that held by the pastor or presumed to be held by me. These considerations may indeed have softened or otherwise modified the true picture, but not to an extent that would seriously jeopardize the validity of the research findings. The pattern of recollections and evaluations emerging from the interview responses may be taken, therefore, as a sufficiently accurate approximation of the situation prevailing today.

This seemingly optimistic estimate is based in part on the types of individuals interviewed. These are simple and friendly people, quick to welcome the stranger to the group gathered around the tavern table, eager to volunteer advice or to help him solve any problem that might be troubling him. Co-operation still rules the community relationships, however much outside interests and activities may be operating to loosen the traditional ties. The building of a new *Scheune* (barn), the major social event of the summer of 1961, illustrated this in the extent to which it brought forth a seemingly limitless (certainly not carefully calculated and measured) flow of co-operative effort from the adult population. The men contributed many hours of individual labor in laying out the frame and then all coming together for one day of mass effort in the raising of that frame. The women added their bit by cleaning roof tiles or helping to prepare and serve the meals for the working crew. The climax of the whole affair was something of a community festival highlighted by a gay episode of ritual thievery. The owner and victim-to-be explained the tradition to me weeks before the work on the barn had begun. The young bachelors of the community would arrange to "steal" the main beam and this "theft" would not be "discovered" until the carpenters were ready to lift it into place. The "discovery" would set off a general round-up of all the suspect *Burschen* who would then be tied together and forced to accompany the searching party until the "stolen" beam was found. Incidentally, the scuffling involved in "capturing" these young men is no empty ritual formality; in this particular instance, one of the carpenters ended up with a broken toe and other participants suffered more minor injuries. Anyway, once the search was successfully concluded, everybody joined in a spontaneous celebration of the now completed barn raising. This admittedly extended resume of a local practice is introduced here to illustrate that co-operation, freely given when needed, is the universally acknowledged mark of "the good neighbor" in St. Radegund. And this same spirit of co-operation was extended to me in my efforts to probe into the background and history of their former friend and neighbor. I was to learn later that co-operation was offered me even though some of the people felt that it would have been better not to stir the whole matter up again. For the most part the persons interviewed were men and women who had known Jägerstätter personally as schoolmate, chum, friend, or neighbor. Apart from the series of interviews with Pastor Karobath, the widow, and the daughters of the executed man, twenty-five key interviews were conducted with informants who were assumed to be most knowledgeable concerning the affair. In several cases, the interviews were conducted on a family basis so that, as in one instance involving the head of the local veterans' organization, as many as four people might contribute the information sought. All but three or four of the informants selected for interview were either engaged in the operation of one of the farms of the area, or had been; the exceptions were the "town folk," i.e., the proprietor of a general store, the village clerk, and the schoolteacher. All of the families whose lands border on the *Leherbauer* farm were interviewed, as were the last three *Burgomeisters*; the proprietors of the two Radegund *Gasthäuser*; the head of the local veterans' group; seven former schoolmates and Jägerstätter's three or four closest friends; his godfather; and the aged sister of his stepfather (the last living representative, as she pointed out, of the Jägerstätter family line). A livestock dealer from a neighboring farm was also included, both because he visited the community regularly—sometimes twice a week or oftener—and because he had been personally acquainted with Jägerstätter.

Sometimes several qualifications were combined in a single informant. For example, the first formally scheduled interview was held with an elderly man who was a relative of Jägerstätter's mother, his baptismal sponsor, and the official witness at his wedding (a role usually performed by the father of the groom). In addition, he was one of the immediate neighbors; twice *Burgomeister* (having been removed from the post when the Nazis assumed power, and returned to it by the Occupation authorities); the former head of the *Bauernbund*; and, after he finally resigned his post as mayor, an officially designated *Ehrenburger* ("distinguished citizen") of St. Radegund. In the course of the interview, it developed, too, that he was a man to whom the young Jägerstätter had sometimes turned for personal counsel and advice and with whom Franz had frequently discussed their mutual dislike for National Socialism.

My original research plans had anticipated a more extensive sampling of the population. However, once the first dozen or so interviews had been completed, the similarity of responses made it quite clear that little or no purpose would be served by going further afield—especially in view of the fact that those already interviewed had been the individuals most closely associated with Jägerstätter during his lifetime.

Most of the interviews took place in the informants' homes. Life in the typical Upper Austrian houses centers about the *Stube*, an all-purpose family room, one corner of which—furnished with a heavy wood table and benches along the walls—serves as both an eating and visiting area. All social activities take place in the Stube, which did not make for privacy in interview sessions. Even in those instances where the interview began with no one but myself and the intended informant in the room, it rarely happened that it was concluded without one or more members of the family joining us—and, often enough, contributing amplifying or confirmatory comments to the statements made by the person I had come to interview. To further complicate the situation, I was obviously receiving the hospitality of the informant and his family, a factor that excluded all possibility of objecting to the presence of the others or doing anything to structure the interview differently.

In retrospect, it can be said that the nature of the information sought was such that the presence of persons other than the principal informant was not, except in a very few cases, harmful. Once or twice when the pastor was present (usually because he had generously arranged to take me to one of the more remote farms on his motorcycle), it was quite obvious that the informant was tailoring his replies to suit what he knew were the pastor's own ideas and attitudes. The results of these interviews had to be dismissed as being of little or no value.

A few interviews were conducted in the *Gasthaus*. Obviously this was most convenient as far as the interviews with the two rival innkeepers and their mothers were concerned. The interview with the man who had served as *Burgomeister* under the Nazis was also undertaken, "spontaneously," one evening when he and I were the only guests at the tavern table; I had feared (with some supporting evidence drawn from other discussions with this man) that he might shy away from a formally scheduled research session. As it developed, the relaxed setting proved quite helpful, and the interview was most productive. Two interviews were held in the pastor's rectory office at his suggestion; in both cases he absented himself by going across the way to the *Gasthaus* until the interviews were completed.

One other format, unorganized and truly spontaneous, deserves to be mentioned in this description of the research methods. On several occasions, when a group of local residents and I were gathered around the table at the inn to enjoy the customary evening refreshments, snacks, and talk, the conversation turned to the progress of my study. Usually, it should be added, the issue was introduced by one of the others; on the rare occasions when I saw fit to do so it was in the hope of pursuing some line of information that seemed best suited to such a general discussion. These sessions often proved quite valuable in the information obtained and, even more significant, in the hints they gave to underlying evaluations and attitudes that had not been expressed by the same individuals in the more direct interview sessions.

"More direct" is not to imply that the interviews in the home setting were "structured interviews" in the usual sense of the term. Taking into consideration all the factors already noted, I decided upon a highly informal discussion based on a few "opening" questions followed by whatever probing for specifics might be indicated as the most suitable, if not the only practicable, approach. Thus, after the usual amenities of greeting and self-introduction were completed, I would give a brief and very general summary of my interest in the Jägerstätter case, stressing its highly unusual character and relating it to my sociological interest in social control and social deviance—or, as I would put it to the informant, "men

258

who take a stand all by themselves and opposed to the stand taken by everyone else." This proved enough to justify the inquiry, for the person being interviewed usually picked up this lead with some statement of agreement that such a description certainly did apply to Jägerstätter.

The next step was for me to describe the difficulties associated with the fact that there were no documents in existence which could enable one to fill in the details essential to a full understanding of the man and the stand he took. This meant, I would continue, that the kind of information necessary for such a study could only be obtained by talking with the people who had known the man personally. Assurances were given that a level of anonymity would be preserved which would make it difficult or impossible for anyone to identify the source of any particular item of information or expression of opinion—in most cases, this included the specific assurance that "not even the pastor" would be told anything about the course and content of the interview. It is not known whether such assurances actually accomplished anything beyond setting a more relaxed tone for the following discussion; the informant would frequently volunteer the statement that he had no objection to anyone knowing what he had to say, and it is quite probable that this was indeed the case.

The four general "cue" questions were: What sort of a person was this man Jägerstätter? What was the basis for his refusal to serve and where did he get the ideas which cost him his life? What was the attitude of the people of the community toward him and his stand at the time? (This was always expanded to ask specifically about the attitude toward his family.) What do the people of the community think about the whole affair today? It should be noted again that these questions merely served to open the major phases of the discussion; the probes that followed varied from interview to interview depending upon the direction of the individual responses. Phrasing the last two questions in terms of what "the people of the community" thought then and now seemed advisable on two grounds. First, it was intended to relieve the informant of whatever pressure a more direct request for his personal evaluation might have placed upon him; in most cases, the answers

259

led quite easily to a voluntary or easily given indication of that personal evaluation anyway. Second, in a closed community like St. Radegund, each member of the community would be a highly competent judge of what "the community" thought; and this, after all, was a primary focus of my research interest.

The Younger Generation

Not all of the research objectives were achieved with equal success, however. One of the anticipated points of special focus had been the extent to which the Jägerstätter story was known to the younger generation of Radegunders. This had been suggested by the impression given me on my earlier visit—a false impression as it turned out—that the young girl who had driven my taxi on that occasion was totally unfamiliar with the case. To test this impression and, more important, to discover the pattern of community recollections and evaluations as it would be reflected in the accounts passed on by their elders to the children, I planned to interview a representative number of residents who were either too young to have known the man personally or, if they had any recollection of him at all, would remember him only as the strict sexton who had "kept them in line" when they attended church as children.

This phase of the research effort proved to be a complete disappointment. Few interviews were held, and these were most unproductive. In the first place, it proved almost impossible to reach the youngsters who were to provide the information desired. This inaccessability was partly a matter of physical arrangements. As already noted, it rarely occurred that one could interview a particular informant in private. The interviews usually took place in the family room; and, even when I was not faced with the problem of several individuals actively participating by adding their responses to those of the principal informant, there were always likely to be some onlookers and listeners present. The presence of children while elders were being interviewed was not considered a serious hindrance; however, it was quite obvious that the presence of parents or other elders while one of the younger generation was being interviewed would have seriously jeopardized any real hope of reaching the essential levels of rapport and freedom of response. Part of the problem lay in getting an informant aside for the interview, a factor which simply eliminated the possibility of setting up any interview sessions with girls and which severely limited the occasions for interviewing the boys as well. When the latter were at home, they would either be working in the fields or engaged in more attractive forms of recreation than that offered by the prospect of answering questions about someone they had never known. In their case, the device of having them come to the rectory office for a private interview would have been self-defeating; even if they could have "spared the time," they would have been so much "on guard" that the desired rapport would have been all but impossible to achieve.

Even in a less structured situation, it would have been difficult to establish the psychological accessability of this particular group of intended informants. Whatever restraints or reserve the parent generation may have felt in talking to the foreign professor were multiplied for their children in that the block to communication associated with both the "foreign" and "professor" designations was complicated by the additional obstacles presented by the age difference between us. The few interviews that were attempted proved to be extremely tense and uncomfortable, even embarrassing, to all parties. This undoubtedly accounts for the fact that only one of these interviews was at all productive—and even in this instance the information, when it was finally given by the young man involved, was "blurted out" by him and not at all the product of a free and easy exchange.

The Family

Similarly disappointing, but for quite different reasons, were the informal interview sessions with Mrs. Jägerstätter and her daughters. The difficulties here stemmed more from the personalities involved and the immediacy of their involvement in the events under study. There was no opposition on their part to the research being done. Indeed, I had made a point of getting the widow's approval before I formulated definite research plans and proposals. In the one "formal" interview session scheduled with Franz's widow just before the end of my research activities in St. Radegund, she showed no reticence about answering any of my questions. In fact, it was at this meeting that she brought me the prison letters and the commentaries—material of whose existence I had not been aware.

There were some difficulties, nonetheless. Mrs. Jägerstätter's reserve, the obvious value she places upon privacy, her tendency to "keep everything inside her" (as the Radegunders see it), combined to place the interviewer at something of a disadvantage. It was almost impossible to elicit sufficiently specific and detailed information concerning her recollections of the community's reactions to, and evaluations of, her husband's action at the time it all took place—or, for that matter, since then. Of course, if the observed cleft extended back to 1943—and there is good reason to think it must have if one considers the responses concerning the nature of the change and the virtually unanimous preference for the "early" Jägerstätter—it is quite possible that she would not have been fully aware of (or too much concerned about) what the community actually thought of her husband's decision and its consequences. The interview with her did reveal some awareness of attitudes prevailing at the time in question, but she may have already been too "apart" or "shut off" from the others to be able to gauge correctly the full depth and scope of the community disapproval. And even if she had been able to do so, it is not certain that she would have unburdened herself of the unpleasantness or injury she may have had to suffer as a result, preferring instead to abide by her husband's admonition that such things are to be accepted as part of the "cross" she had to bear and to be forgotten as well as forgiven by her.

Admirable as this principle is in a spiritual context, it obviously presented an obstacle for the researcher in his efforts to get behind that barrier and reserve to learn what her experiences could reveal about the community consensus then and now. It was at this point that the second consideration entered as a restraint. Except for a few probing efforts which produced necessarily inconclusive results, no systematic effort was made to force questions upon Mrs. Jägerstätter. Perhaps another researcher more thoroughly committed to the ideal of coldly impersonal social science could have accomplished more in this respect. My own decision was that there are always some limits to be respected, and in this case the limits proved to be quite narrow. Whatever Mrs. Jägerstätter may have felt about the research project, no matter how much gratification she might take in knowing that her husband's sacrifice was finally receiving some serious attention, the fact remained that the inquiry could not avoid restoring to their full intensity all the old sorrows and hurts that she had somehow managed to bring under control and make bearable in the course of years. Such unpleasant effects were certain to occur whenever the family was approached directly for information and insights only they could provide. This may be illustrated more directly by her response to an article of mine based on some of the material gathered for this study ("The Mind of a Conscientious Objector," *St. Anthony Messenger*, Vol. LXIX, No. 11, pp. 25–28; translated and reprinted in *Werkhefte*, Vol. XVI, No. 8–9, pp. 327–335). After expressing her gratitude, she wrote that, in spite of the joy it had brought her, "I had to cry anyway when I read it. Whenever I read my husband's letters, everything comes back to my mind as if it all took place a few months ago. But when I look at my grandchildren, I can see that many years have already gone by, for my children were then as small as these." In my interviewing, a line had to be drawn; and in this case it was drawn so as to exclude any serious or direct probes into areas of inquiry that were clearly too sensitive.

There were times when this line may have been crossed. Certainly the fact that the widow broke down in tears toward the end of my questioning in the course of our one scheduled interview is evidence enough of this. At other times, too, I was troubled by the thought that any attempt at all to question this woman or her children was already exceeding the bounds of scholarly propriety. Yet the risk had to be taken or else the story of this man and his heroic act of rebellion would probably never be made known to others. In this context, then, one must be grateful for the information the widow and her daughters were willing to give at such a deep personal cost to themselves and not be dismayed by the fact that they were not prepared or able—or even asked—to go into greater detail than they did.

Except for the one formal interview with Mrs. Jägerstätter, the meetings with the immediate family took the form of frequent "visits" to the home, in which the progress of the study was described and any requests for information could be introduced as directly or as indirectly as substance or circumstance seemed to dictate. Once again, the setting was one which did not lend itself to individual interviews since it was customary for several family members—if not all three daughters and Mrs. Jägerstätter—to be present. Only in the case of the second eldest daughter was the opportunity presented for individual discussions. Physically incapacitated as she was, she stayed at home caring for her sister's children while the others were out working in the fields. Several such discussions did take place under the "cover" of the researcher assisting her with her correspondence school study of English.

It would have been possible, of course, to schedule separate formal interviews with each of the three daughters but this was not done for a variety of reasons. Most important, of course, was the fact that they had been too young at the time of their father's death to have any real recollections of how he and his action had been regarded by the community. Since the informal sessions offered sufficient opportunity to introduce questions about any subsequent experiences of theirs that might relate to that action, it was felt that whatever additional information they might give would not be of sufficient importance to justify putting them through the ordeal of a more focused investigation. Again, this decision may reveal too sensitive or timid an approach on my part; if so, my only defense would be to insist that it is better to have erred in this direction than to have gone ahead and caused them unnecessary additional sorrow.

It is, of course, entirely possible that a more prolonged stay in St. Radegund and a more thorough and systematic survey of its population by means of more highly structured interviews would have produced deeper insights and revealed other, more profound, dimensions of the Jägerstätter history. Unfortunately, this was not possible in view of my academic schedule and the limited funds available. Even granting such possibility, however, I am completely satisfied that the essential elements of the story did emerge through this study and that any improvements in method would merely serve to embellish and confirm the pattern that has been presented here. In a very real sense, any social science research project necessarily assumes something of the character of a jig-saw puzzle in which the task becomes one of identifying and assembling all the pieces and relating them to one another in their most meaningful context. A study such as the one reported in these pages presents some special problems in that many of the most crucial pieces have been destroyed or mislaid and there is no way of knowing how many are missing or what relationship the missing pieces bear to those at hand. One can only proceed in the hope that by picking up one item here and another there, by moving from the obviously important sources to those more indefinite "leads" which may or may not prove to be of value, enough of the puzzle can ultimately be assembled to furnish a level of understanding sufficient to justify having made the attempt in the first place.

The central pieces of this puzzle, the insights into the motivations and values which produced his heroic refusal to serve, were provided by Jägerstätter's own writings. The interviews and other sources cited added different and sometimes oddly-shaped pieces which, if they have been assembled properly, should combine to reveal much of importance concerning the setting and circumstances which contributed to the formation of the man and his unique definition of his responsibilities as a Christian in Hitler's Third Reich.

In the last analysis, of course, it must be remembered that the most crucial dimension to Jägerstätter's action may be something above and beyond mere human understanding, even where that understanding is aided by the full range of sociological conceptualization and techniques. For there are no sociological tools adequate to the task of analyzing the workings of grace and the power of revelation. Any such pieces to the puzzle, then, had to be put aside as far as this study is concerned and it must be left to the reader to judge for himself what part they play in completing the final picture.

2 A NOTE ON SECONDARY SOURCES AND BIBLIOGRAPHY

Official Documents

Inquiries at the military archives in Vienna concerning Franz Jägerstätter's case produced nothing beyond the original 1939 *Wehrstammblatt*, a military registration form, which provided a minimum of personal background information and noted that the conscript had been called and found eligible for the draft in April, 1939, and classified for service in the motorized corps. All further records would have been in the Berlin archives, which were destroyed by Allied bombings toward the end of the war.

A personal interview with Attorney Feldmann, who had been assigned to defend Jägerstätter at his trial before the *Reichskriegsgericht* (Reich's Military Tribunal) produced no further documentation. His files contained only a few notes, apparently taken down from memory.

Jägerstätter's widow possesses a formal notice of his execution, which consists of nothing but the bare statement of the fact.

Finally, the village records contain a *Kriegstodesnachricht* ("report on war death"), in which Jägerstätter's death is reported. This report, interestingly enough, was not submitted until March, 1950, almost seven years after the fact.

Though it is possible that other documentation exists, there is little likelihood that that is indeed the case.

Newspaper Reports

A review of 1943 issues of publications likely to carry news of Jägerstätter's execution produced nothing at all bearing on his case. Periodicals reviewed for this purpose were: *Neue Warte am Inn* (Braunau); *Oberdonau Zeitung* (Linz); and *Verordnungs- und Amtsblatt für den Reichsgau Oberdonau* (Linz). These issues did contain reports of other executions involving capital crimes, such as:

266

war-profiteering, listening to enemy broadcasts, defeatist talk, etc. A review of the 1946 editions of *Neue Warte am Inn*, the regional newspaper published in Braunau, revealed no mention of the ceremonial burial of the Jägerstätter ashes at St. Radegund on the third anniversary of his execution. In the November 6, 1946, issue of the paper (p. 3) there is a description of a meeting of the Braunau chapter of "former political victims." In this article twenty-two people from the area, "murdered" during the Nazi period, are listed. This listing includes: "Jägerstätter, Franz, of St. Radegund, August 3, 1943—executed by shooting in Braunschweig." However, the date as well as manner and place of execution are inaccurate.

Secondary Sources

To two priests, Heinrich Kreuzberg, Dean of St. Margarethe's Church in Brühl (Germany), who had been chaplain at the Berlin-Tegel prison at the time of Jägerstätter's imprisonment, and Fr. Josef Karobath, pastor of the parish church in St. Radegund, must go the major credit for attempting to keep the memory of Jägerstätter and his martyrdom alive.

In 1953 Kreuzberg published a biography of an Austrian priest of the Pallotine order who had been executed for refusing to take the military oath requiring that he swear unconditional obedience to the person of Hitler. His biography, *Franz Reinisch: Ein Martyrer unserer Zeit* ("Franz Reinisch: A Martyr for our Time") contained an appendix with a brief description of the martyrdom of Jägerstätter, who is referred to as "Franz II."

The tone of this appendix, like that of the book itself, is predominantly didactic and inspirational. It mentions Jägerstätter's early desire to enter a religious order, his marriage in 1936, and the honeymoon trip to Rome—a trip which "left a great impression and strengthened the happy pair in their love for the Holy Mother Church." It traces his return to the family farm where he led an exemplary religious life, receiving communion daily and reading regularly in the Bible and books of the lives of the saints. With the Nazi takeover and its acceptance in the plebiscite of 1938, a new

267

phase in the Jägerstätter story opened: he distinguished himself as the only man from St. Radegund not to vote for *Anschluss*, and by his continuing refusal to co-operate with official collections or to share in the subsidies and other benefits offered by the Nazi regime. One day, as Kreuzberg writes of it, he told his wife that should he be ordered into military service, he would not be able to obey. The order came; he refused, as he had said he would, and the inevitable consequences of arrest, imprisonment, and execution took their course.

There follows a brief description of the visit made to the Berlin prison by Jägerstätter's wife, accompanied by a priest from St. Radegund. Kreuzberg draws a parallel to the martyrdom of St. Thomas More in that he, too, had to face the appeals of his wife and daughter, on a similar visit to prison, to save his life by obeying the king. Finally, Kreuzberg tell of his own attempts to persuade the peasant to abandon his position. When these appeals proved unsuccessful, he recalls, he congratulated Jägerstätter on the courage and constancy of his stand, and then told him about a priest (Reinisch) who had taken much the same position a year before. "Even while I was telling him this, his eyes lit up and, after a deep sigh as if a heavy burden had fallen from his soul he joyously declared, 'But this is what I have always told myself, that I cannot be following a false path. If a priest made such a decision and went to his death, then I may do so too.' "

Perhaps the most significant contribution made by Kreuzberg to the development of the Jägerstätter story was his request that the condemned man set down in writing a full statement of his position. The result of this effort, a truly remarkable document, is now in the possession of the St. Radegund pastor. Kreuzberg's appendix to the Reinisch book quotes excerpts from this prison statement and from the farewell letter addressed by Jäggerstätter to his family and his friends on the day of his death. The chaplain's summary records the fact that the execution took place on August 9, 1943, and calls attention to the interesting coincidence that this was the feast day of St. Jean Baptiste Vianney, the Curé of Ars, a man who had chosen to become a "draft-dodger" in preference to accepting military service under Napoleon. His account concludes with the note that Jägerstätter's ashes were later removed from their original resting place in the Brandenburg cemetery and given a ceremonial burial in St. Radegund.

Kreuzberg has also published several articles dealing with Jägerstätter in which he offers substantially similar treatments. These include a 1954 article in *Der Pflug*, a magazine for rural youth, and an article found in Pastor Karobath's collection of materials, which is unidentified as to source or date. Several articles predate the publication of his book on Reinisch, including a 1948 article in *Mann in der Zeit*, an influential national publication for Catholic men. From this, one can conclude that the appendix to the Reinisch book was not, as it might at first seem, an afterthought.

The second priest, Josef Karobath, pastor of St. Radegund and personal friend of Jägerstätter, wrote one article intended for the official Linz diocesan paper, but its publication was apparently blocked by the personal intervention of the bishop. Despite this disappointment, his effort was not entirely wasted. It is quite clear that the notes he compiled on his parishioner later served as the basis for at least three, possibly more, reports that were published elsewhere by other authors. Pastor Karobath has also kept a file of clippings and various other materials concerning Jägerstätter.

Perhaps the most "official" publication containing such a report is *Prälat* Jakob Fried's *Nationalsozialismus und katholische Kirche in Oesterreich* ("National Socialism and the Catholic Church in Austria"), published in 1947. As Fried described the events to me in a personal interview in 1961, he had occasion shortly after the war to have a personal meeting with Pope Pius XII. In the course of this meeting, the discussion turned to the struggle between the Nazi state and the Austrian church and led to the Pope's expressing his wish that Fried would undertake the task of compiling a systematic record of these events so that the many heroic incidents that had taken place might not be forgotten over the passage of time. Fried remembers answering him that, despite his lack of preparation for such a task, he would be willing to take on the papal assignment—to which the Pope repeated that he would prefer that it be considered more a request than an assignment. In any event, upon Fried's return to Austria, he wrote to the various dioceses asking for reports of any incidents that would warrant inclusion in such a history. With specific reference to the Jägerstätter case, he was not certain of his exact source, but he said he assumed the information had come to him from some Upper Austrian chancery official. (Actually, his book is more specific, since it refers to Pastor Karobath as his source.) It is interesting, too, to note that he was not familiar with Kreuzberg's writings on the case.

Fried characterizes Jägerstätter as a "typical example, albeit of a special kind," of Catholic opposition to Hitler. Based as it is on the pastor's longer personal acquaintance with the man, the brief account adds a few significant touches to the story already drawn from the Kreuzberg account. Fried notes, for example, that "in his younger years, he was quite a lively fellow, and at times even jumped over the traces," but that after making a retreat at Altötting in 1934, he became very serious in matters of religion. After his marriage, he took over the family land, "managed the farm work efficiently, was a good father to his family, and a happy man. He received Holy Communion almost daily." The Nazi victory in 1938 was viewed by him to be "the greatest misfortune because of the godlessness of these new heathens." Again we encounter the fact that Jägerstätter did not vote in favor of *Anschluss*, though there is a slight discrepancy, since Fried reports that the peasant turned in "an invalid ballot," whereas Kreuzberg reported that he cast an openly negative vote. There is agreement on the point of the peasant's refusal to contribute to official collections—with Fried adding the further item that the man performed personal acts of charity where there was need.

The actual refusal to serve is given a more complete, and apparently more accurate, description in the Fried account as follows:

In his [Jägerstätter's] eyes Hitler's war was unjust, and one in which one might not co-operate. In 1940 he had to report, but he returned home a few days later. In 1941 he was obliged to report again for service. When, however, he went as a soldier to church, he was severely harassed and made the object of scorn. He again succeeded in winning his release and returned to the village. He declared that he would definitely not report a third time. His friends, priests and lay, argued that he surely could not risk his life and put his family in the gravest danger by making such a refusal. He always had one answer: "I may not co-operate in an unjust war. God will certainly take care of my wife and children in such a case."

When, therefore, he was ordered to report again at the end of February, 1943, he did not comply. As the police came to him (still before he was due to report, however) he went to the bishop. The latter brought all the fundamentals of morality to his attention [pointing out] that he had no responsibility for the secular ruler, that he had to obey, and that he had an absolute responsibility toward his family. The bishop could see that the peasant thirsted after martyrdom and explained that he could take that path only if he knew that he was called to it through an exceptional revelation from above and not for reasons of his own. Jägerstätter accepted this.

Even though his spiritual advisors continued to warn him against refusing military service, he reported to the designated induction center six days late. On June 6, 1943, he was sentenced to death. Before the sentence was confirmed, he was still begged to reconsider and change his mind. He stood firm. On July 13 his wife visited him. She was supposed to try to convince him otherwise, but he told her, "I am completely happy (though one could see the signs of maltreatment and hunger on him); I will not weaken. I am happy that I have come this far." His brave wife did not argue too much. He expressed the wish that he might already be with the Mother of Heaven on August 15 [the Feast of the Assumption]. Shortly before his death he wrote his final letter: ". . . may God accept my life as a penance not only for my sins but for those of others as well."

On August 9, 1943, he was beheaded in Brandenburg and his body was cremated. His ashes were cared for by friends; and on August 9, 1946, three years after his death, they were buried in the presence of the whole parish community.

At this point one should note that the Fried account has been challenged in some respects. In a letter to the present author, Mrs.

Jägerstätter has offered some "corrections" to this and the other reports. For one thing, she writes, her husband reported *four* days, not six days, late. This checks with the documentation: A letter from Franz to Fr. Karobath said the induction order called on him to report on February 25; his letter from Enns, dated March 1, told his wife, "Today I am going to take the difficult step." The other corrections are interesting as evidence of the widow's own humility. The reports that they had both gone to communion every day and read the Bible together every evening were not true; the tasks involved in caring for three infants often made it impossible for her to get to morning Mass or to join him in the Bible readings. In general, Fried's account appears to be reliable in most respects. There is only one factual error. He (and this applies to Kreuzberg, too, incidentally) gives June 6 as the date of sentencing; the defense attorney's letter suggesting that the wife come to Berlin to make one last effort to save her husband's life, and the official report of the execution, both establish July 6, 1943, as the actual date.

An article by "L.A." and entitled "Heldenhafte Konsequenz" ("Heroic Consistency"), published in the Vienna periodical, *Der Fels,* is also traceable to the notes compiled by Pastor Karobath. The approach here is less to provide an historical narrative than to preach the moral lesson to be drawn from the example given by Jägerstätter's action. The author, Leopold Arthofer, is the pastor of Kronstorf, another relatively small town in the vicinity of Linz, and a personal friend and former classmate of Karobath. Like Jägerstätter (and Karobath), Arthofer was a staunch opponent of the Nazis, a fact which earned for him an extended internment in Dachau. In his article, Arthofer claims a personal acquaintance with the peasant, but in the course of an interview he said he could not recall ever having met him. One interesting note that was not encountered in any of the other material dealing with this case is provided by Arthofer's statement that, while in prison, Jägerstätter succeeded in converting to Catholicism two men who had also been sentenced to death.

Two other articles, clippings of which are to be found in the parish "Jägerstätter file," deserve to be mentioned. The first translates as "Rather Death than Fight for Nazism: The Resistance of an

Innviertel Farmer to the War," and appeared in a paper identified as "the official journal of the Austrian People's Party." Although neither the newspaper's nor the author's name is shown on the clipping, it, too, is obviously based on the information compiled by Karobath. Like the Arthofer treatment, it seeks to point up a lesson, but this time it is more a political lesson: "It should not jeopardize a favorable judgment of our homeland if people—including those in the outside world—learn through these lines that, in all the insanity and the indescribable blindness of the past few years, one man out of the total rural population found it possible to maintain a truly amazing strength of character; from the very beginning, a simple man of the people reached a clear and unconfused judgment about the completely objectionable nature of this anti-folk, anti-homeland, and anti-Christian idea, and acted accordingly in spite of his full awareness that it would cost him his life."

The other article, "Was dir zum Frieden dient" ("That Which Will Bring You Peace"), is essentially a homily based on the Gospel for the Ninth Sunday after Pentecost which appeared in an independent, but apparently Catholic-oriented paper published in Innsbruck. It refers to Jägerstätter largely as an illustration of a point. Its author does not cite his sources, but its contents again clearly follow the pattern set in the Fried and Arthofer writings. In the article itself, the author discusses war as a punishment visited upon man by God, but goes on to say that this is true only in the sense that, by giving men free will, God made it possible for them to "punish" one another in this fashion. He then goes on to discuss the responsibility of all men for all wars and makes specific reference to Austria's share of the guilt for World Wars I and II. He continues:

Peace would have been served if the mass of Austrian Catholics had done what the heroic peasant, Franz Jägerstätter of St. Radegund in Oberösterreich did: He refused military service on the grounds of his Christian conscience. He submitted to imprisonment and went knowingly to his death. "I may not contribute to an unjust war," he said, and in his last letter he wrote, "May God accept my life as a penance for my sins and those of others." How

273

many Christians understood that at the time? Who was ready to bear like witness? If it was folly, then it was the same folly that Jesus Christ placed on the day and demanded of us.

Two other passing references serve to bring this survey of the secondary literature dealing with Franz Jägerstätter to its close. The volume of letters compiled by Gollwitzer and others, *Du hast mich heimgesucht bei Nacht*, contains the text of Jägerstätter's farewell letter in a slightly edited form and prefaced with a brief summary identifying its author as a peasant who was executed for refusing military service. This, too, must have been obtained from Pastor Karobath.

Finally, Walter Hammer mentions Jägerstätter in the course of a summary of cases involving peasants among the (according to his count) 1800 persons executed at Berlin-Brandenburg. This article is of particular interest because it appeared in a periodical licensed by the Soviet Military Administration. The tone of the article is quite frankly "leftist"; despite this, however, the author credits Jägerstätter with assuming "martyrdom for his faith."

Such, then, is the published record of the case. The emphasis of most of these articles is on the lessons to be drawn from Jägerstätter's heroic act of self-sacrifice, and whatever references are made to his early life or to the reasoning behind his stand are chosen to serve that didactic purpose.

The following is a listing of published books and articles devoted to, or referring to, Franz Jägerstätter and written before the completion of this study:

ARTHOFER, LEOPOLD ("L.A."). "Heldenhafte Konsequenz," *Der Fels*, Vol. I, No. 16.
FRIED, JACOB. *Nationalsozialismus und katholische Kirche in Oesterreich*. Vienna 1947.
GOLLWITZER, HELMUT, *et al*. *Du hast mich heimgesucht bei nacht*. Munich, 1954. English translation: *Dying We Live*. New York: Pantheon, 1956.
   The English translation does not include the Jägerstätter material.

HAMMER, WALTER. "Sie starben für Frieden, Freiheit, und Fortschritt," *Der Freie Bauer*, Vol. IV, No. 37 (September 11, 1949), p. 9.

JANTSCH, FRANZ. "Was dir zum Frieden dient," *Der Volksbote*, No. 31 (July 31, 1955), p. 11.

The following issue of *Der Volksbote* included a mild dissent from a reader and a "clarification" by the editor.

KREUZBERG, HEINRICH. "Einer der für den Frieden starb," *Der Weg*, Vol. IV, No. 2 (November, 1949), pp. 35–36.

——. "Er verweigerte den Eid," *Mann in der Zeit*, Vol. I, No. 8.

——. *Franz Reinisch: Ein Martyrer unserer Zeit*. Limberg/Lahn, 1953.

——. "Der tapfere Bauer von St. Radegund." Publication date and place unknown.

——. Untitled article in *Der Pflug, Zeitschrift des Jungen Landvolks*, Vol. VI, No. 12.

"Lieber sterben als für den Nazismus Kämpfen: Der tapfere Widerstand eines Innviertler Kleinbauer gegen den Krieg."

This article was found in the St. Radegund Jägerstätter files. Periodical and author not known, but the clipping bears the date, March 9, 1946.

Since this study was begun—indeed, to some extent, as a direct result of it—other articles have appeared, including some by the author:

BALDINGER, FRANZ. "Er folgte seinem Gewissen," *Linzer Kirchenblatt*, Vol. XIX, No. 34/35 (August, 1963), pp. 4–5.

"Enthauptet, weil er seinem Gewissen folgte," *Linzer Volksblatt*, Vol. XCIII, No. 154 (July 15, 1961), p. 3.

ERB, ALFONS. "Er verweigerte den Dienst im Hitler-Krieg," *Pax Christi*, XV (September–October, 1963) pp. 8–9.

"Menschlichkeit auf dem Schafott," *Nachrichten für den Sonntag*, Vol. XI, No. 28 (July 15, 1961), pp. 1, 4.

ZAHN, GORDON C. "A Christian Protest," *Jubilee*, Vol. XI, No. 5 (1963), pp. 8–14.

——. "He Would Not Serve," *America*, XCIX (July 5, 1958), 388–390.

——. "The Mind of a Conscientious Objector," *St. Anthony Messenger*, Vol. LXIX, No. 11, pp. 25–28.

The following brief list indicates some recent publications dealing with the issue of the relationship between the Catholic Church and Nazi Germany:

AMERY, CARL. *Die Kapitulation, oder deutscher Katholizismus heute.* Hamburg, 1963.
BÖCKENFÖRDE, ERNST-WOLFGANG. "Der deutsche Katholizismus im Jahre 1933," *Hochland*, LIII (March, 1961).
———. "Der deutsche Katholizismus im Jahre 1933: Stellungnahme zu einer Diskussion," *Hochland*, LIV (February, 1962).
    The original Böckenförde article provoked an extensive and often controversial discussion. Böckenförde's second article, which constitutes a rejoinder to the criticism against his interpretation of historical data, includes citations of such additional discussions.
BUCHHEIM, HANS. "Der deutsche Katholizismus im Jahre 1933," *Hochland*, LIII (1960/61).
    A rejoinder to the Böckenförde article.
BULLOCK, MALCOLM. *Austria 1918–1938: A Study in Failure.* London, 1939.
CORSTEN, WILHELM (ed.). *Kölner Aktenstücke zur Lage der Katholischen Kirche in Deutschland, 1933–1945.* Cologne, 1949.
DEUERLEIN, ERNST. *Das Reichskonkordat: Beitrage zur Vorgeschichte, Abschluss und Vollzug des Konkordats zwischen dem Heiligen Stuhl und dem Deutschen Reich vom 20. Juli 1933.* Düsseldorf, 1956.
———. "Zur Vergegenwärtigung der Lage des deutschen Katholizismus, 1933," *Stimmen der Zeit*, CLXVIII (April–June, 1961).
DIAMANT, ALFRED. *Austrian Catholics and the First Republic: Democracy, Capitalism, and the Social Order 1918–1934.* Princeton, N.J.: Princeton University Press, 1960.
GULICK, CHARLES A. *Austria. From Hapsburg to Hitler.* 2 vols. Berkeley, Cal.: University of California Press, 1948.
GURIAN, WALDEMAR. *Hitler and the Christians.* Tr. by E. F. Peeler. New York: Sheed & Ward, Inc., 1936.
HOFER, WALTHER. *Der Nationalsozialismus, Dokumente 1933–1945.* Frankfurt a.M., 1957.
LEWY, GUENTER. *The Catholic Church and Nazi Germany.* New York: McGraw-Hill, 1964.
MEINECKE, FRIEDRICH. *The German Catastrophe: Reflections and Recollections.* Tr. by Sidney B. Fay. Cambridge, Mass.: Harvard University Press, 1950.

MÜLLER, HANS. *Katholische Kirche und Nationalsozialismus: Dokumente von 1930–1935.* Munich, 1963.

RITTER, GERHARD. *The German Resistance: Carl Goerdeler's Struggle Against Tyranny.* Tr. by R. T. Clark. New York: G. Allen, 1958.

SHIRER, WILLIAM L. *The Rise and Fall of the Third Reich: A History of Nazi Germany.* New York: Simon and Schuster, 1960.

SHUSTER, GEORGE N. *Like a Mighty Army: Hitler Versus Established Religion.* New York: Appleton, 1935.

WEINZIERL-FISCHER, ERIKA. "Oesterreichs Katholiken und der Nationalsozialismus," *Wort und Wahrheit,* XVIII (1963).

ZAHN, GORDON C. *German Catholics and Hitler's Wars: A Study in Social Control.* New York: Sheed & Ward, Inc., 1960.

About the Author

Gordon C. Zahn is now Professor Emeritus of Sociology at the University of Massachusetts-Boston. One of the relatively few U. S. Catholic conscientious objectors to World War II, he was assigned to alternative service from 1942-46. He is a 1949 graduate of the College of St. Thomas and received his Ph.D. from Catholic University in 1952. He has held fellowships for post-doctoral study and research at Harvard and at the Universities of Wuerzburg (Germany) and Manchester (England). He has received honors and awards from LaSalle University, St. John's University (Collegeville), the Washington Theological Union, as well as the Pope Paul VI "Teacher of Peace" citation from Pax Christi USA.

It was during his Fulbright research in Germany in 1956-57 (which led to the publication of his first book, *German Catholics and Hitler's Wars)* that he happened upon the Jägerstätter case. With the assistance of a grant from the Penrose Fund, he was able to return several years later to do the research upon which this book is based.

He is the author of *War, Conscience and Dissent; The Military Chaplaincy: A study of Role Tension in the R.A.F.;* and, most recently, *Another Part of the War: The Camp Simon Story.* He also edited *The Nonviolent Alternative,* a collection of Thomas Merton's writings on peace and has published numerous articles in a variety of journals, both popular and scholarly.

Since his retirement from active teaching he has served as National Director of the Pax Christi USA Center on Conscience and War and has lectured widely under the Center's auspices. Information concerning his availability (or about *The Refusal,* the Austrian docudrama based on this book) can be obtained by writing the Center at Box 726, Cambridge, MA 02139.